A DICTIONARY OF
GLOBALIZATION

by Jens-Uwe Wunderlich and
Meera Warrier

FIRST EDITION

Routledge
Taylor & Francis Group

LONDON AND NEW YORK

First Edition 2007
Routledge
Albert House, 1–4 Singer Street, London EC2A 4BQ,
United Kingdom

Routledge is an imprint of the Taylor & Francis Group,
*an **informa** business*

© Routledge 2007

ISBN-13 978 185743 332 6
ISBN-10 1 85743 332 7

Development Editor: Cathy Hartley
Copy Editor and Proof-reader: Simon Chapman

Typeset in Times New Roman 10/13.5

The publishers make no representation, express or implied,
with regard to the accuracy of the information contained
in this book and cannot accept any legal responsibility for
any errors or omissions that may take place.

Typeset by
Taylor & Francis Books
Printed and bound in Great Britain by
MPG Books Ltd, Bodmin

For Atchan, Wolfgang, Regina, Martin, Maya and Richard

FOREWORD

The purpose of this DICTIONARY OF GLOBALIZATION is to present an interdisciplinary overview of some of the key concepts, theories, ideologies, global organizations, activists and thinkers connected with globalization. Needless to say, given the range and diversity of discourses on globalization today, the introduction and the entries provided here can only aspire to be indicative. They point to the diversity of emergent theories, debates and concerns, but are far from being exhaustive. The entries serve as introductions, and if they whet the appetite and stimulate the interest of at least a few readers, our purpose will have been served.

It may come as a surprise to some that this dictionary lacks an entry on globalization itself. As the introductory chapter highlights, however, it would be impossible to do justice to globalization in the form of a short dictionary definition. Indeed, more than the term itself, it is the many competing approaches to it, its manifestations, contradictions and symptoms, that make it an interesting and challenging concept.

The introduction is followed by the alphabetically organized and cross-referenced entries. A concluding bibliography offers a list of references that have informed the various entries and which can be used for further reading on the subject. The volume works best as a quick reference or a companion to some of the existing and emerging works on globalization in a variety of disciplines.

Jens-Uwe Wunderlich
Meera Warrier
June 2007

ACKNOWLEDGEMENTS

This project began in autumn 2004. Given the scope of the task involved, it is perhaps no surprise that so much time has elapsed between the initial idea and the finalized manuscript. In completing this enormous task, we have been fortunate to have had the support of numerous friends and colleagues. In particular we would like to acknowledge Chris White from the University of Reading who contributed to the entries on the Bush Doctrine, Capitalism, Clash of Civilizations, Collective Security, Conservatism, Communitarianism, Deterritorialization and End of History. A debt is owed to Michael Sutton of Aston University, Chris Rumford from Royal Holloway, University of London and Ron Skeldon, Mick Dunford and Ben Rogaly at the University of Sussex for their constructive and insightful comments on the introductory chapter. Just as significant an influence were the many undergraduate and postgraduate students at the University of Reading, Royal Holloway and Aston University, whose constant questioning and desire to learn provided the stimulus and challenge for this work. Finally, we want to thank our editor, Cathy Hartley, for her enthusiasm for the book and for her patience in seeing the project through to completion. All shortcomings or mistakes remain the authors' own.

Jens-Uwe Wunderlich
Meera Warrier

CONTENTS

THE AUTHORS

Jens-Uwe Wunderlich is a lecturer in International Relations at Aston University. He has a multi-disciplinary academic background and holds degrees from the Otto-von-Guericke-University Magdeburg in Germany and the University of East Anglia in Norwich. He has held teaching appointments at the University of East Anglia, the University of Reading, at SOAS (the School of Oriental and African Studies, University of London) and at Royal Holloway, University of London. His research interests focus on regionalism and regional integration, international relations theory, globalization, the European Union and East Asia. He is the author of *Globalisation, Regionalism and International Order—Europe and Southeast Asia* (Ashgate, forthcoming 2007) and several articles.

Meera Warrier has degrees in English Literature, Sociology and the History of Science. She completed her doctoral degree in Development Studies at the University of East Anglia in Norwich. She is currently Research Manager for the Development Research Centre on Migration, Globalization and Poverty, based at the University of Sussex, Brighton.

Introduction
Globalization: The Word and the Debates

Few terms have evoked the range of responses, or been quite so used, and abused, as the term 'globalization'. It has been variously described as a process, a period, a force and a condition. The resulting ascriptions and attributions are diverse and invariably invite confusion. There are those who would enthusiastically argue for globalization's merits, setting it up as a panacea to all the ills of contemporary political, economic and social organization. Others argue equally vociferously and convincingly that it has done more harm than good, exacerbating and entrenching inequalities. For still others, there is no point in arguing for or against globalization; 'progress' (and by implication the neo-liberal logic) inexorably leads us into more intensely global settings, and we must either adapt to it and move forward, or be left to languish by the wayside.

Even though the term globalization is used liberally in political rhetoric and in the press, its meaning is somehow assumed to be intuitively known; it is rarely spelt out. Indeed, 'globalization' is often both the term being explained and the explanation itself. In contrast, the academic literature offers an amazing variety of different theories and definitions, with almost every researcher in the social sciences having something to add to the ongoing debates and discussions. However, here again, nothing about globalization is uncontested—there is little consensus on what globalization actually is, what drives it, whether it is a qualitatively new phenomenon, and whether it is a primarily beneficial or damaging process. Some define it as the development of a global society, characterized by the denationalization of markets, politics and legal systems. Other scholars tend to focus on the 'symptoms' of globalization, such as transnational migration, global cultural flows or external environmental effects. Globalization's critics regard it as something of a myth, created by the neo-liberal school in order to spread capitalism around the globe, divert attention from the suppression of local cultures, and eventually to effect the 'Americanization' of the international political economy. Yet, also visible around the world is a greater involvement in grass-roots organizations and movements, regionalism, and efforts for greater local autonomy, making any universal statement about globalization, let alone its effects, quite untenable.

This introduction will draw out some of the key trajectories of thinking on globalization, highlighting the complex nature of the subject, and offering a framework for navigating through the rest of the volume. It flags up some of the usages that dominate academic and non-academic discourses, applied to various dimensions of economic, political, social, environmental, technological and cultural transformations. We begin by asking whether there is something substantively new about globalization—a discussion that leads on to the etymology of the term 'globalization' and the evolution of its finer nuances and contemporary connotations. Following from there, this introduction seeks to understand some of the ways in which globalization is currently theorized, looking at what globalization is seen to be doing in its economic, political, cultural and social incarnations. Thus, the following sections look at the globalist arguments for the triumph of the market and the end of the nation state; the challenges posed by deterritorialization, including the perceived threat of cultural homogenization; to conclude by asking whether globalization is 'good' or 'bad'. Posing this question is necessary in so far as most of the arguments for or against globalization look at its perceived effects or outcomes. As will be seen, it is equally important to understand where, or from which positionality, these arguments are coming, as these in turn determine particular understandings of globalization and arguments for or against it.

Globalization—Old or New?

There is nothing intrinsically new about philosophical ideas about global interconnectedness or economic interdependencies, trade in commodities, or intellectual and cultural exchange. From the 16th century onwards, European colonization and industrialization established the foundations of the contemporary global political economy. Marxist scholars, for instance, have long argued that contemporary globalization is simply a more advanced stage in this process—the latest stage in the development of capitalism, itself a product of historical evolution. Capitalism, or the exploitation of the many by the few, Marxists would argue, is built on the back of the industrial revolution and the subsequent European imperialism of the 19th and early 20th centuries, which has created the contemporary division of the global political economy into a developed global North and an underdeveloped global South.

Many a writer has been tempted to draw up historical checklists of the key developments that have preceded today's stage or phase of globalization. For instance, Roland Robertson (1992) distinguishes five phases. The first phase (1400–1750) witnessed the age of European exploration, the global spread of the Roman Catholic Church, the emergence of the Westphalian state system and the advent of modern geography. The second phase (1750–1875) saw the consolidation of the state system based on sovereign nation states in Europe and North America. Relations between sovereign states were increasingly structured by international regimes based on diplomatic norms and conventions. The Enlightenment and the first stage of industrialization transformed European societies and economies alike. European colonialism spread and the first international non-governmental organizations emerged with the foundation of the Red Cross in 1863. In the third phase (1875–1925) globalization went through several significant changes. It roughly coincided with the beginning of a second industrial revolution—a revolution in communication and transport technology, leading to a significant increase in the volume and speed of communications. Steel-hulled ships were surpassing sailing vessels in tonnage and speed. There was a massive expansion of railroad networks. The period also heralded the introduction of the factory system, industrialization and mass production. Other innovations included the telegraph, the first transatlantic cable, the introduction of the telephone, the widespread use of electricity, the radio and the airplane. Global trade flourished. Phase four of globalization (1925–late 1960s) witnessed the creation of international regimes and institutions with global reach, such as the United Nations (UN), the International Monetary Fund (IMF), the World Bank, and the General Agreement on Tariffs and Trade (GATT).[1] The Bretton Woods system, set up in this phase, was designed to manage the global political economy. Contemporary globalization (1969–to date) is distinguished from the previous stages by new patterns of migration and the global impact of information and communications technologies, which have increased the speed and volume of the circulation of goods, capital, services, ideas and people.

Writers such as Keohane and Nye (2003) argue that while globalization itself may be an old phenomenon, its degree and intensity have varied. They distinguish between 'thin globalization', such as the time when trade through the Silk Route connected diverse parts of the world but affected only a comparatively limited amount of trade and a small number of people, and 'thick globalization', which has created a dense network of extensive and overlapping relationships and an intensification of economic, social, cultural and political interdependencies, which is the way globalization manifests itself today.

Others see the roots of globalization in antiquity. Stoic philosophy and the idea of the cosmopolis, it is argued, were some of the earliest conceptualizations of a community of humankind across political and cultural borders. Today, elements of Stoic philosophy can be found, for instance, in modern conceptions of universal human rights. Thus, it is argued that the idea of links, of certain rights and duties transcending political communities, predates the nation state and the formulation of notions of sovereignty.

It is probably important here to take a step back and look at the basis of the term 'globalization'. While this term itself might have been in use only for the last 45 years, it is derived from the words 'globe' or 'global', which have a much longer history. Both terms derive from the Latin 'globus', meaning a round body, a sphere, or a ball, and came into usage in English in the 16th century. However, in English usage, the term 'global' was used more in the sense of 'all-inclusive' or 'comprehensive' in the sense of 'relating to or embracing the whole of something, or a group of things' (*Concise Oxford Dictionary*, 10th edn).

The meaning of 'global' as 'of or relating to the whole world; worldwide', is relatively new. This was not a term Adam Smith, for instance, had access to; instead he wrote 'in the whole globe of the earth'. The English translator of Marx's and Engels' work 70 years later did not have recourse to it either; he was still writing of 'the whole surface of the globe' (Sheil 2001). 'Global' as relating to the whole world came into usage only at the end of the 19th century; no coincidence here that by now the physical discovery and mapping of the world was complete.

In the early 1940s, American military authorities combined the older sense of 'total' with its newer interpretation as 'world-wide' in the concept of 'global war' (Sheil 2001). The war of the 1940s now came to be known as the Second World War, and the Great War of 1914–18 was retrospectively renamed the First World War. But the sense of 'global' as 'world-encompassing' needed another impetus to enter the wider imagination, and that came with Marshall McLuhan's conception of the 'global village' in 1960.

The usage of the term since then has conflated the senses of something experienced instantly and simultaneously across the world, attracting media attention, and, as if by implication, something very significant or important. Other events speeded up the take-up of the term. For instance, 'global economy' came into use when national controls on international movements of capital and currencies began to be relaxed in the mid-1970s.

The term 'globalization' first entered the English lexicon through *Webster's Dictionary* in 1961, where it was used to describe the interconnectedness of social events and relationships (Waters 1995). By and large that definition has not changed. For instance, according to the British political theorist David Held's much-cited definition:

> Globalization is best understood as a spatial phenomenon, lying on a continuum with 'the local' at one end and 'the global' at the other. It denotes a shift in the spatial form of human organisation and activity to transcontinental or interregional patterns of activity, interaction and the exercise of power. [...] Globalization today implies at least two distinct phenomena. First, it suggests that many chains of political, economic and social activity are becoming interregional in scope and, secondly, it suggests that there has been an intensification of levels of interaction and interconnectedness within and between states and societies (Held 1997: 3).

Equally quoted today is British sociologist Anthony Giddens' definition of globalization as 'the intensification of world-wide social relations which link distant localities in such a way that local happenings are shaped by events occurring many miles away and vice versa' (Giddens 1990: 64). The term entered common parlance following the fall of the Berlin Wall and the collapse of the bipolar world. The first reference to the word in the *Oxford English Dictionary* speaks of its use in the *Spectator* magazine of October 1962, which had declared that 'globalization is, indeed, a staggering concept' (Cerami 1962).

Over time, 'globalization' has acquired political meanings and nuances not quite captured in that earliest definition of globalization in *Webster's Dictionary*. The most dominant strands of thinking around globalization might be discussed in terms of two words, both with their roots in the word 'global'—'globality' and 'globalism'. 'Globality' comes nearest to *Webster's Dictionary* meaning of globalization. It is a social concept referring to the emergence of a global society in the sense that the notion of closed spaces has become illusory so that nothing that happens on earth is only a limited local event (Beck 2000). It evokes the emergent and contradictory condition of global-ness (Shaw 1999). 'Globalism', on the other hand, is much more politically charged in that it is endowed with neo-liberal meanings and values. For advocates of globalism, the 'world market' is now powerful enough to take the place of (local and national) political action; indeed, it suggests that the nation state is on the verge of becoming a thing of the past.

Today, the term 'global' summons up the planet as a physical entity, but it also hints at something more than just the sum of its parts. It suggests a transformation of the spatial content of social relations, as it evokes something over and above just the territorial. Indeed, its usage today might be said to evoke the self-consciously common framework of human society world-wide (Shaw 1999). Thus, quite apart from the physical 'shrinking' or 'compression' of the world due to the impact of information and communication technologies and improved transport systems, there is also seen to be an enhanced consciousness of the world as a whole, of a common global fate, and as such, it is also suggestive of conscious global-oriented action.

It is perhaps this 'global' consciousness, and action directed at the 'global', which makes globalization as we understand it today something 'new'. This is manifested in our use of terms to encompass the whole, such as 'global economy' or 'global factory', meant to convey the world-wide proliferation of activities, where events or actions in one part of the world, or changes somewhere along the production chain in one location, can have consequences throughout the globe. Thus, globalization is both a spread of tangible, physical global forces and relations, as Immanuel Wallerstein (1979) would have it, and also the spread of an idea, an intensification of consciousness of the world as a whole through the ever-increasing proliferation of global connections, as Roland Robertson (1992) would argue.

A number of writings on globalization see it as a set of projects that require us to imagine space and time in particular ways. Thus, for David Harvey (1989), the technologies of globalization, particularly electronics and telecommunications, together with the ease of travel, have rendered it possible to reorganize time such that space is no longer a constraining factor, and vice versa. His phrase, 'time-space compression', suggests a speeding up of economic and social processes which has experientially shrunk the globe so that neither distance nor time are any longer major constraints on the organization of human activity. A related but different connotation might be attributed to that other favourite phrase: 'time-space distanciation'. This phrase, coined by Anthony Giddens (1990), suggests the stretching of social relations across distances, and reducing their consciousness of their own local status, as technologies speed up communications and start to connect distant localities. Here, social relations are 'disembedded', or lifted out of their local contexts of interaction, to be restructured across time and space.

Among the globalization theorists who argue that the extent and pace of globalization today is unprecedented are those who see this world as characterized by borderless worlds. These are the voices of the 'hyperglobalizers', who tom-tom the triumph of the market and the death of the nation state. Let us examine the arguments for seamless global markets and the end of the nation state.

Seamless Global Markets or the March of Western Capitalism?

For hyperglobalizers, the contemporary phase of economic globalization began in 1944, when the Bretton Woods system established a new way of managing the international economy based on binding rules and a fixed exchange rate system. The Bretton Woods agreements also created new international economic institutions to oversee the international political economy—the International Monetary Fund (IMF) and the World Bank. This was followed in 1947 by the establishment of the predecessor of the contemporary World Trade Organization (WTO), the General Agreement on Tariffs and Trade (GATT). The aim of these international organizations was to prevent an economic recession that could potentially give rise to conflict.

Social and economic policies espoused at the time followed a welfare state model, based, in the widest sense possible, on a Keynesian compromise, which included raising wages and assuaging class conflicts, at least temporarily. States could not trust markets to always get it right, hence the need to intervene. However, when the Bretton Woods system of fixed exchange rates ran into problems in the 1960s, and collapsed in the early 1970s, a prolonged structural crisis of the global economy paved the way for a new economic and social order (Duménil and Lévy 2005). Following a decade of inflation, high unemployment and low economic growth in the Western world, a more neo-liberal approach began to replace the Keynesian compromise, as illustrated by the social and economic policies ushered in by US President Ronald Reagan and British Prime Minister Margaret Thatcher (Palley

2005). These policies championed entrepreneurial and individual freedom, unregulated and free markets, and private property rights as the best routes to economic development and improved human well-being (Harvey 2007).

Meanwhile, the World Bank and the IMF managed to consolidate and enhance their weight in international economic affairs in the aftermath of the debt crisis of the developing world in the early 1980s. The IMF, in particular, gained a new role with the formulation of the so-called Washington Consensus, focusing on market liberalization, fiscal austerity and privatization, replacing a critical role for governments with a strong focus on the free market. As such it might be said to represent the triumph of economic neo-liberalism as the favoured paradigm for economic development. In return for much-needed development loans, the IMF and the World Bank demanded the implementation of structural adjustment programmes, which gave these institutions unprecedented influence over the domestic economic and social policies of sovereign nation states.[2]

Trade liberalization had long been on the agenda of successive GATT rounds of multilateral negotiations, aimed at reducing tariffs on cross-border merchandise trade. Several factors converged towards the end of the 1970s to usher in a new phase of globalization as the deregulation of interest rates and the removal of credit and capital controls significantly increased the transborder flow of capital. An entirely new financial infrastructure began to emerge from the 1980s, aided by satellite dishes, fibre optic cables and internet-based technologies, and the innovation of new financial products. Large sums of money could now be transferred in nanoseconds across the globe. The development of e-businesses and dot.com companies are among the latest signposts of this new economy.

A key feature of this phase has been the growing amount of foreign direct investment (FDI). Indeed, from the 1980s, FDI grew four times faster than world gross national product (GNP). However, FDI was by no means universally distributed across the globe. It was concentrated in developed countries, with significant amounts now also being directed to the dynamic emerging economies in East and South-East Asia and Latin America. The number of countries acting as sources of FDI has since diversified considerably, with a number of the newly industrializing countries also becoming sources of FDI between 1985 and 2000. Today, for instance, Indian and Chinese firms are said to be starting to give their rich-world rivals a run for their money. So far in 2007, Indian firms, led by Hindalco and Tata Steel, have bought some 34 foreign companies for a combined US $10,700m.

Coming into the forefront here were transnational companies (TNCs). Aided by technological innovations and financial and trade liberalization, TNCs[3] were increasingly concentrating control over a large share of global capital, technology and market access. They account for about two-thirds of world exports of goods and services, with a significant share within that held by intra-firm trade. The power held by these large corporations, and the transnational, and in some cases global, nature of their operations, has enabled them to bypass trade unions, labour laws and to actively influence government legislation in both developed and developing countries.

Throughout this period, and particularly from the late 1980s, a neo-liberal orthodoxy had been taking hold. It was argued that international economic institutions, multinational enterprises and transnational activities distributed common values and benefits through the spread of market-oriented economic policies, which in turn would encourage more democratic and representative governments and human rights. Markets were best given free rein to sort the world out; the state was an inconvenience. If markets were allowed to function without undue state intervention, economic globalization would be able to unfold its real potential. Milton Friedman (1962), for example, advanced the idea of organizing society through the mechanisms of private enterprise. Economic activity would be decentralized and states would be restricted to providing the legal framework for economic activities. In the same vein, Jagdish Bhagwati (2004) sees globalization as the most powerful force for social good today, when properly managed. Neo-liberal globalization, in this view, is a process that increases economic efficiency, individual freedom and overall living standards, and alleviates poverty. The many problems faced by the developing world are not the result of too much liberalization but of too little, it is argued. Protectionism, for instance, is still rampant, both in the developing and in the developed world. The Common Agricultural Policy (CAP) of the European Union (EU) is just one notorious example of how misplaced protectionism impedes the chances for developing countries. Thus, neo-liberalism in practice often diverges widely from neo-liberalism in theory, leaving its true potential unrealized (Munck 2005, Navarro 2006, Harvey 2007).

Market liberalization is perceived as further supporting the spread of human rights and democracy throughout the world. Indeed, for some writers, liberal democracy and free market capitalism are synonymous terms. In his 1989 essay 'The End of History' and in his 1992 book *The End of History and the Last Man*, Francis Fukuyama argued that with the end of the Cold

War, historical progress, defined as the quest for human freedom, has reached its final stage. Communism, the last great ideological challenge to liberal democracy, has failed and liberal democracy based on the principles of liberty and equality, together with capitalism as the organizing principle, has triumphed.

The Demise of the Nation State?

For hyperglobalizers then, globalization is primarily driven by economic and technological forces (Ohmae 1996). As such, hyperglobalizers pronounce the dawn of a 'borderless world' and the decline of territorial sovereignty as the important reference point for political, economic and social organization. The crumbling nation state is seen very much as an artefact of the 18th and 19th centuries. It is described as:

> an unnatural, even dysfunctional unit for organizing human activity and managing economic endeavour in a borderless world. It presents no genuine, shared community of economic interests; it defines no meaningful flows of economic activity. In fact, it overlooks the true linkages and synergies that exist among often disparate populations by combining important measures of human activity at the wrong level of analysis ... On the global economic map the lines that matter now are those defining what might be called 'region states' (Ohmae 1993: 78).

States have thus been usurped and/or sidelined by global markets (Strange 1996). Or, as Philip Bobbit (2002) contends in his provocative book, *The Shield of Achilles*, nation states are transforming themselves into market states. Indeed, the only role left for the state is to provide a legal framework for the market system to operate effectively. Furthermore, political power will be located in 'global social formations and expressed through networks rather than through territorially based states' (Steger 2003: 61).

The hyperglobalizers are not without their detractors. The opposition believes that the retreat or disappearance of the state has been grossly exaggerated. They highlight the importance of politics in unleashing the economic forces that characterize globalization. The rapid expansion of economic activity in the last 20 years is not so much the result of the 'quasi-natural' forces of economic activity. Rather, it has been driven by political decisions creating a framework for free market economies to flourish, they argue. In particular, the neo-liberal policies of the USA and Great Britain in the 1970s and 1980s have been instrumental in liberalizing international trade and capital flows and in unleashing the forces of economic globalization. Or, as Hay (2006) would argue, it was states, after all, that put the current neo-liberal infrastructure that facilitates globalization in place. And at least the larger, wealthier states, or their governments, remain in a position to determine the 'rules of the game'.

Governmental policies, and not economic activities are, therefore, behind the globalization process:

> [G]lobalisation is not the global release of an imminent desire of individuals and businesses to truck, barter and exchange, it is rather a neoliberal project, based on a conviction that markets manage resources in a superior way to states, but that public institutions are required to impose and maintain those markets (Harrison 2004: 154).

Alan Milward (1993) goes a step further, arguing that the state has actually grown stronger as the result of global forces. The pressures of globalization driving European integration, for instance, have ironically rescued the state rather than undermining it, by allowing it to operate more effectively, he argues.

Indeed, states still hold enough power to influence their domestic economies (and in some cases the global economy) decisively. Among international actors, the nation state will remain in a key position, at least for the foreseeable future. There is no apparent alternative which could command or enforce the same amount of respect, loyalty and authority and, hence, focus and organize social energies in the way governments still can and do by appealing to a sense of shared identity (Maull 2000). States are able to restrict and manage transnational flows such as international migration through stricter border controls, and to stifle the flow of capital through the imposition of capital controls. National security measures, especially following the 9/11 attacks on the World Trade Center have further enhanced the power of national governments and restricted civil liberties and freedoms. Nation states continue to define, discipline, control and regulate populations, whether these are on the move or in residence.

However, it is important to recognize that the nation state's normative character may have been challenged: globalization is changing traditional conceptions around the practice of national sovereignty. One of the main features of the Westphalian nation state is an explicit connection between sovereignty and territoriality.

> [...] sovereign states rooted in territorial notions of social space have been the prime unit for facilitating, impeding and mediating interaction between the social groups, organisations, and citizens and other categories of collective and individual social units contained within their borders (Hughes 2000: 5).

But the Westphalian model might no longer be so relevant. For instance, Jan Aart Scholte (1997: 21) argues:

> [...] owing to globalization, the Westphalian system is already past history. The state apparatus survives, and indeed is in some respects larger, stronger, and more intrusive in social life than ever before. However, the core Westphalian norm of sovereignty is no longer operative; nor can it be retrieved in the present globalizing world. The concept of sovereignty continues to be important in political rhetoric, especially for people who seek to slow and reverse progressive reductions of national self-determination in the face of globalization. However, both juridically and practically, state regulatory capacities have ceased to meet the criteria of sovereignty as it was traditionally conceived.

There has been a reduction in the capacity of national governments to set independent national objectives and to impose their own domestic policies. Devolutionary pressures, regional integration and international organizations have forced national governments to transfer some of their traditional powers and functions, often from the national to the municipal and the provincial level. Thus, globalization has resulted in direct transborder links between different sub-state authorities, sometimes in association with central state authorities, but also often bypassing them. For instance, 'global cities' such as London, Tokyo or New York tend to have very close links with each other. Within Europe, several sub-national regions are increasingly involved in forging transnational alliances with other regions, creating new cross-border regional entities.

This 'top-down' transfer of policy-making power has often also been supplemented by a 'bottom-up' movement of other state competencies to the international level, evidenced in the steady growth in the number and scope of international organizations and intergovernmental networks in every part of the world. Examples range from regional organizations such as the EU, the North American Free Trade Agreement (NAFTA) and the Association of South-East Asian Nations (ASEAN) to institutions with a global reach, such as, for instance, the UN, the IMF, or the World Bank, which must all, however, answer to their governing councils, made up of representatives from various states.

Global governance is also increasingly shaped by the emergence of a 'global civil society' characterized by numerous non-governmental organizations (NGOs),[4] such as Greenpeace, Amnesty International or Oxfam International. Global civil society organizations are distinct from official and commercial structures and include, apart from NGOs, consumer protection bodies, academic institutions, environmental campaigns, farmers' associations, trade unions, peace activist groups, human rights advocacy networks and more. Taken together, global and regional governance and sub-national governance structures tend to break the formal institutional framework of the nation state and exclusive national sovereignty, replacing it with a more fluid multi-level governance structure where sovereignty is increasingly shared in many areas (Bullman 1997). These dynamics are causing many structural changes, including a rethinking of the role of national governments (Lipsey 1997). Globalization is seen here as leading to a reworking of the nature of national sovereignty and national borders. It transforms the organization of society and opens up new political spaces, creating new challenges.

Theories of hyperglobalization seem to constitute a package built around the premise that markets need to be free to function, and that markets will ensure well-being all round. For hyperglobalizers, globalization is new, in that this global economic interconnectedness, together with the death of the socialist challenge and the unipolarity thus established are all new. Indeed, it is in this context that we must view the arguments by those who would not concede that there is something completely 'new' about globalization (e.g. Hirst and Thompson 1996, and Hay 2006). By arguing that today's world market is not unprecedented, they are able to defend certain political responses to globalization—such as European social democracy—as still viable; options that hyperglobalizers (and neo-liberals) have already banished into history. It is also in this context that we must understand Hirst and Thompson's (1999: 6) words, that globalization is 'a myth suitable for a world without illusions, but it is also one that robs us of hope. ... for it is held that Western social democracy and socialism of the Soviet bloc are both finished. One can only call the political impact of "globalization" the pathology of over-diminished expectations'.

The Challenges of Deterritorialization

The increasing movement and operation of people, goods, businesses and services in markets beyond national borders are said to have led to the erosion of any 'natural' relation of a culture with a geographical and social territory. The deregulation and liberalization of markets has immensely contributed to this process of deterritorialization. Sovereign national states are now 'criss-crossed and undermined by transnational actors with varying prospects of power, orientations, identities and networks' (Beck 2000: 11). As such, any 'natural' relation of a culture or process with a geographical and social territory is sundered, and the connections between cultural structures, relationships, settings and representations are torn apart. While there are those who hark back to an older world and bemoan deterritorialization, it also creates new opportunities. For instance, it creates new markets for businesses that thrive on the need of deterritorialized populations to keep in touch with 'home'. Thus, both deterritorialization and greater connectedness are consequences of globalization.

However, this deterritorialization of culture is not seen by all as a benign matter. Fears around deterritorialization stem from the fear of cultural imperialism—a fear that the world is being made over in the image of the West, spreading a shallow, 'inauthentic' homogeneity and uniformity throughout the world. The use of English as the global medium of communication is thought to ensure the global transmission of Western-style consumerism. The influence and reach of Western media and entertainment industries (like CNN and Time Warner), and the values they espouse, are seen to be encroaching on and destroying the variety of traditions in the world in insidious ways, primarily by spreading, and validating as superior, Western ways of seeing and knowing.

This purportedly homogenizing and universalizing trend is seen to be creating a 'global culture', slowly obliterating and replacing local and regional cultural practices. Westernized/largely Americanized culture in the form of pop music and Hollywood blockbusters is seen to have created a global culture that binds together young people of different national, linguistic and cultural backgrounds. According to this view, global culture is directly related to the restructuring of the global political economy, in particular to the spread of capitalism.

Indeed, the outcome of economic globalization is portrayed as being both negative and limited, largely benefiting the developed world and already powerful TNCs, and leading to 'corporate globalization' or 'globalization from above' (Steger 2003). This proliferation of global capitalism is seen as a form of neo-colonialism, undermining the political, social and economic fabric of many societies, making them vulnerable to the volatility of markets, systematically destroying the environment, endangering the rights of minorities and, ultimately, rendering ineffective democratic principles. Globalization, from this perspective, is another name for Westernization, and the systematic exploitation of the global South by Western capitalism.[5]

The term 'McDonaldization' is used to capture the process of the dissemination of Western consumerism. According to Ritzer, who coined the term, it is 'the process by which the principles of the fast-food restaurant are coming to dominate more and more sectors of American society as well as of the rest of the world' (Ritzer 1993: 1). The term also evokes the ubiquity of brands, industrial giants and entertainment icons such as Coca-Cola, Disney, Benetton, Unilever, BP, BASF, Shell, Nike, Adidas, Hollywood or Levi's, all of which shape desires, create new needs, establish brand-awareness and contribute to capital accumulation.

The fears of a homogenizing global culture have, however, been criticized as being largely unfounded. They are seen to be built upon rather simplistic constructions of Third World subjects as passive consumers of the West's exports, rather than actors who creatively engage with these cultural forms, interpreting and adapting them to local circumstances, or sometimes simply rejecting them. Roland Robertson (1992), for instance, points to a much more complex local/global connection (glocalization). It would be far too simplistic to reduce the relationship between global and local culture to a one-dimensional one of domination and subordination. First, while global culture might be dominated by Western ideas, global cultural flows are always interpreted in local contexts. Imported commodities are often indigenized in order to cater to local tastes. McDonald's, for instance, adapts its menu to suit local tastes. Similarly, non-Western cultures localize Western cultural influences. Indian women, for example, may change between wearing a traditional saree and Western-style clothing according to occasion and context. As Anna Tsing (2001) argues, there has been a tendency to naturalize the notion of a global culture, with very little exploration of the possibility that different manifestations of capitalism and governmentality are themselves born of particular contexts, are culturally circumscribed, and are often contradictory. While the homogenizing tendencies are certainly very powerful, they do not necessarily extinguish cultural differences.

Second, cultural flows are by no means unidirectional, from West to East or from the global North to the global South. As diverse and remote cultures become accessible, both as signs and as commodities, the flows move in both directions as well. Indeed, a deterritorialized world is said to have engendered a 'new cosmopolitanism' uniting the cultural, financial and political flows within and between Western and non-Western countries into a single conceptual whole. And, third, Westernization invites a reaction when advocates of marginalized cultures feel their identity being threatened. Benjamin Barber (1996) points out that the colonizing and imperialistic tendencies of 'McWorld' provoke cultural and political resistance in the form of 'jihad'. This finds expression in the efforts of fundamentalist orthodoxy in the Third World and in xenophobia and right-wing nationalism in many developed countries. Other expressions of resistance against these homogenizing forces may take the form of the ban on satellite dishes in some Middle Eastern countries or the censorship of the internet in China.

Cultural imperialism theorists also fail to consider circuits of culture that bypass the West. This could take various forms, such as the movement of capital into China from Taiwan, Hong Kong or south-east Asia. Or it could be a cultural influence—while CNN and Time Warner might boast an extensive reach, there is no gainsaying the hold Bollywood has on large parts of Asia, the Middle East and even Africa, or the triumph of Cantopop in the West.

Deterritorialization has been accompanied by other changes. The very notion of citizenship, for example, conventionally based on political rights and participation within a sovereign state, is now understood differently. Arjun Appadurai (1996), for instance, argues that diaspora populations around the world comprise emerging 'post-nations' that deterritorialize states. Transnational ties, and their legalization through, for instance, dual citizenship regimes, are seen to raise new challenges for the construction of national identities and processes of decision-making. At the same time, managers, technocrats, and professionals on the move often seek to both circumvent and benefit from different nation state regimes by selecting different sites for investment, work and family relocation. The term 'flexible citizenship' is often used to capture both these strategies and the effects of such manoeuvres (see, for instance, Ong 1998, 2006). As such, globalization is seen to have made economic calculation a major element in diasporic subjects' choice of citizenship, as well as in the ways in which nation states redefine immigration laws.

A number of writers on global governance maintain that globalization will facilitate the emergence of a transnational cosmopolitan democracy where rights and obligations become detached from national and, ultimately, territorial contexts. Such a cosmopolitan model of democracy requires the creation of regional (or global) parliaments connected to states, regions and localities; the extension of the authority of regional bodies such as the EU; the setting-up of a new International Court of Human Rights which entrenches a new charter of rights and duties in different national parliaments, the separation of political and economic interests and a working global legal system, including effective enforcement mechanisms (see, for instance, Archibugi and Held 1995, Kaldor 2003 a and b, Held 1995, and Archibugi et al 1998).

Deterritorialization has led to new ways of conceptualizing relations in the world. The centre-periphery model, set out by Frobel, Heinrichs and Kreye in their work on the international division of labour (1980) and Wallerstein's world systems theory (1979), and variations on that theme, had for long defined the contours for the discussion on relations between different parts of the globe. The newer model is that of flows or circulation, evoking very different images, and a profoundly different understanding of globalization. While flows or circulation conjure up images of markets and trade, they might equally suggest the breaking down of barriers among cultures, races and nations. Appadurai's 'scapes' (1996), for instance, exemplify this new imagery—ethnoscapes, the landscape of persons who constitute the shifting world in which people live; technoscapes, the global configuration of technologies moving at high speeds across previously impermeable borders; financescapes, the global grid of currency speculation and capital transfer; mediascapes, the distribution of the capabilities to produce and disseminate information and the large complex repertoire of images and narratives generated by these capabilities; and ideoscapes, ideologies of states and counter-ideologies of movements, around which nation states have organized their political cultures. For Appadurai (1996), the movements of people are increasingly making it difficult to neatly distinguish between core and periphery or here and there as the core becomes 'peripheralized' with the reverse traffic in people and culture setting itself up at the heart of the West.

Meanwhile, a new entity that has entered discussions of deterritorialization is cyberspace, a simulated space spawned by computers and online networks. It has become a site that holds the potential to simulate innumerable spaces of action, with its own agendas, interests and values, which are beyond the containment of the nation state. It has become a 'new imaginary location of escape, promise and profit' (Eisenstein 1998). Time too is transfigured here, shifting away from the linearity of past-present-future, 'becoming either a static, frozen moment that breaks time down into discrete instances, or an automatic, continuous flow, similar to a video monitor with its screen switched on and waiting for an event to happen' (Boyer 1996).

Several countries have made attempts to secure, regulate or even 'handcuff' cyberspace, and bring it in line with national laws and concerns (including the US government's National Strategy to Secure Cyberspace in February 2003). China and Saudi Arabia are two examples of countries that have placed significant restrictions on their citizens' access to parts of cyberspace. There are also efforts to start a global dialogue to effect comprehensive and harmonized laws in this domain.

Conclusion: Is Globalization 'Good' or 'Bad'?

As we have seen, the concept of globalization can be approached from various different directions. It is a highly contested concept and the standpoint one takes depends ultimately on one's ideological disposition. It concerns questions of governance, as also the distribution of wealth and resources, and it tends to often pitch 'tradition' against new symbols and images that are 'imported' primarily through the media. Although some authors present globalization as a largely apolitical process, almost everything related to it is political in one way or another. Indeed, as we have seen, claims to its neutrality are value-laden in themselves, and represent a particular position of interest in the contemporary global political economy.

It should come as no surprise then that the most vocal proponents of neo-liberal globalization as a force for social, political and economic progress have been stakeholders in the contemporary global political economy. Support is evident in the neo-liberal policies of many international organizations, such as the World Bank, the IMF or the WTO, but also in the foreign and domestic policies of the G8 countries. Other advocates include the chief executives of large transnational enterprises, corporate managers, corporate lobbyists, investment banks and large insurance companies, as well as journalists and academics, bureaucrats and politicians, propagating the merits of free market capitalism and consumerism, all suggesting that the distribution of wealth and power is central to one's position in the whole globalization discourse.

While there may be increased opportunities for the movement of people, goods, businesses and services in markets beyond national borders, and trans-national diaspora are producing conditions for new hybridized cultures and identities, this is hardly weakening existing relations of power or in any way threatening Western hegemony. Indeed, there is increasing 'inter-culturalism' (as opposed to multiculturalism), including processes of both 'dis-integration' and 're-integration' at both the state and global levels. There are processes of homogenization or integration such as, for instance, unifying commodity and consumer cultures such as Coca-Cola, the Big Mac, Dallas or Lost, while processes of differentiation or fragmentation could take the form of ethnic resilience, fragmentation and the re-emergence of powerful national-ist sentiments associated with the myths, memories and symbols of local places rather than global spaces.

Moreover, the movement of people is still restricted, with better-off states and economies fast developing a siege mentality, nervous about large-scale immigration from poorer parts of the world. A security dimension has now been added to these concerns since the events of 9/11, taking fear to new dimensions.

Neo-liberal globalization, it is argued, has subordinated both nature and social values to the drive for economic growth. The increase in international trade and the liberalization of markets have environmental implications as they promote unsustainable patterns of production and consumption and potentially hasten an overall lowering of environmental regulations and stan-dards (race to the bottom). Anthropocentric notions are deeply enshrined in the current neo-liberal globalization discourse. Industrial development, unrest-rained consumption and population growth have placed an unprecedented strain on natural resources and atmospheric conditions, resulting in large-scale pollution of rivers and oceans, deforestation and desertification. However, we are also very conscious of the conditions we are creating. We live in what Ulrich Beck calls a 'risk society', reflexively aware of the damages we our-selves are causing the environment, such as the loss of biodiversity, and global warming, and aware of the imminent threat these pose to life not just locally, but across the globe. Yet, concerted political will to effect change has been lacking. The USA, the largest producer of carbon emissions, for instance, has refused to ratify the Kyoto Protocol. And despite large commitments of funds from the EU and other sources, without US participation, and with no clear enforcement mechanism, it is unclear how effective this treaty will be.

Neo-liberal globalization is seen to be generating new inequalities while exacerbating the gap between the richest and the poorest:

> [It] reinforces patterns of global exclusion and disempowerment while also making globalization ethically, if not politically, unsustainable. ... This architecture, which divides humanity into elites, the bourgeoisie, the marginalized and the impoverished, cuts across territorial and cultural boundaries, rearranging the world into the winners and the losers of globalization (Held and McGrew 2002: 81).

It would be a mistake, however, to believe that globalization sceptics represent a united front. Indeed, there are arguments from many different quarters that point to the negative sides of contemporary globalization. For instance, Samuel Huntington's foreboding concerning a 'clash of civilizations' in the post-Cold War world is relevant in this context since it predicts violent conflict around the politics of religion, culture and identity (Huntington 1993).

The ideological opposition to globalism comes from the left and the right of the political spectrum. On the right are particularist protectionists, critics who blame neo-liberal globalization for many of the economic and social problems faced by national societies. They are motivated by a fear of reduced living standards, a loss of national identity and culture due to unwanted foreign influences and the loss of national sovereignty. Proponents of this view denounce free trade agendas, the power of TNCs and international institutions, the perceived 'Americanization' of national cultures and the general permeability of national borders to transnational influences. On the left is the so-called 'anti-globalization movement', a group of loosely organized universalist-protectionist networks challenging neo-liberal globalism. Sporadic anti-globalization struggles occurred throughout the 1990s in the developing world. A significant event was the 1994 Zapatista uprising in the Mexican state of Chiapas when a constitutional amendment following the ratification of the North American Free Trade Agreement (NAFTA) abolished communal land rights and opened the economy to market forces. However, a large-scale confrontation between supporters of globalism and its challengers did not erupt until the WTO meeting in Seattle in 1999, when an alliance of human rights groups, trade unions, labour groups, environmentalists, animal rights activists, consumer rights proponents, feminists and advocates of Third World development and debt relief gathered in Seattle to raise their voices against the WTO, free market capitalism and corporate globalization.

The term 'anti-globalization', however, does not quite capture the spirit of this movement. Most protesters are not against globalization as such but against a neo-liberal vision of globalization. They actively voice their support for a bottom-up form of globalization where democracy, labour rights and environmental standards would not be marginalized by the market. Furthermore, campaigners employ the technologies that characterize globalization with great efficiency and effect. Indeed, modern communications such as the internet, mobile phones and laptop computers have made the global co-ordination of protest possible. Several commentators, such as Noam Chomsky, have therefore suggested that 'global justice movement' or 'global social movement' may be more appropriate names.

There have also been several regional and local movements that might be termed 'anti-globalization'. Though varying widely in their aims and political complexions, they share a common sense of injustice. While challenging processes whose origins lie beyond their immediate localities, they profess the aim of establishing greater control over their own lives and spaces.

It appears then that globalization remains a controversial and highly contested term. Given such a wealth of differing opinions, almost everything related to globalization let alone the definition of the concept, or its social, political, economic and cultural implications, is notoriously difficult to pin down.

The aim of this short introduction has been to alert the reader to some of the literatures at the centre of the debate, and provide a framework for the rest of the volume.

Notes

1 However, any such periodization also invites challenges. For instance, there are those who see 1925 as a rather arbitrary dividing line, seeing more coherence in taking the period from 1914 to 1945, which might be viewed as one of retreating globalism.
2 However, it ought to be mentioned here that 'conditionalities' in return for IMF help long predated the Washington Consensus.
3 FDI is only one measure of TNC activity. As Dickens (2003) points out, FDI is based on ownership of assets and is therefore not able to capture the many intricate ways in which TNCs engage in transnational operations.

4 Though questions remain as to who or what NGOs represent, and whether they might be termed democratic in their own internal functioning.
5 These arguments do not, however, convince many economists, who are able to delink globalization from Westernization, modernization or any cultural context. Globalization for them is very firmly based on trade and markets. As such, there could potentially be globalization without modernization or Westernization (e.g. Turkey and Japan).

A

Accountability

The term accountability describes the requirement for answerability regarding the exercise of functions, powers and duties. It is an incremental element of representative **democracy** and good governance. Accountability implies restriction, careful monitoring and vigorous scrutiny of governmental powers. Competitive elections are deemed the ultimate measure of governmental accountability in democratic political systems. The elected representatives exercise decision-making powers on behalf of their electorate, to whom they are subsequently accountable. Transparency is, therefore, an essential part of government accountability. Institutional arrangements ensuring accountability in political systems include ministerial responsibility, collective responsibility, etc., and where these are seen to have failed, they give way to other mechanisms that allow for accountability, such as parliamentary investigations and public inquiries.

The globalization process can have positive and negative implications for accountability. On the one hand, technologies associated with globalization have made it much easier to disseminate and transmit information (for instance, via the **internet**). **Civil society** actors, for instance, are able to keep governments under much closer scrutiny than ever before. On the other hand, economic globalization is also seen to have led to the extension of the governance powers of intergovernmental organizations such as the **International Monetary Fund**, the **World Bank** and the **World Trade Organization**, to give but three prominent examples. With the growing powers of these organizations, questions of accountability and transparency in decision-making processes have been raised repeatedly. This is an issue that has also been raised in the context of the **European Union**. Critics argue that these international institutions operate primarily on an intergovernmental basis, providing insufficient access for civil society organizations. It is claimed that decision-making within these institutions is non-transparent and non-representative. At the centre of these arguments, therefore, are the intergovernmental character and the growing powers of international organizations. Another line of critique pursued by radical liberals points to a massive democratic deficit at the global level. These critics argue that the structure of the international system is determined by only a small number of states, often referred to as the 'West', in which a significant amount of economic and military power is concentrated. The power exerted by the so-called West perpetuates structural inequality. Scholars such as Danielle Archibugi, **David Held**, Mary Kaldor and Jan Aart Scholte have called for the democratization of global politics. (See also **Global Governance**.)

Acid Rain

Acid rain is a widespread form of **air pollution** that cannot be territorially contained. It refers to rain containing a larger concentration of acid than would normally be present in the atmosphere. The primary cause of this phenomenon is the release of sulphur dioxide and nitrogen oxides into the atmosphere, where they react with water, oxygen and other chemicals resulting in mild but dangerous concentrations of sulphuric and nitric acid. Principal sources of the emission of acid-producing gases can be natural (e.g. volcanic activity) or man-made (e.g. the burning of fossil fuels in power plants and vehicles). Acid rain has a variety of effects, damaging forests, fish stocks, and human health.

In recent years, acid rain has dramatically increased in many parts of Europe, Asia and America. It creates a **collective goods** problem since the deposition of acid rain usually occurs far away from the actual source of the pollution, being influenced by wind direction, atmospheric conditions and rainfall, and thus often crossing national boundaries.

Acid rain has been the subject of several bilateral and regional arrangements. Canada and the USA and several European states have agreed to limit air pollution for mutual benefit. However, industrial growth in parts of Eastern Europe, Russia and China will continue to be a significant source of acid rain as coal with a high sulphur content is burned there in order to generate electricity. (See also **Climate Change**.)

Acquired Immune Deficiency Syndrome (AIDS)

AIDS is a disease caused by the **Human Immunodeficiency Virus (HIV)**. HIV is transmitted through the exchange of body fluids. The most common known ways of infection are sexual intercourse, blood transfusion and contact with infected blood (e.g. through intravenous needles), but also include prenatal contact between an infected mother and her child and infected breast milk.

AIDS was diagnosed for the first time in 1981 in the USA. During the past 20 years the number of infections has increased dramatically. In many ways the spread of globalization has facilitated the spread of HIV. The increase in **migration** flows and tourism facilitated by the transport revolution has resulted in the spread of HIV across the planet. According to the joint United Nations Programme on HIV/AIDS (UNAIDS), in 2004 39.4m. people were infected with HIV and 3.1m. died as a consequence of AIDS. Since 1980 approximately 19m. deaths have been caused by AIDS (for recent figures, see http://unaids.org).

AIDS has become a global health problem with tremendous social and economic consequences, particularly in the **Third World**. The AIDS pandemic is among the most pressing and immediate problems of the international community, for it cannot be efficiently addressed by individual governments alone. In response to the pandemic, the **World Health Organization** has initiated a Global Programme on AIDS containing three main objectives: to prevent the spread of HIV; to provide a caring environment for those who are already infected; and to co-ordinate national and international research efforts, treatment and prevention.

The pattern of the pandemic is very different across the world. In some African countries, for instance, more than 25% of the adult population of working age are infected. In fact, AIDS has overtaken malaria as the dominant killer disease in Africa. In many ways, AIDS is a disease of **poverty**. Poverty creates the conditions for greater susceptibility and limits the options for effective treatment due to limited savings, declines in household productivity and the absence of effective public health systems. Consequently, poverty structures the pandemic and the outcome of the sickness in developing countries. Indeed, AIDS is now viewed as one of the biggest obstacles to **development** in the **Third World**.

Advertising

Advertisements are messages that aim to inform or influence their recipients, and form a crucial part of commercial enterprises in a capitalist system. They intend to sell either a product or a service, to seek support and participation, to raise awareness, or to provide information.

Most **multinational companies** have developed global marketing strategies in order to reach consumers dispersed across the world. Thus, the emergence of global markets for products and services has fostered the **deterritorialization** of business strategies. Through advertising, international and global commodities have successfully penetrated the daily lives of people across the globe.

Advertising is closely linked to **consumerism**. It aims to generate and satisfy material desires. Potential customers are induced by advertisements to purchase commodities and services, some of which might otherwise have been regarded as non-essential. Design, **branding**, packaging and display have become major preoccupations in contemporary markets, and are as important to the success of commodities as their utility. As such, they constitute an important part of surplus accumulation through the creation of a unique selling point. Global communication in the form of advertising has facilitated the spread and intensification of **commodification** and consumerism around the world.

So great is the influence of international advertising through the **mass media**, particularly television, that some governments have attempted to restrict and control the flow of communication and commodities across their national borders in order to protect their national space.

Advertising is also crucial for the emergence of international culture. Many multinational companies have linked their products and services with the performance of actors, artists and athletes. Global sporting events such as the Olympic Games have effectively become important branding events and many international sport or music broadcasts are nowadays unthinkable without advertising sponsorship.

Global advertising has constituted a critical ground for arguments regarding the nature of **capitalism**—as to whether corporations are presenting potential buyers with 'choice', or seducing their customers with tyranny. For those who favour the latter view, advertising is considered a key technology for deluding consumers into thinking they are the agents, while masking the real source of agency, the producers themselves.

African Union (AU)

The African Union is a pan-African organization (see **International Organization**; **International Governmental Organization (IGO)** and **Regionalism**). It was launched in Durban, South Africa, in 2002 as the successor of the

Organization of African Unity (OAU) and includes the African Economic Community (AEC). The OAU was founded in 1963. It was driven by the various **decolonization** processes that dominated Africa in this period. This was reflected in its mandate, which emphasized the enhancement of **sovereignty** of the member states, non-intervention in domestic affairs and respect for post-colonial borders.

In 1991 the Abuja Treaty established the AEC on the basis of a commitment to achieve full African economic integration, including the free movement of people, goods, services and factors of production, the creation of a single market, economic and monetary union, including an African central bank and a single African currency, and the establishment of an African parliament. The original treaty stipulated that the AEC is to rely on the creation of Regional Economic Communities (RECs).

The commitment to the AEC has been reasserted by the AU. To date the AU has 53 member states and includes seven RECs. These are the Arab Maghreb Union, the Economic Community of West African States, the Economic Community of Central African States, the Common Market for East and Southern Africa, the Southern African Development Community, the Intergovernmental Authority on Development and the Community of Sahelian-Saharan States. Thus, the mandate of the AU goes beyond political union, emphasizing economic **development** and economic integration. In addition, it includes a **security** dimension, reflecting serious concerns about the stability of Africa.

Its organizational structure comprises the AU Assembly of Heads of State, the Executive Council (of ministers), the AU Commission, the Pan-African Parliament and the African Court of People's and Human Rights. As such it has certain parallels with the organizational structure of the **European Union**. However, the AU remains an intergovernmental organization. There are also parallels with the **United Nations**, in particular with the UN Security Council. The AU Peace and Security Council recognizes the destabilizing effect of the numerous internal conflicts that plague many AU member states. While the AU is based on the principle of sovereignty, non-intervention is subject to certain exceptions. The AU Assembly of Heads of States can decide to intervene in the domestic affairs of member states in case of 'war crimes, genocide or crimes against humanity'. AU peace-keeping forces have been deployed in Burundi, in the Darfur region of Sudan and in Somalia. (Website: http://www.africa-union.org.)

Agribusiness

Agribusiness is a term used to refer to the various businesses involved in the modern food production chain, and describes the vertical integration of large-scale agriculture and farming. The term **corporate farming** is also often used.

Agribusinesses bring together such diverse agricultural activities as farming, seed, agrochemicals, farm machinery, wholesaling, food processing, distribution and retail sales. The benefits of vertical integration in the agricultural sector include economies of scale, larger market shares, control over the whole production chain, as well as enhanced competitiveness.

Corporate farming has been criticized from several quarters. From a consumer perspective, the concentration of market power has potential negative outcomes. The absence of competition, for instance, could help monopolists keep prices high. In addition, large-scale farming and vertical integration has caused many undesirable environmental side effects, including the loss of **biodiversity** and natural habitat, affecting the overall quality of agricultural produce and food products.

Aid

Foreign aid and **development** assistance describe financial and other forms of support (including the provision of goods and services), made available by one international actor in order to help another. This can also include loans and grants from public and private sources. Depending on its purpose, aid aims either at political and economic development or at humanitarian assistance.

Financial aid has become a major source of currency for many **Third World** countries. It is given by national governments, private donors, international aid agencies, multilateral institutions such as the **World Bank**, or by development **non-governmental organizations** (such as **Oxfam**). International aid provided by national governments is often explicitly or implicitly linked with foreign policy aims. The promise and granting of aid, or its obverse, the threat to withhold or cut aid, are important instruments in the foreign policy mix of a **nation state**. A classic example of financial aid as a foreign policy instrument was the Marshall Plan, which was the economic face of the Cold War strategy of the Truman Administration. It had political and economic implications and was aimed at strengthening Western Europe as a potential ally against the Soviet Union. An oft-quoted critique of financial aid as a foreign policy instrument is the potential establishment of a donor-recipient relationship, ultimately empowering the donor and creating a dependency culture.

Financial aid is often subject to conditions. The **International Monetary Fund**, for instance, can influence the economies of the states receiving its aid packages, as the aid is often tied to certain political and economic conditionalities.

Aid also includes offers of humanitarian assistance by individuals, international institutions, national governments, relief organizations and private actors in order to respond on a temporary basis to natural disasters or emergency conflict situations. Humanitarian assistance is not a duty under current international law; it is more a moral obligation. There are moves to make humanitarian assistance a legal requirement rather than a form of voluntary assistance. Those in a crisis, natural or man-made, could, therefore, demand humanitarian assistance from the international community, at least in the form of the provision of a minimum level of subsistence.

Air Pollution

Air pollution describes the modification of the natural characteristics of the atmosphere by chemical and biological agents. The causes of air pollution may be natural or induced by human activity (anthropogenic causes). Natural causes include volcanic eruptions, dust from natural sources, methane (emitted by animals), smoke and carbon monoxide from wild fires, or radon gas from minerals and pine trees, which emit volatile organic compounds and oxygen. Anthropogenic sources include industrial activity in general, the use of vehicles with internal combustion engines, incinerators and power plants. Oil refining, landfill sites, aerosol sprays and refrigeration and military activities (chemical, biological and nuclear weapons) also fall into this category.

In globalization discourse air pollution is connected to enhanced industrial activity. Widespread industrialization and the increase in the burning of fossil fuels to generate electricity are said to have contributed to a dramatic increase in levels of air pollution, with potentially disastrous consequences for human life and the environment. **Acid rain** and **global warming** are but two examples of the negative consequences of human industrial activity in this context.

Al-Jazeera

Al-Jazeera is a Qatar-based Arabic television network with an estimated 50m. viewers world-wide. Since its launch in 1996 it has gained a wide international audience due to its controversial broadcasts. It has presented programmes critical of autocratic governments in the Persian (Arabian) Gulf. In 2001, Al-Jazeera broadcasted videos of Osama bin Laden and other al-Qaeda leaders justifying the attacks on the World Trade Center on 11 September. Since then the network has remained in the public eye due to its news coverage of the Middle East and the wars in Afghanistan and in Iraq. Some of the broadcasts from these war zones have accused the USA of committing war crimes, and have made a powerful impression on already alienated Muslim populations around the world.

The USA has repeatedly accused Al-Jazeera of engaging in a world-wide propaganda war by broadcasting videos and messages of various terrorist groups, in order to deliberately undermine the position of the USA in the Middle East, and to incite hatred and terrorism in the Muslim world and among Muslim populations in the West. In response, Al-Jazeera has highlighted its independence, its lack of bias and the impartiality of its coverage. It aims to make information and different opinions available to its predominantly Muslim audience. Its real impact is difficult to measure but the controversy surrounding Al-Jazeera bears testimony to the power and global reach of the media and contemporary information technology. (See also **Mass Media**.) (Website: http://www.aljazeera.net.)

Americanization

Globalization is often described as being another name for Americanization, a process by which the USA extends its economic and cultural influence globally. The global reach and influence of US companies such as Microsoft, McDonald's, CNN and Coca-Cola are cited as among the most vivid expressions of Americanization. The overwhelming political and economic power of the USA, particularly following the end of the Cold War, makes this a plausible view. Many large **multinational companies** are based in the USA. US corporate interests and US preferences have, furthermore, dictated much of the neo-liberal agenda of the global political economy. In that sense the Americanization thesis seems to hold more water than the neo-liberal **hyperglobalization** thesis, which suggests the end of the **nation state** as multinational companies begin to assume powers exceeding those of states.

An extension of the Americanization thesis is the notion of **Westernization**, whereby the world is slowly being transformed to conform with American/ Western values. Thus, globalization is seen as a dynamic process spreading the structures, institutions and culture of 'Western modernity', such as **liberal democracy**, **consumerism**, **free trade**, **capitalism**, the English language and American/Western-dominated **mass media**, and this is seen as leading eventually to **cultural homogenization** (see **Appadurai, Arjun**). The process of homogenization works simultaneously at several levels of social, political, economic and cultural interaction, obliterating particularities and traditions, obscuring local cultures and suppressing local self-determination. Modernization theory is implicated in this view as all particularities are brought together in a symbolic hierarchy, with movement up the hierarchy being symbolized by the increasing adoption of American culture and value systems. The term has also been used to describe new forms of **colonialism**, exercised through **cultural imperialism**, in particular when related to the loss of cultural diversity.

While the Americanization thesis is very popular, particularly among various critics of contemporary globalization, it needs to be pointed out that neither the USA nor American corporations are all-powerful. Indeed, half of the largest multinational companies are Japanese. Nor is the flow of cultural norms and ideas entirely one-directional. Japanese management techniques, for instance, are being taught at most Western business schools. (See also **Coca-Colonization**.)

Amnesty International

Amnesty International is an international non-governmental organization focusing on **human rights** issues. It was founded in 1961 by the British lawyer Peter Benenson as a protest movement, but has transformed into a fully-fledged non-governmental organization with an organizational structure, goals and tasks. It purports to be independent of any government, political ideology, economic interests or religion. Amnesty International has more than 1.5m. members and supporters in over 150 countries.

Amnesty International is essentially a monitoring organization that sends researchers to investigate claims of human rights abuses. It publicizes its findings and mobilizes its members to lobby to stop activities infringing on human rights. It depends on the responsiveness of an attentive public throughout the world and uses tactics of direct lobbying by writing letters, protesting and demonstrating, organizing fundraising activities, and education and information measures. It has a reputation for impartiality and has monitored and criticized human rights abuses world-wide, including in the USA, Germany and France. The organization is driven by three broad goals: to release all prisoners of conscience, to put an end to all forms of torture and the death penalty, and to ensure fair and prompt trial for all political prisoners. It opposes all human rights abuses whether by governments or any other groups. In order to achieve its goals, Amnesty International employs a wide variety of instruments.

Amnesty International is governed by an international executive committee, a secretary-general, who implements policy decisions, and an international secretariat, headed by the secretary-general. The headquarters of Amnesty International are located in London. The organization is represented in the **United Nations** and is officially recognized by the Council of Europe, the **European Union**, the Organization of American States and the Organization of African Unity. (Website: http://www.amnesty.org.)

Andean Group

Founded in 1969, the Andean Group is a regional organization compromising Bolivia, Colombia, Ecuador, Peru and Venezuela. Its member states have made major efforts to develop an economic union through trade **liberalization**, **development** programmes and investment creation. Although Chile was among the founding members, it withdrew later. Since 1995, the member states have been establishing a **customs union**. (See also **Regionalism**.)

Antarctic Treaty System

The Antarctic Treaty System constitutes an important and wide-ranging international regime dealing with military, resource and environmental issues. It is an example of **global governance**, the main purpose of which is to regulate the international relations of the Antarctic. It comprises the Antarctic Treaty and several related conventions and protocols. The Antarctic Treaty was concluded in 1959 between 12 states (Argentina, Australia, Belgium, Chile, France, Japan, New Zealand, Norway, South Africa, the Soviet Union, the United Kingdom and the USA). It sets the Antarctic continent aside as a scientific preserve and bans any military activity on it. As such it was the first disarmament agreement involving the Cold War adversaries, the Soviet Union and the USA, and designated Antarctica as a nuclear weapons-free zone.

Subsequent agreements have dealt with environmental issues, including measures for the conservation of the flora and fauna and marine life in

Antarctica, as well as the regulation of mineral resources, and environmental protection.

The Antarctic Treaty System is based on five communal norms: the acknowledgement of an 'Antarctic community' for the use and management of the continent, non-militarization, scientific co-operation, environmental protection and abeyance of territorial claims (see **collective goods**). The international forum for the management of the Antarctic region conducts the yearly consultative meetings of the Antarctic Treaty System. Currently, 44 countries are part of the Antarctic Treaty System. However, only 27 states participate in the consultative meetings. These include the original 12 signatories and 15 other countries (Brazil, Bulgaria, the People's Republic of China, Ecuador, Finland, Germany, India, Italy, the Republic of Korea, the Netherlands, Peru, Poland, Spain, Sweden and Uruguay). The non-consultative parties are Austria, Canada, Colombia, Cuba, the Czech Republic, Denmark, Greece, Guatemala, Hungary, the Democratic People's Republic of Korea, Papua New Guinea, Romania, Slovakia, Switzerland, Turkey, Ukraine and Venezuela.

The Antarctic Treaty System is currently outside the **United Nations** framework and there are calls from non-signatory states to relocate the regime in the Common Heritage of Mankind Principle or to create a world wilderness reserve in order to prevent the exploitation of the Antarctic continent by the signatories. (For further information, see: http://www.antarctica.ac.uk.)

Anti-globalization (Movement)

Opposition, or resistance, to globalization has taken various forms. It has been highly fragmented, and has included such different groups as the **Zapatista Movement** in Mexico, American militias, Aum Shinrikyo in Japan, environmental NGOs, the women's movement, New Ageists, and religious fundamentalists. It has come from the left and the right of the political spectrum, from the particularist protectionists and the universalist protectionists. Uniting the many different hues and views of the anti-globalization movement is its opposition to neo-liberal globalization, or corporate globalization. It broadly aims to fight the hegemony of finance, the monopolization of knowledge, **mass media** and communications, the destruction of cultures, and the degradation of nature. It claims to fight for equity, social justice, **democracy** and **security** for everyone.

Particularist protectionists are firmly on the right of the political spectrum. They blame neo-liberal globalization for many of the economic and social problems nation states are facing today. Prominent representatives of particularist protectionist agendas include such people as Patrick Buchanan, Jörg Haider and Jean-Marie Le Pen. Motivated by a fear of reduced living standards, loss of national identity and culture through the diffusion of powerful foreign influences, particularly through the media, and the loss of national **sovereignty**, this anti-globalist rhetoric denounces free trade agendas, the power of **multinational companies** and international institutions, the perceived threat posed by transnational **migration** and imported labour, and the perceived **Americanization** of national cultures and the general permeability of national borders to transnational influences. This form of anti-globalization is not restricted to the global North. In the global South, opposition to American-style neo-liberal globalization has also given rise to nationalist populism and religious **fundamentalism**. Examples in that context include Hindu nationalist parties in India or Osama bin Laden's al-Qa'ida.

On the left of the political spectrum, a group of loosely organized universalist protectionists is challenging neo-liberal **globalism** (see **Global Justice Movement**). They claim to be guided by the ideals of equality and social justice for all people in the world, not just for the citizens of their own countries. One of the main arguments of this group is that globalization is widening the gap between the haves and the have nots, benefiting the rich (and the richer nations) disproportionately. They include activists and political parties aiming to achieve a level playing field and more equitable relations between the global North and the global South. Also included here are **non-governmental organizations** and campaigners concerned with the environment, **fair trade**, labour standards, **exploitation** and **human rights** issues. These universalist protectionists aim to construct a new international economic and political order based on a global redistribution of wealth and power.

Those countering the argument of increasing disparities argue that **free trade** helps promote growth. They argue that within the developing world, those who have opened up to the market economy are improving their lot through increased trade and **foreign direct investment**, while the 'non-globalizing' group trades less and less, falling into greater **poverty**. The Indian and Chinese examples in recent years are cited to make a case for countries improving their lot by opening up to trade, and the anti-globalization argument for increasing inequalities in these countries is countered by attributing these to bad domestic policies, taxes and social policies.

Appadurai, Arjun

One of the most influential theorists today on globalization, Appadurai is most quoted on his theorization of 'flows', describing the complex movements of people, images, finance, labour technology and culture in a highly unsettled world, and captured in his conceptualization of the five 'scapes', namely ethnoscapes, ideoscapes, financescapes, technoscapes and mediascapes. For Appadurai, understanding globalization entails understanding these complex, dynamic and interactive processes or 'flows'. These 'flows' or 'scapes' are carried on by a variety of agencies. They are not objectively given relations that look the same from every angle, but are constructs deeply influenced by the perspective taken, inflected as they are by the historical, linguistic and political situatedness of different sorts of actors, whether nation states, multinationals, sub-national groups, or religious, political or economic movements, or villages, neighbourhoods or families. There are also disjunctures between the flows, each subject to its own constraints and incentives, and each following increasingly non-isomorphic paths. Thus there are deeply disjunctive relations between human movements, technological flows and financial transfers. Indeed, the most significant flows, Appadurai argues, occur *between* the flows. For instance, the 'new cosmopolitanism', brought about by movements of people and capital, unites cultural, financial and political flows within and between Western and non-Western countries in a single, conceptual whole. Appadurai coined the term 'alternative modernities' to link this with the increased **deterritorialization** of the globe and the movement of people, capital and political movements across cultural and national boundaries. He is also distinctive in not conflating the notions of 'nation' and 'state', arguing that **diaspora** populations around the world comprise emerging 'post-nations' that deterritorialize states.

In a major departure from theories of cultural convergence, Appadurai contends that globalization does not entail **homogenization**; indeed, there is no single cultural or economic hegemon. The processes of standardization and diversification, convergence and fragmentation occur simultaneously. The articulation of cultural domination is site- and region-specific. Thus, **Americanization** might be one embodiment of cultural power, but Japanization might be more worrying than Americanization for Koreans, or Indianization imminently more threatening for Sri Lankans.

Globalization, for Appadurai, is marked by a new role for the imagination in social life. The global media have no small role to play here, blurring the distinction between the realistic and the fictional, so that people are able to live and share in many imagined lives. Imagination is no longer a matter of individual genius, escapism or aesthetics, but a faculty that informs the daily lives of ordinary people in myriad ways, whether it is individuals weighing up their **migration** options, or resisting state violence, seeking social redress or designing new forms of civic association across national boundaries. The imagination thus has a split character—while it is in and through the imagination that the modern citizen is disciplined and controlled, it is also the faculty through which collective patterns of dissent and new designs for collective life emerge.

Arms Control

Arms control refers to international agreements designed to regulate levels of armaments by limiting the acquisition and deployment of military capabilities. While global interconnectedness might act as a disincentive to war, and the growth of governance at a suprastate level brings greater possibilities of controlling arms, spending on defence and armaments continues to grow (see **Global Governance**). Examples of attempts at arms control through conventions and treaty ratifications include the nuclear non-proliferation treaty regime, the Chemical Weapons Convention, and global controls for biological weapons and land mines. Suprastate governance has also led to the emergence of new forms of conflict management and arms control, such as peace-keeping operations.

Arms control differs from disarmament. The former is based on the premise that armaments will continue to exist while the latter aims to abolish arms in general. Both arms control and disarmament have a long history, and have aimed to reduce the risk and the impact of military conflict by limiting the use and availability of military assets. However, disarmament has rarely been successful. Most examples of disarmament are enforced reductions imposed by victorious parties on defeated enemies.

There are two primary forms of arms control: bilateral and multilateral agreements. The record of bilateral arms control agreements diverges substantially from multilateral ones. This might, in part, be accounted for by the fact that bilateral arrangements are much easier to negotiate, control and enforce than multilateral agreements. Both face many obstacles and depend on the improvement of relations between the involved parties. Since they tend not to address the source of underlying conflicts and tensions, rivalry can easily resurface. In addition, a lack of mutual trust and incentives to 'cheat' and gain subsequent strategic advantages can potentially undermine arms control agreements. Consequently, until recently arms control agreements have controlled mostly obsolete weapons or ones with little strategic use for the negotiating parties. (See also **Arms Trade**; for examples of arms control efforts, see http://www.fas.org./nuke/control.)

Arms Trade

While much international effort has been directed to control and restrict the proliferation of **weapons of mass destruction**, i.e. nuclear, biological and chemical weapons, the amount of market transactions in conventional arms has grown substantially. In fact, according to some sources, global military expenditure and arms trade constitute the largest spending in the world. The increasing number of small arms in circulation at legal and black markets has become a pressing issue for developed and **developing countries** alike.

As world trade globalizes, so does the arms trade. The international market for armaments has become an important source of income for some states. Major arms traders include France, the People's Republic of China, Russia, the United Kingdom and the USA. However, established patterns of arms trade are changing as arms manufacture and arms trading have increased substantially in some **Third World** countries. Examples include Argentina, Brazil, India, Israel and South Africa. Attempts to restrict the flow of arms are as old as they are numerous. In the 1990s, in the aftermath of the first Gulf War, several major international initiatives were launched in order to control the flow of arms into crisis regions and countries. Examples include a comprehensive International Code of Conduct proposed by a group of Nobel Peace Laureates in 1995 and the **European Union** regional Code of Conduct (1998). However, there are many obstacles. Centres of instability arguably provide potentially good markets for small arms, pointing to the incentive to sell armaments and to obscure restrictions or to block initiatives in international multilateral organizations. Financial transparency of sales has remained yet another abiding problem. (See also **Arms Control**.)

ARPANET – *see* Internet

ASEAN Regional Forum (ARF)

Established in 1994, the ASEAN Regional Forum (ARF) is a multipurpose institution designed to introduce structure into the post-Cold War Asia-Pacific, to prevent misunderstandings, and to facilitate regional confidence-building. The end of the Cold War left members of the **Association of South East Asian Nations (ASEAN)** concerned about the rise of China and the dis-engagement of the USA from the Asia-Pacific. ARF is the principal forum of **security** dialogue in the region, bringing together ASEAN member states (Brunei, Cambodia, Indonesia, Laos Malaysia, Myanmar, the Philippines, Singapore, Thailand and Viet Nam) and a number of dialogue partners (Australia, Canada, the People's Republic of China, the **European Union**, India, Japan, New Zealand, the Democratic People's Republic of Korea, the Republic of Korea, Mongolia, Papua New Guinea, Russia and the USA).

ARF draws from the ASEAN experience and is characterized by a process of consensus decision-making and minimal institutionalization. In 1995, the ARF Concept Paper envisioned the development of the forum to proceed in three stages, starting from confidence-building, moving to preventative diplomacy, and culminating in the creation of a conflict resolution capability. At the eighth ARF in July 2001 the principles of preventative diplomacy were adopted.

The achievements of ARF to date are modest. However, the forum has provided ASEAN with the possibility of presenting itself as a relatively coherent regional organization. In addition, it has contributed to fostering a sense of strategic community in the Asia-Pacific. (Website: http://www.asean regionalforum.org/.)

Asia-Europe Meeting (ASEM)

The Asia-Europe Meeting (ASEM) is an inter-regional dialogue bringing together the Heads of State of the member states of the **Association of South East Asian Nations**, Japan, the People's Republic of China, the Republic of Korea and Heads of State of the member states of the **European Union** as well as the president of the European Commission.

ASEM was an initiative originating from ASEAN's 1995 Bangkok summit to strengthen Asia-Europe linkages in political, economic and cultural terms. The inaugural meeting was held in Bangkok, Thailand, in March 1996. ASEM is envisaged as an informal gathering of national leaders to discuss topics of mutual interest. The institutional framework for the dialogue is being provided by the Asia-Europe Foundation and the Asia-Europe Business Forum, a private-sector initiative. (Website: http://www.aseminfoboard.org/.)

Asian Financial Crisis – *see* Global Financial Crisis

Asia-Pacific Economic Co-operation (APEC)

Asia-Pacific Economic Co-operation (APEC) is a forum bringing together economies from both sides of the Pacific. APEC was founded in 1989 as a response to growing economic interdependencies in the Asia-Pacific region. APEC's objective is to react collectively to changes in the international economic order brought about by the globalization process and the end of the Cold War, and to promote stability, economic growth and prosperity. Although APEC began as an informal dialogue group with limited participation, it has evolved to become the premier forum for facilitating economic growth, trade, co-operation and investment in the region. APEC has no treaty obligations required of its participants and operates on the basis of non-binding commitments, open dialogue and consensus, reflecting the diversity of its member economies and the preferences of some of its Asian members. Currently APEC has 21 members: Australia, Brunei, Canada, Chile, the People's Republic of China, Hong Kong (China), Indonesia, Japan, the Republic of Korea, Malaysia, Mexico, New Zealand, Papua New Guinea, Peru, the Philippines, Russia, Singapore, the Republic of China (Taiwan), Thailand, the USA and Viet Nam.

APEC contains three processes: economic and technical co-operation promoting economic and human resource development, a trade and investment **liberalization** agenda and a **sustainable development** agenda. In the 1994 Bogor Declaration, APEC members committed themselves to establish a **free trade** area by 2010 for industrialized economies and by 2020 for **developing countries**.

APEC faces a variety of challenging problems, partly arising from the political and economic diversity of its members. One issue is the fear of Western domination of the APEC agenda, and the possible marginalization of the **Association of South East Asian Nations**. Thus, the vision of an East Asian Economic Group, limited exclusively to Asian members, has been promoted by leaders such as Mohamed Mahathir. In a way, this reflects a 'clash' between Western values (see **Americanization**) and so-called Asian values. More seriously, different economic ideologies are competing within APEC (e.g. **neo-liberalism** and the Asian version of state-led **development**), resulting in clear differences about how far trade liberalization should go. (Website: http://www.apec.org.)

Association of South East Asian Nations (ASEAN)

The Association of South East Asian Nations (ASEAN) is the most prominent international intergovernmental organization in south-east Asia. It was formed in 1967 when Indonesia, Malaysia, Thailand, Singapore and the Philippines signed the Bangkok Declaration. Subsequent enlargements brought Brunei (1984), Viet Nam (1995), Laos (1997), Myanmar (1997) and Cambodia (1999) into the organization. ASEAN's original aims were to counter the political influence of Communist countries, such as North Viet Nam and China, to avoid superpower involvement, to reconcile Indonesia with the rest of the region and to create a stable regional environment allowing the member states to concentrate on their respective state-building efforts. Among the core principles of ASEAN are non-intervention, consensus, consultation and minimal institutionalization, underlining the importance of **sovereignty** for the five founding members.

Although little happened in terms of co-operation in the years following 1967, the reduction of US commitment in the region following the Nixon Doctrine, the Communist victories in Indochina and an increasing uneasiness regarding China forced the ASEAN governments to put aside their differences and to adopt a compromise which would accommodate their diverse interests and preferences. This compromise came in 1971 in the form of the Declaration on a Zone of Peace, Freedom and Neutrality, re-emphasizing the non-alignment of ASEAN in the superpower conflict and the non-aggressive nature of the Association. In February 1976, the leaders of the ASEAN member states met at the first ASEAN Heads of Government Conference in Bali, Indonesia. During the summit, two major agreements were signed: the Treaty of Amity and Co-operation in South East Asia and the ASEAN Concord.

An important stepping stone in the development of ASEAN's organizational maturity was the invasion of Cambodia by Viet Nam in 1978. Despite differences among individual member states, ASEAN was able to speak with one voice internationally and proved to be successful in rallying international opinion in various fora, most notably in the **United Nations.**

Following the end of the Cold War, ASEAN faced a fundamentally changed international environment. It responded with the Singapore summit in 1992, which resulted in several major initiatives. The first was an agreement that laid down the foundation of the **ASEAN Regional Forum** in order to tackle broader regional **security** issues. The second major initiative was the commitment to establish the ASEAN Free Trade Area (AFTA). This was partly driven by the development of **regionalism** in other parts of the world (see **North American Free Trade Agreement**). Furthermore, ASEAN members agreed to hold formal Heads of Government meetings every three years. In 1995, at the Bangkok summit, ASEAN's member states made commitments to create a South East Asian Nuclear Weapon Free Zone and to engage in a regular inter-regional dialogue with Europe through the mechanism of the **Asia-Europe Meeting**.

The **Asian financial crisis** of 1997/98 struck some of ASEAN's member states particularly hard. ASEAN's failure to respond collectively in an effi-cient manner to the crisis and the ensuing turmoil in Indonesia and East Timor have undermined the credibility of the organization and thrown ASEAN into disarray. ASEAN members have attempted to revitalize the organization and issued the ASEAN Vision 2020 in 1997. Furthermore, a series of measures was adopted at the Hanoi summit in 1998, including the acceleration of the AFTA process.

The terrorist attacks on the World Trade Center in New York and on the Pentagon in Washington, DC, on 11 September 2001, and the subsequent 'war on terrorism', led to the ASEAN Declaration on Joint Action to Counter Terrorism in November 2001, the ASEAN-USA Joint Declaration for Co-operation to Combat International Terrorism in 2002, and the Joint Declaration on Co-operation to Combat Terrorism between the **European Union** and ASEAN in 2003.

At the October 2003 summit in Bali, ASEAN leaders signed a Declaration of ASEAN Concord II. Among other things, this document discusses the setting up of an ASEAN Security Community, an ASEAN Economic Com-munity and the establishment of an ASEAN Socio-Cultural Community.

At the same meeting, the People's Republic of China and ASEAN agreed to work faster toward a mutual trade agreement, which was eventually signed in 2004. Japan has also signed an agreement to reduce tariff and **non-tariff bar-riers** with ASEAN. This reflects the idea of broader co-operation in the Asia-Pacific region, which finds its expression in ASEAN Plus Three (to include Japan, the People's Republic of China and the Republic of Korea) and the East Asian Economic Group. (Website: http://www.aseansec.org.)

Autarky

The term autarky describes a closed and self-sufficient economy, or a country which has only very limited interaction with the rest of the international system. It is doubtful, however, whether it is possible to achieve complete autarky. No nation state and no economy can detach itself completely from the rest of the world and the geopolitical and economic system they are embedded in. Examples of attempts at autarky might be found in the period following the economic turmoil of the 1920s and the rise of Communism and Fascism, when a drive for self-sufficiency was observable in Germany and the Soviet Union.

According to neo-liberal economic theories, closed economies are inefficient due to limited markets, limited investment and low levels of productivity induced by the lack of competition (see **Neo-liberalism**). Today, there are hardly any examples of closed economies. The exception is, perhaps, the Democratic People's Republic of Korea (North Korea), with its government ideology of *Juche* (self-reliance). Even so, North Korea conducts a small amount of trade with the People's Republic of China and Japan.

Automatic Teller Machine (ATM)

Also referred to as cash dispenser or cash point, an ATM is an electronic device allowing bank customers to withdraw cash from their accounts and to make balance enquiries. The first ATM was installed by Barclays Bank in London in 1967. Since then the use of ATMs has spread around the world. Nowadays, most ATMs are connected by inter-bank networks, thus enabling customers to access their accounts from an ATM which belongs to a different bank and to withdraw foreign currency while abroad.

The spread of ATMs has revolutionized the global circulation of currency and contributed significantly to the **deterritorialization** of money. The widespread international usage of ATMs has facilitated the electronic global circulation of major currencies.

B

Ballistic Missile Technology

'Ballistic' refers to the science of the propulsion, flight, and the impact of projectiles. Ballistic missiles are closely linked to **weapons of mass destruction** since they can carry nuclear, conventional, biological, or chemical warheads, and come with their own warning and acquisition radar systems. They are categorized by range and basing mode, and include short-range, medium-range, intermediate-range and intercontinental ballistic missiles, as well as submarine-launched ballistic missiles. Ballistic missiles can also be launched from a ship or an aircraft.

Ballistic missile technology has now been around for more than 50 years. This technology was first deployed by Germany during the Second World War. Today, the know-how and infrastructure to manufacture and deploy ballistic missiles is widely dispersed, with more than 25 countries in possession of ballistic missiles. These include countries such as the USA, Russia, the United Kingdom, France, China, the Democratic People's Republic of Korea (North Korea), Iran, Iraq, Israel, India, Pakistan and Libya. Many of the countries that are acquiring ballistic missiles also have programmes to develop nuclear, biological, or chemical warheads. Most countries also possess short- or medium-range missiles for battlefield use. While these pose threats within the regions of their deployment, the development of longer-range missiles and the capability to use these to deliver nuclear, biological or chemical warheads, creates a threat to global **security**.

Two factors related to globalization have accounted for the wide dispersal of ballistic missile capabilities. First, technologies that facilitate engineering design and testing, including computers, are much more capable and widely available than they were a generation ago. And second, many nations now possess and manufacture missiles, components, production facilities, and expertise, and are willing to sell or trade these on the international arms market. The international arms market is much less regulated now than during the Cold War, when stringent export controls were in place (see **Arms Trade**).

Among the many contrasting approaches to dealing with threats from existing missiles and missile proliferation are some coercive ones, such as developing missile defences or imposing missile technology export controls, and collaborative approaches such as space launch technology sharing or **arms control** and disarmament.

Bank for International Settlements (BIS)

Established on 17 May 1930, and headquartered in Basel, Switzerland, with representative offices in Hong Kong and Mexico City, the Bank for International Settlements (BIS) might be deemed the first multilateral institution devoted specifically to monitoring transborder financial flows and supervising financial institutions. It is the world's oldest international financial organization and operates under the auspices of **international law**.

In the first instance, following the First World War, BIS was responsible for the collection, administration and distribution of reparations from Germany, as agreed upon in the Treaty of Versailles. After the Second World War, BIS turned its attention to the defence and implementation of the **Bretton Woods system**. Through the 1970s and 1980s, BIS monitored cross-border **capital flows** in the wake of the oil and debt crises, which in turn led to the development of regulatory supervision of internationally active banks.

Today BIS is a supraterritorial institution that fosters co-operation among central banks and other agencies in pursuit of monetary and financial stability. It is based on the 1988 Basel Committee's Capital Accord. Its banking services are provided exclusively to central banks and international organizations. By focusing on providing traditional banking services to member central banks, BIS aims to give the 'lender of last resort' a shoulder to lean on. BIS also acts as a forum to promote discussion and facilitate decision-making processes among central banks and within the international financial community. It is also a centre for economic and monetary research, a prime counter party for central banks in their financial transactions and an agent or trustee in connection with international financial operations.

The bank thus has four main tasks. First, it provides a forum for central bank co-operation. Second, it conducts research contributing to global monetary and financial stability, gathering a wide range of economic data from all countries of the world to provide detailed statistical analysis of economic conditions, and conducting policy-related research aimed at producing recommendations for the structure, functioning, and regulation of the world's financial system. Third, the bank provides traditional banking functions, such as reserve management and clearing of gold transactions for the world's central banks. And finally, the bank acts as a lender of last resort to countries that are facing acute economic crises. It bailed out the central banks of Germany and Austria during the financial crisis of 1931–33, propped up the Italian lira in 1964, helped Mexico out of its **debt crisis** in 1982 and, most recently, contributed significant resources to bailing out Brazil in 1998. The BIS's unit of account is the **International Monetary Fund**'s special drawing right, which is based on a basket of convertible currencies. The reserves account for approximately 7% of the world's total currency.

More recently, doubts about the bank's mandate, including its programme, its effectiveness, and, indeed, the desirability of any existing institution taking the lead role in accounting reform, have been raised. Criticism, particularly from the anti-**capitalism** and anti-globalization camps (see **Anti-globalization (Movement)** and **Global Justice Movement**), have surfaced in the light of serious failures in money-laundering law enforcement, and major breaches of prudence and supervision in the USA, particularly as highlighted in the case of Enron. (Website: http://www.bis.org.)

Beck, Ulrich

A German sociologist who places risk at the centre of his analysis of contemporary social change, Ulrich Beck is widely quoted for his term 'risk society'. Beck sees industrial society as having been replaced by a society riven by insecurities. But characteristic of this emerging global society is also its reflexivity. Like **Giddens**, Beck's view of **modernity** and the risk society is built on the notion of self as a project, the individual's reflexivity being central to these discussions.

Risk is seen primarily in ecological terms. The full import of industrial modernization's legacy of environmental side effects and its repercussions is only becoming apparent now (see, for instance, **Climate Change** and **Global Warming**). In a globalized world, ecological threats are no longer anchored in, or limited to, particular localities. It is a universalizing influence, as perpetrators and victims, rich and poor alike, everywhere in the world, are affected by global ecological problems. Furthermore, these ecological problems multiply over time, leading to what Beck calls a 'boomerang effect'. In a risk society, everyone pursues a 'scorched earth' policy against everyone else. While industrialized nations have put in place stringent measures to curb ecological damage, industries have simply relocated to poorer countries.

For Beck, globalization is a blanket term describing processes by which sovereign states are criss-crossed and indeed, undermined, by transnational actors of varying degrees of power, orientations and identities (see **Transnationalism**). Globalization is not an automatic, unilateral or one-dimensional process, but it can be grasped in the cultural symbols in even the smallest and most mundane aspects of one's everyday life, as all these bear the signature at once of the global and the local, or the glocal. The processes of **glocalization** involve the cultural 'de-' and 're-' location of local cultures as they are justified, shaped and renewed through exchange, dialogue and conflict within a global context.

These interactions, however, do not rule out a process of **cultural homogenization** taking shape in so far as it is becoming a 'single commodity world', with local identities being replaced by symbols and images from the publicity and image departments of **multinational companies**. Beck views this as fundamentally a process of **Americanization**. Indeed, for Beck, contemporary cultural globalization is reflected in a surrender to the values of **commodification** and **consumerism** sold by the purveyors of culture—the media, advertising and communications industries, which find this a promising route to the 'profit paradise' (see **Advertising** and **Branding**). Also consumed are possible or imagined lives, as individuals are presented with a repertoire of images by the media, or the 'global imagination industry' (see **Appadurai, Arjun**).

Beck introduces two other variations to the theme of globalization—globality and **globalism**. The first refers to a sense of everything affecting the whole world, with nothing confined any more to just the level of the local. The latter encapsulates the view that the world market is powerful enough to supplant political action, be it at the local or the national level.

It is not a completely bleak world though; there is potential for the growth of something like a global **citizenship**, as informed opinion and concerted action at a global level is possible with the growth of **civil society**—what Beck terms 'globalization from below'.

Beck's most recent research activities include a long-term empirical study of the sociological and political implications of 'reflexive modernization', and work on a sociological framework to analyse the ambivalences and dynamics of 'cosmopolitan societies'.

Beggar-thy-Neighbour Policies

Governments often try to pursue strategic economic policies that are designed to enhance domestic welfare by promoting trade surpluses that can only be realized at the expense of other countries. Such policies are referred to as 'beggar-thy-neighbour' policies since they increase welfare in one country by worsening economic conditions abroad. While such strategies might be tempting and beneficial in the short term, they are ultimately self-defeating in the long term as other countries will ultimately follow suit or retaliate. They can, therefore, result in trade wars and in a general breakdown of the international trading system.

Examples of beggar-thy-neighbour policies include efforts by one country to counter domestic unemployment through competitive currency devaluations, the imposition of tariffs and quotas on imports, export subsidies and other strategies that adversely affect trading partners and neighbouring countries. These measures are designed to achieve a trade surplus by enhancing the competitiveness of exports, while at the same time limiting imports.

Strategic economic policies were very popular in the 1920s and 1930s when rising unemployment rates and declining productivity levels tempted many capitalist states into undertaking measures to enhance exports and to minimize and substitute imports. Among the measures adopted were, for instance, unilateral currency devaluations. These made exports cheaper and more competitive in international markets. The imposition of tariffs and quotas on imports reduced the amount of imports and stimulated domestic production by favouring domestic goods. Export subsidies further enhanced the competitiveness of exports abroad. In the end the effort to generate trade surpluses by cutting imports for the benefit of domestic economies led to a breakdown of the entire **international trade** system. The disastrous implications of beggar-thy-neighbour policies where addressed at the Bretton Woods conference in 1944, where the reconstruction of the international economy was discussed (see **Bretton Woods System**). Part of the responsibility of the **International Monetary Fund** was to create and ensure economic stability. The introduction of a fixed exchange rate system was supposed to stop countries from devaluing their currencies to gain a competitive edge over their neighbours. The problem returned with the breakdown of the fixed exchange rate system in the 1970s. However, at that time countries were more reluctant to use **exchange rates** to export unemployment, as such policies would have resulted in an increase in domestic inflation.

Beggar-thy-neighbour policies continue to loom as a danger in the international economy. Trade surpluses are a constant cause of friction between states. It is often described by the term neo-mercantilism, a policy whereby a state seeks to maintain a positive balance of trade, or a trade surplus, to promote domestic production and employment by limiting imports through various protectionist measures, stimulating domestic production and actively encouraging exports.

Beijing Declaration

The Beijing Declaration and its Platform for Action (PfA) were the documents adopted by 189 countries at the Fourth World Conference on Women, held in Beijing, People's Republic of China, in September 1995. It reaffirms the fundamental principle that the rights of women and girls are 'an inalienable, integral and indivisible part of universal human rights'. Most countries have subsequently developed national plans of action linked to the PfA. In June 2000, a special session was held in order to follow up on the progress made at the national level in implementing the PfA.

Much preparatory work and lobbying preceded the conference in 1995, both at the governmental level (international, regional and national levels) and at the level of **civil society**. The Action Plan adopted in Beijing is a document of intent that came out of consensus and reflects the detailed negotiations that went on between governments. Critical areas affected by the negotiations included issues around women's reproductive rights, affirmative action to promote more women into positions of power and decision-making, and issues surrounding the girl-child. However, several other issues that were discussed did not find their way into the final document, such as the issue of sexual orientation.

The Beijing Declaration includes six components on different aspects of commitments made by governments in adopting the final outcome, from financing to **accountability** mechanisms. These are its mission statement, its global framework, critical areas of concern, strategic objectives and actions, and institutional arrangements to effect these, including financial arrangements.

The most important aspect of the PfA was its commitment to integrating a gender perspective into all aspects and spheres of society. This commitment to integrate, and take into consideration, women's and men's diverse roles, responsibilities and opportunities has been labelled 'gender mainstreaming'. This is seen today as the only way to achieve the goal of gender equality. (For further information see: http://www.un.org/womenwatch/daw/beijing/platform/declar.htm.)

Biodiversity

The term 'biodiversity' emerged in 1985 as a contraction of the term 'biological diversity', and has since taken on a life of its own. The term broadly refers to the diversity of life on Earth, including the many species that populate the Earth, with their diverse forms and functions, at the genetic, species and habitat levels. The survival of each is dependent on the health of the other two, and together they comprise the ecosystem. This diversity, which is the product of billions of years of evolution, forms the web of life of which human beings are an integral part and on which they depend. Today, the term is used emotively to connote 'life' or 'wilderness' or, indeed, 'conservation' itself.

At issue in debates on globalization today is the loss of biodiversity, which is seen as reducing an ecosystem's ability to recover from natural or man-induced disruption. However, international response to the crisis facing the world's biodiversity has been inadequate and slow in coming. Environmentalists have argued that the increasing integration of the global economy is leading to various irreversible environmental ills, such as tropical deforestation and biodiversity loss (see **Ecologism** and **Environmentalism**). The 1992 Earth Summit in Rio de Janeiro, Brazil (see **United Nations Conference on Environment and Development**), was designed as a joint global effort to prevent further damage to the world's biodiversity. World leaders agreed there on a comprehensive strategy for '**sustainable development**', and adopted the Convention on Biological Diversity. The convention put forward three goals: the conservation of biological diversity, the sustainable use of its components, and the fair and equitable sharing of the benefits from the use of genetic resources. It established some rules for the use of genetic resources and biotechnologies. All parties committed themselves to achieve a significant reduction of the current rate of biodiversity loss at the global, regional and national level by 2010. This target was subsequently endorsed by the World Summit on Sustainable Development.

Bond-rating Agencies

These have been a means of governing global finance, shaped by non-official initiatives. Bond-rating agencies have regulatory authority with respect to financial management, rating creditworthiness not only of companies but also countries. Amongst the prominent bond-rating agencies are Moody's Investor Services and Standard and Poor. While northern countries and firms are able to access bond markets through favourable credit ratings, few southern countries have a credit rating that allows them access to global bond markets. (See also **Credit-rating Agencies** and **Capital Flows**.)

Bové, José

Prominent French farmer, agricultural unionist and anti-globalization activist, José Bové has become an important symbolic figure for the **Global Justice Movement** in the struggle against neo-liberal economic globalization, the unchecked power of international institutions and big business (see also **Neo-liberalism**).

In 1987, José Bové founded an agricultural union, the Confédération Paysanne, or Peasant Confederation, to protect small-scale farmers and agricultural workers against the concentrated power of agribusinesses (see **Agribusiness**). He is a prominent opponent of the introduction and use of genetically-modified crops and hormone-treated meat. Bové has gained an international reputation for his militant methods of direct action against such crops and large multinational businesses (see **Multinational Companies**). He is most famous for his destruction of a McDonald's outlet in Millau, France, in 1999. His aim was to raise awareness of the dangers of globalization. McDonalds, for Bové and his supporters, is a very visible sign of economic globalization representing industrialized agriculture (see also **Americanization**). In 1997, Bové was responsible for the destruction of a Novartis seed production facility and in 2001 he led a protest of Brazilian farmers against the American biotechnology firm Monsanto during which genetically-modified crops and seeds were destroyed.

In 1995, Bové participated in the **Greenpeace** protests against the resumption of French nuclear testing in the Pacific by boarding the Greenpeace ship *Rainbow Warrior*. He was also present at the Seattle protests against the **World Trade Organization** in 1999. While often associated with the **anti-globalization movement**, Bové and his supporters point out that they are not against globalization per se. Rather, their protest is directed against a particular form of economic globalization, largely epitomized by the so-called **Washington Consensus** policies, that promotes the global spread of unchecked **capitalism**.

Brahimi Report

The Brahimi Report, also called the Report of the Panel on UN Peace Operations, is considered a landmark document, recommending drastic changes in the manner in which **United Nations (UN)** peace-keeping and post-conflict peace-building are conceived, planned and executed. The report identified serious shortcomings in the UN's ability to 'confront the lingering forces of war and violence', and helped launch an ongoing effort for institutional change within the UN.

The report is named after the chairman of the panel, Lakhdar Brahimi, a former Algerian minister of foreign affairs and, since 1997, the Under-Secretary-General for Special Assignments in Support of the Secretary-General's Preventive and Peacemaking Efforts. Brahimi and the nine other respected experts on various aspects of conflict prevention, peace-keeping and peace-building on the panel were asked by UN Secretary-General Kofi Annan to outline the processes and changes which would enable and allow the UN to be better prepared to meet the challenges of peace-keeping facing both the member states and the UN in the 21st century. The panel was set up in response to UN member concerns that the UN did not have adequate management and financial systems to support the sharply increased number of peace-keeping operations and peace-keepers it deployed.

The Brahimi Report provided a tangible and implementable set of recommendations on how to improve UN peace-keeping and related activities. It examined shortcomings of the existing system, made realistic recommendations for change, and addressed key political and strategic issues as well as operational and organizational issues. (For further information, see: http://www.un.org/peace/reports/peace_operations/.)

Branding

Brands are augmented products that are differentiated and well positioned versus other products in the category. In order to dominate, a global brand must be a leadership brand in all the important markets in the world. A brand is usually marked by a logo, symbol, trade mark, brand name, colours or shapes, its positioning, its marketing mix, distribution, strategic

principles and **advertising**. Often price, rather than appearance or function-
ality, can constitute the key differentiator, marking a branded product as a
status symbol (e.g. Nike shoes).

The most fundamental innovation of enterprises is often the creation of a
market—the construction of a convincing world of symbols, ideas and
values harnessing the desires of individuals to the consumption of their
products. Global brands, while global in reach, originate in particular countries. The majority of global brands today are based out of the USA. In
non-Western societies, consumption of the brand may help make aspira-
tional American/Western lifestyles slightly more approachable.

No global brand, however, is fully globally standardized in terms of
brand name, packaging and advertising throughout the world. Instead,
global brands simply share the same strategic principles, positioning and
marketing, and comparable brand loyalty in every market throughout the
world, though the marketing mix may vary. For instance, at one end of the
spectrum are Marlboro cigarettes, positioned as a premium brand, a global
brand symbolized the world over by the 'Marlboro man' and 'Marlboro
Country'. Knorr soups, at the other extreme, is not standardized at all. In
yet another variation, a global brand may not carry the same brand name
everywhere. Unilever's detergents are a case in point—they are called Surf
and Wisk in the USA, Persil in the United Kingdom, Skip in Spain, Pollena
in Poland, etc. An oft-cited reason for this is that when companies acquire
other companies that have invested years in building a brand locally, the
acquiring company will retain the same name if it has a popular resonance.

Branding is considered a symptom of an advanced or post-modern consumer culture, where minute differences between products, or minute
improvements in them, can determine variations in demand. Consumption
thus becomes differentiated on the basis of signifiers—their 'brand names'.
Here consumption, or the capacity to consume, is also reflexively consumed,
captured in terms such as 'taste', 'fashion' and 'lifestyle', which become
critical sources of social differentiation, displacing class and political
affiliation. (See also **Consumerism**.)

Bretton Woods System

In July 1944, delegates from 44 countries met in Bretton Woods in the USA
and managed to reach a series of multilateral agreements on the post-Second
World War international economic order. The new framework was based on

a stable, co-operative international monetary system, which would prevent financial crises. The key feature was a system of fixed **exchange rates**. Floating exchange rates had proven to be inherently instable, with devastating consequences not only for individual countries but also for the international system. The new international economic order was to be in stark contrast to the inter-war years. Exchange rates were fixed against the US dollar and the US dollar was fixed to gold at a rate of $35 per ounce. The strength of the US economy, the fixed relationship of the dollar to gold, and the commitment of the US government to convert dollars into gold at that price implied that the US dollar was as good as gold. Thus, the Bretton Woods system managed to secure the advantages of the gold standard without its disadvantages. Countries were committed to ensure the convertibility of their currencies into foreign currencies and to **free trade**.

These agreements were the outcome of lengthy negotiations between the USA and the United Kingdom. There were considerable differences between both positions. The US proposal was drafted by Harry Dexter White and the British plan by the famous economist John Maynard Keynes. Keynes envisioned the establishment of a world reserve currency administered by a central bank with the authority to issue money and to take large-scale action. In case of imbalances in the balance of payments, creditors and debtors could change their policies. Countries with payment surplus would increase their imports from deficit countries and, thus, facilitate the creation of a trade equilibrium. However, the overwhelming political, military and economic power of the USA ensured that White's plan was implemented at Bretton Woods. Consequently, the institutions created as the result of Bretton Woods were born with an underlying neo-liberal economic outlook (see **Neo-liberalism**), which stressed controlling inflation and budgetary austerity rather than actively eradicating **poverty**.

The Bretton Woods system is of historical rather than contemporary relevance. Although the institutions set up as a result of the Bretton Woods agreements are still in existence, they have changed substantially since their inauguration. The fixed exchange rate system collapsed in the 1960s due to economic recovery in Western Europe and Japan and the unwillingness of those countries to revalue their currencies against the US dollar. As a result, US President Nixon decided to sever the link of the US dollar with gold in 1971 and changed the international monetary system.

The Bretton Woods agreement created multilateral international institutions to manage the new international economic system: the **International**

Monetary Fund (IMF) and the International Bank for Reconstruction and Development (IBRID—see **World Bank**), and it is these that continue to play a major role in the global political economy. The underlying neo-liberal ideology that shaped the Bretton Woods agreement has left the World Bank and the IMF as objects of severe criticism.

Bush Doctrine

The Bush Doctrine refers to a set of foreign policy guidelines that were developed in response to the attack on the World Trade Center on 11 September 2001 and formalized in policy terms in a document entitled *The National Security Strategy of the United States of America*, published in September 2002. It encompasses a dramatic redefinition of threats to US **security**, its own interests and its definition of strategy. The doctrine constitutes a significant departure from existing policies of deterrence and containment to preventative war. 'Pre-emptive' military action is justified on the grounds that a threat is 'emerging' or 'sufficient', challenging the traditional assumption that war is only justified when a threat is 'imminent'. The perceived new threat by 'rogue states' and 'terrorist groups' is seen to justify the change as neither are deemed to act rationally or abide by the rules of law. That these agents may gain **weapons of mass destruction** is seen as a crucial and novel factor, justifying where necessary a unilateral response.

In addition to a novel reworking of the doctrine of pre-emption and a stress on unilateral action—reflecting scepticism about the efficacy of institutions such as the **United Nations** Security Council—there is also a utopian dimension to the doctrine, which talks of the need to promote the values of **democracy** and freedoms abroad, through both regime change and the promotion of **free trade** and free markets. Intervention is therefore guided by a mixture of *realpolitik* security interests, together with a more 'idealistic' appraisal of the possibility of creating democracies abroad.

The Bush Doctrine must be assessed within the context of the so-called war on terror. It can also be interpreted as a response to the security challenges arising out of contemporary processes of globalization. Some analysts, for instance, have interpreted the attacks on the World Trade Center as a protest by the **Third World**, which feels increasingly marginalized by neo-liberal globalization (see **Neo-liberalism**). Others regard it as the opening gambit in a **clash of civilizations** between the West and an increasingly assertive and radicalized Islam.

Criticism of the war on terror and the Bush Doctrine has come from several quarters. Critics argue that, far from dealing with the root causes of **terrorism** and insecurity, the Bush Doctrine makes the world an even more insecure place. It has generated an intense debate as to whether it is another form of **imperialism** and whether the USA is in the process of transforming itself into an **empire**.

C

Cable News Network (CNN)

CNN is a cable television network that is widely credited for introducing the concept of 24-hour news coverage, which gained the spotlight in 1991 during the Gulf War. It was founded on 1 June 1980 in Atlanta, USA, by Georgia businessman Ted Turner, together with Reese Schonfeld, a former manager for UPI Television News. It is a division of Turner Broadcasting System, now owned by Time Warner. Its coverage spans a large part of the globe, with its branded networks and services reaching more than 1,500m. people in over 212 countries, often in their local languages. Its satellite signal is said be within reach of 98% of the world's population.

CNN's 24-hour news coverage was considered a path-breaking style, though critics have lamented the compression of editorial decision-making processes in its rush to air events. As CNN acquired a global reach, there were those who labelled this the **Americanization** of global media and bemoaned a new form of **cultural imperialism**. The cultural influence of the Anglo-Saxon region was seen to have been growing rapidly since the Second World War. Most of the largest cultural firms are based on the **commodification** of Anglophone culture, which is seen to flow out of the West. As such, CNN was viewed as another powerful influence from this part of the world. Even CNN International was said to have a high proportion of American news, and very little international news. The channel has sometimes been regarded as a mouthpiece of the USA, presenting news from an American perspective. During the 1991 Gulf War, for instance, the Pentagon managed to use television news images for its own purposes by controlling access to the front lines.

CNN has 42 news bureaux around the world and more than 900 affiliates world-wide. It began its web presence with the launch of CNN.com (or

CNN Interactive) in 1995. The influence of its news coverage is such that observers sometimes speak of the *CNN effect* or the *CNN factor*, as CNN's coverage in turn affects political, diplomatic and military decision-making. The network is even considered to be able to shape events by virtue of its broadcasting and live coverage and, accordingly, it has a considerable impact on international relations. Indeed, some observers have gone so far as to argue that the network was crucial to the end of the Cold War. It broadcasted visions of capitalist prosperity into households in Eastern Europe, and these instant and global communications are believed to have fostered the uprisings across Eastern Europe in 1989, with news pictures of one uprising inspiring the next.

Other TV channels attempting to emulate the success of CNN include the British Broadcasting Company (BBC) and Rupert Murdoch's STAR TV. (Website: http://www.cnn.com.)

Capital Controls

The reduction or outright abolition of capital controls is often cited as evidence for globalization. Capital controls are a set of measures and regulations aimed at restricting or controlling the inflow and outflow of capital ('real' assets and portfolio capital) across national borders. These measures may be imposed for a variety of reasons. For instance, they may aim to prevent the inflow of highly volatile speculative short-term capital. Capital controls may also be imposed as part of wider macro-economic management of the national economy or to attain certain **development** goals.

The main purpose of regulating the outflow is to protect the national currency; in case of a crisis, massive financial outflows can put pressure on currencies and **exchange rates** with devastating consequences as illustrated in the **Asian financial crisis** (see **Casino Capitalism** and **Global Financial Crisis**). The inflow of capital can also create problems. It may put pressure on national currencies, forcing their values to appreciate. Rising exchange rates, in turn, make exports more expensive and less competitive in international markets.

Since the 1970s and 1980s there has been a global tendency for capital to move faster and in larger volumes between countries. Among the reasons to which this is attributed are technological advances, the innovation of new financial products and a trend towards economic **neo-liberalism**, including the **liberalization** of capital markets. Indeed, aided by the dominance of neo-liberal economic paradigms in the **G8** countries and global financial institutions (see

International Monetary Fund and **World Bank**), financial liberalization through the removal of capital controls has facilitated the development of a global financial market.

The USA and the United Kingdom were among the first to start eliminating capital controls, thereby allowing individuals and corporations to move financial capital in and out of their countries. This liberalization of financial activity constituted the core of the so-called **Washington consensus**, which stipulated that a combination of financial and trade liberalization is best for economic development, in line with conventional neo-liberal logic. A number of states have already established rules to permit the entry of global banks and global securities firms. Furthermore, the proliferation of offshore financial facilities has meant that governments have had to construct enabling statutory frameworks.

Capital controls are seen to be impeding the decision-making process of potential investors unnecessarily and reducing the incentives for investment. Furthermore, proponents of financial liberalization maintain that capital controls undermine economic discipline. Without capital controls, they argue, economic mismanagement would automatically be punished by the market. And, lastly, neo-liberals argue that capital controls not only inhibit consumer choice, but also potentially reduce trade flows and limit imports.

While neo-liberal policies have removed statutory restrictions on foreign exchange transactions, **capital flows**, foreign ownership of financial assets, etc., the regulation of global finance has by and large tended to ignore the question of structurally unequal access between richer and poorer countries. Furthermore, during various debt crises, multilateral financial agencies have tended to point the finger of blame at domestic laws and institutions in the affected countries, underplaying the rule of liberalized transborder capital flows.

Supporters of capital controls continue to be wary of the extreme volatility of short-term speculative capital inflows that aim to take advantage of exchange rate fluctuations without generating any value. Increasingly, a case is being made for timing and sequencing the liberalization of cross-border flows, with arguments that short-term controls could be beneficial, and regulatory measures could protect vulnerable markets from transborder speculative runs.

Capital Flows

As economies have become more open and integrated with the rest of the world through globalization, countries have received high levels of capital flows. During the 1970s and 1980s, capital flows were mainly directed to governments or to the private sector through the banking system. A dramatic rise in capital flows occurred in the 1990s, taking the form of **foreign direct investment** and, increasingly, portfolio flows, including both bond and equity flows, as **developing countries** liberalized their domestic financial markets and opened them up to foreign investors. In 1997 the **World Bank** stated that the proportion of emerging stock markets allowing free entry to foreign investors roughly doubled to nearly 60% between 1991 and 1994. During this period developing countries also privatized public-sector or government enterprises, and developed deeper and more liquid financial markets.

A critical reason for the growth in capital flows has been advances in **information and communication technologies,** making it much easier to evaluate and monitor investments around the globe. The management of risk has also been rendered easier with technological advances and with the development of new financial instruments and financial products.

Standard models of capital asset pricing suggest that investors seeking to diversify their portfolios should hold equities in different markets roughly in proportion to the share of these markets in total market capitalization. However, even though there was a significant increase in capital flows in the 1990s, international portfolio diversification is far from complete, with shares of foreign assets still lower than those held in domestic assets, creating what is called a 'home bias'. Part of the reason for this is that capital flows to developing countries tend still to be concentrated around a few 'emerging markets'. Between 1990 and 1997, about 75% of private capital flows went to a dozen countries, of which 60% went to six countries: the People's Republic of China, Brazil, Mexico, Thailand, Indonesia, and the Republic of Korea (South Korea).

Capital flows are influenced by both global and domestic factors but their relative importance tends to vary over time. While capital flows provide significant benefits to investors and recipients, their sensitivity to economic conditions makes recipient countries vulnerable to sudden reversals, as evidenced in recent 'boom and bust' cycles (see **Capital Controls** and **Global Financial Crisis**). The challenge for developing countries is to design economic policies that secure the most benefits from capital inflows while reducing their vulnerability to sudden reversals. Adopting more flexible **exchange rates** and strengthening domestic financial systems have been some of the ways countries have sought to reduce their vulnerability.

Capitalism

Capitalism might be described as an economic system, or mode of production, in which the means of production are privately owned and controlled. The capitalist system is grounded in a belief in the sanctity of private property rights and the efficacy of the free market, and its advocates regard 'capital' as a 'factor of production', together with land (earning rent) and labour (earning wages). Each combine through the process of production, distribution and exchange via the market, and in the process generate wealth through the incentive of the capitalist—the owner of capital—earning profits. Profit maximization is regarded as the primary motivation for economic activity and the economy is organized according to the market, i.e. the forces of demand and supply.

The drive to maximize profits leads capitalism to become 'global' as it expands to exploit new markets with new products. From the appropriation of the surplus value by an owner from a worker, capitalism expands to an appropriation of the surplus value of the whole world by some core areas. As such, capitalism is regarded as producing a truly global system. Globalization is thus considered to be linked to the dynamics of capitalism and, by implication, the forces of **imperialism**. Globalization is variously regarded as an outcome of capitalism in the modern period, or the product of the 'disorganized capital' of post-industrialism or **post-modernity**.

Capitalism emerged in the 17th century in Europe. The growth of capitalist market economies aided the breakdown of feudalism and the rise of **liberalism**. With its emphasis on individualism and the role of property, capitalism is sometimes regarded as the economic side of liberalism. In the classical theoretical model of capitalism rational individuals, with perfect information, pursue their interests, free of governmental or geographic obstacles. Freedom and liberty are central values for liberalism and capitalism. Both seek to limit the power of the state and maximize the choice of the individual, enshrined in the writings of Adam Smith, the founding father of economic liberalism, and also those of John Locke and John Stuart Mill. Capitalism, therefore, was and still is regarded as a condition for liberal **democracy**.

There are many different forms of capitalism. The two best known are *laissez-faire* or free market capitalism, and **Keynesianism**. In its most extreme version, free market capitalism advocates market **liberalization** and the retreat of the state from the economic sector. The market is perceived as a self-regulating mechanism that should not be encumbered by external forces. These ideas find their expression in the works of Adam Smith (1723–90) as well as in contemporary economic **neo-liberalism**. A second perspective, generally attributed to John Maynard Keynes (1883–1946), accepts capitalism as the most reliable mechanism for the generation of wealth. However, far from being self-regulating, Keynes views unregulated capitalism as chronically unstable. Market adjustments can take a long time, labour is not as flexible as market forces demand it to be, and economic crisis and market failure can cause social unrest and instability. Hence, he argues, the state ought to actively intervene and regulate the market. This system of capitalism offers the foundation of the **welfare state** and dominated economic policies in the developed world from the end of the Second World War until the 1970s.

With the collapse of the Communist states in Eastern Europe, capitalism and liberalism are seen to have emerged as global systems without any credible ideological challenge (see **End Of History**). An economic system operating along capitalist lines now encompasses most of the world, and economic motives constitute an important (though by no means the only) reason for creating global linkages. The capitalist logic dictates that surplus is accumulated and reinvested in further production for profit. The contexts for accumulation have slowly spread to all aspects of life, with society becoming thoroughly monetized, and with the new communications and financial flows enhancing possibilities for accumulation. Complex networks of international finance exist, and transnational companies or **multinational companies (MNCs)** constitute the significant organizers of capitalism world-wide. Raw materials, capital and labour are now sourced globally.

Since all parties in a capitalist order seek to accumulate, there are perpetual and pervasive contests over the distribution of surplus, between firms, classes, races, sexes, countries, etc. It has been argued that capitalism has led to combined and uneven **development**, with more and more areas in the periphery lured into dependency in an ever-expanding, world-wide consumer society.

The USA has often been viewed as synonymous with capitalism in its global incarnation, although it has been argued that **Americanization** is itself a contingent form of a process that is necessary to global capitalism, namely the cultural ideology of **consumerism**. The domination of MNCs (largely US-based) in a global marketplace has created a new aesthetic based on 'image' industries, with **advertising** representing desires as needs, and fostering the ever-increasing consumption of products.

Today the globalization discourse has become polarized through the ideological debate between the right and the left, often depicted as a clash between capitalism and anti-capitalism, framed in the language of anti-globalization (see **Anti-globalization (Movement)**).

Caribbean Common Market (CARICOM)

The Caribbean Community and Common Market (CARICOM) is an example of regional economic integration (see **Common Market**). It was established by the Treaty of Chaguaramas, which was signed by Barbados, Jamaica, Guyana and Trinidad and Tobago and came into effect on 1 August 1973. Since then CARICOM's membership has increased, with Suriname being the 14th and last member to join, on 4 July 1995. In addition, several Caribbean and Latin American countries are associated members or enjoy observer status in various institutions of the community.

From its inception, CARICOM has concentrated on promoting the integration of the economies of its member states, co-ordinating foreign policies, and facilitating functional co-operation, especially in relation to various areas of social and human endeavour. In 1989, at Grand Anse, Grenada, the heads of state of CARICOM decided to establish the CARICOM Single Market and Economy (CSME). This can be interpreted as a response to globalization and the **liberalization** of **international trade** and economic activities, together with the revival and emergence of **regionalism** and trading blocks in other parts of the world. Among the major objectives of the CSME is the creation of a single economic space that would provide for the free movement of goods and services, labour and capital. (Website: http://www.caricom.org.)

Carnegie Endowment for International Peace

Founded in 1910 by Andrew Carnegie with a gift of US $10m., the Carnegie Endowment for International Peace is a private, non-profit organization set up to advance co-operation between nations and promoting active international engagement by the USA. Today the Endowment receives financial support from a variety of public and private sources.

Through research, publishing, convening, and, on occasion, creating new institutions and international networks, the Endowment associates shape policy approaches. The Endowment offers leading experts on international affairs, particularly in the areas of Russia and Eurasia, the People's Republic of China, the Indian subcontinent/South Asia, globalization, non-proliferation and **security** affairs. Their interests span geographic regions and the relations among governments, business, **international organizations** and **civil society**, focusing on the economic, political, and technological forces driving global change. (Website: http://www.carnegieendowment.org/.)

Casino Capitalism

In the late 1980s Susan Strange coined the term 'casino capitalism' while analysing the unregulated operation of global financial flows. She argued that the high volatility and lack of sensible **capital controls** had turned international financial markets into a global casino where speculators placed bets on the future development of profit margins, commodity prices, **exchange rates** and other economic indicators. Games are played every day involving large sums of money. At night the games continue on the other side of the world. The players, like gamblers in casinos, watch the clicking spin of a silver ball on a roulette wheel, and put their chips on red or black, odd or even numbers.

Technological innovations have increased the speed and amount of transnational financial capital movements. These unregulated transborder **capital flows** are not unproblematic. For instance, a rapid inflow of capital can result in financial bubbles in the host economy caused by overlending, while a rapid outflow of capital could put pressure on exchange rates, stock markets and real assets. Financial crises, such as the **Asian financial crisis**, are good examples of the outcomes of such moves (see **Global Financial Crisis**).

Three factors converged in shaping the character of the current financial system. The first was the **deregulation** of financial markets begun in the 1970s with the breakdown of the **Bretton Woods system** of fixed exchange rates and the move to floating exchange rates. A second factor was the development of new financial products such as Euro currencies, derivatives, options and futures. Together with advances in telecommunications, such as high-speed phone lines, satellite connections and the **internet**, the flexibility, speed and volume of financial transactions increased exponentially. A third factor of considerable significance in facilitating easier international financial movements was the steady removal of capital controls in major industrialized countries. The **Washington Consensus** that followed the **debt crisis** that enveloped the developing world in the 1980s resulted in the triumph of

neo-liberalism as the path to economic growth and **development** propagated by the **International Monetary Fund**, the **World Bank** and other financial institutions. Global financial **liberalization** became an international economic doctrine.

Short-term financial speculation has increased dramatically since the 1980s. Money is being moved around the globe with astonishing speed, taking advantage of fractional differences in exchange rates, leading to casino capitalism. Critics of neo-liberal globalization argue that this kind of activity poses a major threat to the stability of the global economy, with stark social implications such as high levels of unemployment, falling wage levels, the wiping out of savings and pension funds, an increase in **poverty** levels, social fragility and the likelihood of general political and social upheaval in the case of financial crises (see **Anti-globalization (Movement)**). Unfortunately, the biggest costs and risks associated with international financial movements are being faced by those who are not even in a condition to participate in the global casino, let alone share in the winnings.

Centre-Periphery – *see* World Systems Theory

Chomsky, Noam Avram

American theoretical linguist, best-selling author and important left-wing commentator and activist working at the Massachusetts Institute of Technology. Since the 1960s, Chomsky has become widely known for his critical approach to the media, the international political economy, international relations and politics. He is an extremely prolific writer and has made intellectual contributions to a wide range of subjects. His persistent critique of US foreign policy, together with a recurrent concern with an international political and economic order that secures the **exploitation** of the poor by the rich and powerful at the domestic and the international level, has made him a key intellectual figure of the left. Like Michael Hardt and Antonio Negri, Chomsky has taken up the notion of **empire** to describe the current position of the USA in the global system. The USA is the last remaining superpower. The Bretton Woods institutions and their successors, created and fostered by the USA, have generated an international system that exists to facilitate American hegemony and to promote US economic and political interests (see **Bretton Woods System**).

Chomsky has also repeatedly criticized contemporary **capitalism** and the concentration of power in the hands of big business. For instance, the influence wielded by large **multinational companies** can potentially represent a threat to democratic governance. Thus, for Chomsky, contemporary economic globalization is a deliberate endeavour by a privileged élite to expand its power and benefits at the expense of other strata of society. He is actively opposed to economic **neo-liberalism** and to the **Washington Consensus**. The **mass media**, particularly in the USA, are complicit in this project, argues Chomsky, working largely as a propaganda tool of the US government and American companies.

In recent years, Chomsky has made important contributions to the analysis of the so-called 'war on terror'. According to his reading, global **terrorism** and the attacks on the World Trade Center on 11 September 2001 are directly related to American foreign policy. Terror networks, such as Osama bin Laden's al-Qa'ida, are a reaction to US hegemony, American military and economic power and to unchecked neo-liberal globalization.

Citizenship

Although citizenship is conventionally thought of as based on political rights and participation within a sovereign state, the form and meaning of citizenship has been changing with globalization. The increasing mobility of people and the growth in cheaper transport and better communications technologies has led to a **deterritorialization** of social **identity**, posing a challenge to claims of exclusive citizenship by hegemonizing nation states. As such, new ways are being created or necessitated so that citizens can participate in the different levels and dimensions that constitute their lives. For instance, while individuals may take up citizenship in the countries to which they migrate, they often keep in touch and sometimes are even actively engaged with happenings in their country of origin. This dual or transnational existence is often facilitated by 'dual citizenship' regimes, operating in several countries around the globe.

Indeed, globalization is often viewed as having made economic calculation a major element, both in transnational subjects' choice of citizenship, as well as in the ways in which nation states redefine immigration laws. Often the term 'flexible citizenship' is used to describe the strategies of mobile professionals, who seek both to circumvent and benefit from different **nation state** regimes by selecting different sites for investment, work and family relocation.

The notion of 'global citizenship' is also being conceived, though this is seen as a manifestation of the struggle against globalization, as individuals continue to resist both states and corporations, with the hope of moving towards a more cosmopolitan **civil society**, freed from the overarching structures of the contemporary world. Citizenship here would be defined more as an attribute of people in general, in a sociological rather than a juridical sense, and not of the denizens of territorially bounded jurisdictions. This might be seen in the activities of international **human rights** agencies and the development of supranational governance structures like the **European Union**, which are often depicted as signs of an evolving new international order premised on the creation of plural authority. (See also **Cosmopolitanism**.)

Civil Society

The concept of civil society, or indeed the practice of it, dates back to at least 18th century political philosophy, which used the term to describe the state or political society in its broadest sense. The term subsequently lapsed into disuse until its revival in the 20th century. 'Civil society' has been used to express various forms of control and resistance. For Antonio Gramsci, for instance, civil society (churches, schools, etc.) is the space in which the powers that be create and maintain consent. In Eastern Europe under communism, the term referred to a broad sphere of political opposition to the totalizing claims of the state.

There is considerable disagreement, particularly at the margins, as to what constitutes civil society. In a weak, inclusive sense, civil society is society as distinct from the state. In a stronger sense, it is the way society outside the state organizes and represents itself, forming both a source of pressure on and, in another sense, an extension of the state. Civil society is infinitely open; whatever the membership requirements of particular associations, it is always possible to form a new group.

According to a working definition offered by the London School of Economics-based Centre for Civil Society, it 'refers to the arena of uncoerced collective action around shared interests, purposes and values. In theory, its institutional forms are distinct from those of the state, family and market [and hence the references to it as the "third sector"], though in practice, the boundaries between state, civil society, family and market are often complex, blurred and negotiated.' Further, civil society 'commonly embraces a diversity of spaces, actors and institutional forms, varying in their degree of formality, autonomy and power. It is often populated by organizations such as registered charities, **non-governmental organizations (NGOs)**, community groups, women's organizations, faith-based organizations, professional associations, trade unions, self-help groups, social movements, business associations, coalitions and advocacy groups'. Varied conceptual paradigms, historical origins and country contexts make for a wide range of civil society actors.

However, democratic participation within these organizations is far from being a given. There is a need to ensure adequate consultation mechanisms, transparency and public **accountability**. Large-scale participation continues to be ad hoc, usually in response to a humanitarian crisis.

Discussions of civil society tend to see it as contained within the framework of the state; indeed, it is seen as symbiotically linked to the state. However, as the number of issues being posed in global terms has been increasing, and there is greater world-wide recognition of global **interdependence**, there are common grounds uniting an increasing number of civil society organizations based across numerous countries (see **International Non-governmental Organizations—INGOs**). Take, for instance, the labour movement, contemporary environmentalist or feminist movements, or indeed, the trans-state agencies that new social movements are linked with, such as Helsinki Watch, **Amnesty International**, the different organizations spun off by the **United Nations (UN)**, or the World Court (**International Court of Justice**). Many of them have significant financial resources, highly sophisticated management structures and are acutely media-savvy.

The term 'civil society' has acquired an added resonance in a globalizing world, as critics and activists use it as a source of resistance to processes of globalization. In recent times, many civil society groups have tried to shape official policy through suprastate actors, rather than through governments. Ecological campaigns, movements for the rights of indigenous peoples, opportunities for the disabled, and women's struggles offer examples of this.

The description of civil society as endlessly resistant and forever opposing states and corporations, or its role in promoting new forms of democratic practice (for instance, the concepts of 'globalization from below' or '**multilateralism** from below'), is engendering interest in the possibility of a global **citizenship** (see **Cosmopolitanism** and **Cosmopolitan Democracy**). For one unintended consequence of such resistance, opposition and contestation has been to produce the kinds of global dwellingness that escape both the **nation state** and the market. Freeing itself from the overarching structures of the contemporary world, it could trigger a heterogenous and cosmopolitan civil society, albeit constituted by highly different and deeply antagonistic groupings.

Those who see globalization in positive terms see it as engendering classical liberal values, leading to a larger role for civil society. The **World Bank**, for instance, has noted a dramatic expansion in the size, scope and capacity of civil society in recent times, aided by the expansion of democratic governance, telecommunications and economic integration. A significant pointer to this enhanced role of civil society organizations is the increase in the number of INGOs from 6,000 in 1990 to 26,000 in 1999. About 10% of development **aid** is channelled through civil society organizations. They constitute important channels for the delivery of social services and the implementation of **development** programmes. The UN, for instance, is said to rely on the information-gathering and campaigning resources of NGOs.

The role of civil society, as the upholder of democratic values, has come to be seen as an important counter to the excesses of authoritarian states, and to the inequities of capitalist development. Since the end of the Cold War, as donor agencies emphasized liberal **democracy** and market forces as critical to **sustainable development**, there has been enhanced enthusiasm for civil society, or for an intermediary stratum of NGOs, acting as a check upon the state and market. Indeed, civil society is increasingly equated with NGOs, and there is concern that donors are reducing civil society to a technical project fix, thus depoliticizing civil society as a force for social and political change.

Clash of Civilizations

This controversial theory, associated with the Harvard academic and US foreign policy adviser Samuel Huntington, was initially published as an article in *Foreign Affairs* in 1993. The thesis posits that we are entering a new phase in international relations in which conflict will primarily be determined by cultural as opposed to economic or ideological factors. According to Huntington, the clash of civilizations will constitute the battle lines of the future. These clashes are explained in terms of the disputes and rivalries that accompany globalization and the spread of **Westernization**, which lead to difficulties of an intractable nature as conflicts between civilizations question 'what are you', not 'which side are you on' and differ on the most basic distinctions, including the relations between God and man, the individual and the group, the citizen and the state, and so on, as well as differing views of the relative importance of rights and responsibilities, liberty and authority, equality and hierarchy.

Huntington distinguishes between seven or eight major civilizations. These include Western, Confucian, Japanese, Islamic, Slavic-Orthodox, Hindu, Latin American and, possibly, the African civilization. With the cessation of superpower conflict and the end of the ideological confrontation between **capitalism** and liberal **democracy** on the one side and communism on the other, conflict is seen to occur along the fault lines of these aforementioned civilizations. Huntington defines these civilizations in the broadest terms possible as groups of people united by common objective elements, such as history, language, culture, tradition, self-identification, and, most importantly, religion. Conflicts are seen to emerge along the fault lines between civilizations—between Christianity and Islam, Hindu and Muslim, Sinic and Hindu, etc.

While one school sees globalization as engendering closer relations between people, with possibilities for **cosmopolitan democracy**, in Huntington's view, globalization will only increase the prospects for conflict between civilizations as the world is spatially compressed. For the heightened cross-civilizational interactions will serve to enhance **identity** issues, while at the same time undermining the **nation state** as the main source of identity. Religion will subsequently move in to provide a basis for identity that transcends national boundaries and unites civilizations.

Huntington is particularly concerned by the challenge Islam is posing to the West. The rejection of so-called Western values and the opposition to American influence within the Islamic world means that Western civilization, with the USA at its core, and the Islamic world are bound to clash. In the aftermath of the planes crashing into New York's Twin Towers on 11 September 2001 (9/11), this idea has lodged itself in the contemporary imagination, functioning as an increasingly influential idea in the media and political circles.

Many are critical of this thesis, questioning the essentialist view of a civilization as something stable and unchanging, and the idea that non-cultural sources of conflict play a lesser role in conflict situations. There are those who point out that a large majority of wars remain intra-civilizational. Others see Huntington's thesis as less of a description of an existing state of affairs and more as meant to form a basis for future policy prescriptions, leading to criticism that the thesis has the potential to be a self-fulfilling prophesy.

Climate Change

The term 'climate change' is used to describe changes in the average weather, such as temperature, wind pattern or precipitation, that any region experiences. It is an issue that connects subjective lifestyles with the physical condition of the entire planet, with often severe implications for natural ecosystems. Global environmental issues, particularly climate change, have been a source of insecurity and anxiety, bringing the globality of the human condition to the fore. Worries about ecological despoliation have been at the heart of the notion of the '**risk society**' coined by German sociologist **Ulrich Beck**.

During the 1960s and 1970s, evidence of changes in climate and the imperative for action were highlighted by scientists and climatologists who had observed increasing concentrations of carbon dioxide in the atmosphere. Studies further revealed that the average temperature of the Earth's surface had risen by 0.6°C since the late 1800s; it is expected to rise by another 1.4–5.8° by 2100. This rapid and profound change in temperatures has come to be referred to as **global warming**. It is suggested that even if the minimum predicted increase in temperature takes place, it will be larger than any century-old trend in the last 10,000 years.

The increasing temperatures on the Earth have largely been attributed to industrialization, including the large-scale use of fossil fuels, the cutting down of forests, and certain farming methods, which in turn have increased the amount of 'greenhouse gases', such as carbon dioxide, methane and nitrous oxide, in the atmosphere. While these gases are essential for maintaining life on Earth, since they prevent some of the sun's warmth from reflecting back into space, their increasing quantities are threatening to tip that balance, thereby altering the Earth's climate.

The effects of climate change are already being felt. The 1990s turned out to be the warmest decade of the 20th century, and 1998 the warmest year. Already weakened by pollution and loss of habitat, numerous plant and animal species face extinction in the next 100 years. Sea levels are rising, with the threat of overflowing heavily populated tropical coastlines. Altered patterns of disease are also predicted.

The World Meteorological Organization and the **United Nations** Environment Programme set up an Intergovernmental Panel on Climate Change (IPCC) in 1988, which issued an assessment report in 1990, stressing the urgency of the need to do something about global warming and climate change. The IPCC's findings reflect global scientific consensus and are deemed apolitical in character. As such they form a useful counterbalance to the often highly charged political debate over what to do about climate change. During the 1990s various UN conferences were convened and various proposals were mooted to control climate change, particularly global warming, including carbon taxes, tradeable permits in greenhouse gas emissions, and other 'clean' development mechanisms, but with limited concrete results.

The IPCC report spurred governments to create the United Nations Framework Convention on Climate Change, which was ready for signature at the Rio Earth Summit (see **United Nations Conference on Environment and Development**). The IPCC report also played a major role in the negotiations leading to the **Kyoto Protocol**, a more far-reaching international treaty on climate change which sets legally binding targets and timetables for cutting the greenhouse-gas emissions of industrialized countries. The text of the Kyoto Protocol was adopted unanimously in 1997, and it became effective as of 16 February 2005, though the USA has refused to ratify the treaty.

While posing a global challenge, the technologies of globalization could also vastly improve environmental management. Global laws and institutions could provide frameworks for ecological protection and regeneration.

Club of Madrid

This independent organization, dedicated to strengthening **democracy** around the world, was launched following the Conference on Democratic Transition and Consolidation (CDTC) in Madrid, Spain, in October 2001, where 35 heads of state from Europe, the Americas, Asia and Africa, together with more than 100 world-renowned scholars and policy experts, gathered to discuss the issues involved in building democracy from both theoretical and practical perspectives. The Club of Madrid works in partnership with other organizations and governments that share its goal of promoting democracy. A distinguished group of scholars, former policy-makers and political leaders, provides additional advice and assistance on a wide range of issues.

The Club draws on the unique experience and resources of its distinguished members—57 former heads of state and government—and provides peer-to-peer counsel, strategic support and technical advice to leaders and institutions working towards democratic transition and consolidation. The Club is committed to developing practical programmes with measurable results.

The Club of Madrid is supported institutionally by the Fundación para las Relaciones Internacionales y el Diálogo Exterior (FRIDE) and the Gorbachev Foundation of North America (GFNA), the original sponsors of the 2001 conference. (Website: http://www.clubmadrid.org.)

Club of Rome

The Club of Rome focuses on the globalization of problems that pose predicaments beyond the capacity of individual countries, while recognizing the long time it often takes until the impact of action and reaction in this complex system becomes visible. It is a non-profit, **non-governmental organization** and global think-tank that brings together concerned public intellectuals, including scientists, economists, businessmen, civil servants and heads of state, to act as global catalysts for change, taking a global, long-term and interdisciplinary perspective that is aware of the increasing interdependencies between nations. It came into the limelight with its first report, *Limits of Growth*, published in 1972, which was among the first popularized attempts to point out that both population and economic growth are circumscribed by the capacity of the planet to accommodate them. The limits it described were threefold—food, mineral and energy resources, and pollution (see **Environmental Degradation**). The world finds itself in a population-resource trap in which a feedback system operates to exacerbate an already problematic situation. This first Club of Rome report was an early example of raising public awareness of environmental problems, athough awareness of planetary problems has come a long way since then. Among the Club of Rome's current areas of interest are the environment, demography, **development**, values, governance, work in the future, information society, new technologies, education, the new global society and the world economic and financial order. (Website: http://www.clubofrome.org/.)

Coca-Colonization

Like other global brands (see **Branding**), Coca-Cola, sold in more than 195 countries and one of the most powerful brands world-wide, is seen as a product that, coming from the West and carrying invasive connotations of Western success and affluence, attacks local cultural differences, erodes local values, and effects a recolonization of the non-Western world (see **Americanization**;

Cultural Imperialism and **Homogenization**). It is viewed as a vehicle for cultural standardization.

Coca-Cola has used these concerns to good advantage in its **advertising** strategies, in order to build its brand. For instance, it uses the term 'global localization' to describe the process by which its products are embedded in and then promoted within the local culture. Or it makes statements to the effect that it is not a multinational but a multilocal company. At the same time it also succeeds in evoking a consciousness of its globalness, with Coca-Cola seen as the symbol uniting the world, for instance in its advertisement that features young people from different nations singing, 'We are the world ... '.

Coca-Cola's strategy has been to sell a single product in the whole global market, and to promote it in the same way, with the same distribution circuits everywhere. The product mix, however, is varied to suit the local tastes of consumers. For instance, it is sweeter in some parts of Asia.

There have been arguments to counter the standardization thesis. Global brands such as Coca-Cola, Pepsi or McDonald's, it is argued, are made sense of at the local level through local world views and cultural practices and so the question of homogenization or standardization does not arise.

Collective Goods – *see* **Public Goods**

Collective Security

The concept of collective security in international relations is based on the idea that sovereign states can best guarantee their own **security** by entering into collective arrangements with other sovereign states, in which each guarantees the security of the other; a sort of 'one for all and all for one' idea. The idea holds that states can disavow war as a policy tool in favour of a non-aggressive approach to achieve national goals. Instead of relying on balance of power and self-help, the security dilemma nation states face in an anarchical world can best be resolved by legal and diplomatic organization in international institutions. Each state makes the commitment to join communal actions against anyone who threatens the security of another. Such communal actions could range from diplomatic boycotts to economic sanctions and military action. The idea is to deter potential aggressors with the threat of collective punishment. States belonging to such a system will renounce the use of force in their dealings among themselves. The main purpose of a collective security system is, therefore, to maintain peace between the members of the system.

The idea of collective security, especially of common defence, is not new. It can be found in the writings of antiquity and is a common theme in the rich classical political philosophy literature. The notion was to gain renewed momentum in the aftermath of the First World War. The belief, codified in Article 10 of the League of Nations Covenant, and also recognized in a modified form in Chapter VII of the **United Nations** Charter, is in opposition to the view that the anarchic context precludes the development by sovereign states of such a system of binding obligations. However, the universal pretensions of the concept are generally now rejected as too ambitious, critics pointing among other things to the League's failure to provide communal action against aggressions in Manchuria in 1931, Abyssinia in 1935, Austria in 1936, Czechoslovakia in 1939 and Finland in 1940. The effectiveness of collective security systems depends on the idea that peace is indivisible. Aggression against any member ought to trigger a commitment to military action by everyone else. Such an assumption, however, remains somewhat idealistic. National interests play an important role in such decisions and national interests tend to differ. Collective security systems further tend to reinforce a particular territorial status quo. And, finally, collective security systems fail to offer a solution to the security challenges arising out of the globalization process. In the post-Cold War world, security threats are more diverse, ranging from international **terrorism**, civil wars and ethnic cleansing to **climate change**, to give but a few examples.

Colonialism

At the most rudimentary level, the term colonialism implies the extension of a state's authority beyond its own boundaries. The control thus garnered over territories and people facilitates economic domination of their resources, labour and markets. Although colonialism has a long history, it is the period of European expansion into Africa, Asia, the Americas and the Pacific between the 15th and early 20th centuries that is generally associated with colonialism as system of rule.

Colonialism has taken various forms, one of the most common, from the 18th to the 20th century, being prolonged settler colonization, entailing dispossession of the colonized peoples. Distinctions are made between different forms of colonialism, such as informal neo-colonialism, socialist colonialism and so on.

At a broader level, the term refers to the set of beliefs that are used to legitimize and justify this system, especially the belief that the ways of the colonizer are superior to those of the colonized. Race has been a critical defining feature of colonial imaginings, however diversified they have been, and contrasts between the 'primitive' and the 'civilized' or between 'adult' and 'child' have played a key role in ideologies of colonialism. The establishment of control, thus, is presented as a benevolent act, with the colonized being introduced to more 'civilized' ways, and with the colonizer developing the political and economic infrastructure of the colonized to trigger the process of modernization.

This view has, however, been challenged from several quarters. Dependency theorists have argued that colonialism leads to a net transfer of wealth from the colonized to the colonizer, inhibiting successful economic **development** (see **Dependency Theory**). Others have lamented how colonies were 'bled white' as a consequence of the extractive policies of colonizers. Indeed, the damage done to colonized nations is not restricted to the economic; anti-colonial revolutionary thinkers and poets, such as Frantz Fanon and Aimé Cesaire, have argued that colonialism does political, psychological, and moral damage to the colonized.

Colonialism has not always been the homogeneous process that early representations of it have suggested. Frequently it has been characterized by internal divisions and contestations, and more recently there has been a shift from a focus on the colonized to the different agents of colonialism, such as missionaries, traders and the state. There has also been increasing recognition of a plethora of cross-country interests and differences among both colonizing and indigenous populations.

The full development and economic predominance of market trade, the first stage in the development of **capitalism** in the 16th century, went together with the slow colonization of the world, and the appropriation of surplus value from colonized areas by the core colonizing groups. This expansion of capitalism has been critical for the process of globalization (see **World Systems Theory**).

As colonies gained freedom, a large body of scholarship has emerged looking at the impact of colonialism for colonized peoples and societies, the forms of resistance this generated, constructions of the colonized versus the colonizer, and issues around **identity** formation and understandings of the self.

This literature goes by various names, including anti-colonial studies, post-colonial studies or subaltern studies (see **Orientalism** and **Post-colonialism**).

In the post-colonial era, attention has shifted to the notion of **neo-colonialism**. This term, coined in the 1960s, signifies a new form of capitalist subjugation of the **Third World**, which is more economic than political, and more ideologically driven than militarily supported. Symbolic and psychological control, it is argued, are effected through the rapid integration of global telecommunications systems, the proliferation of televisions, etc. (See also **Americanization; Coca-Colonization; Cultural Imperialism** and **Westernization**.)

Commodification

Commodification, in its most basic sense, means to turn into or treat as a commodity or make commercial. Karl Marx used the term to define the transformation of social relations, formerly untainted by commerce, or to which no monetary value could be attached, into commercial relations, or relations that involved buying and selling. As such, commodification expresses a concept fundamental to Marx's understanding of the way **capitalism** develops. Commodities are the objects through the production of which exchange surplus is created, extracted and amassed. A resource becomes commodified when it is incorporated into capitalist accumulation processes.

A key feature of capitalism relates to the kinds of objects that function as commodities. For instance, Marx was critically concerned with the commodification of the labour process, in which an individual worker's real, material activity, his labour, was transformed into a substitutable, abstract activity that could be measured in units of time. Labour, so abstracted, became another cost to the process of production.

Another example is the commodification of women's labour, with work designated 'women's work', such as preparing meals or caring for children or the elderly, being socialized and becoming an abstract activity that could be purchased on the market, for a wage. With commodification, domestic workers could be hired and a monetary value assigned for performing functions that had traditionally remained outside the market.

The range of resources that have become commodified provides a clear indication of the intensity of capitalism in a given social context. The character of commodification has not remained unchanged over the history of capitalism. In the early capitalist period, under commercial capitalism, profit was acquired through trade in agricultural and mining output and the

sale of luxury items. From the 1960s, commodification is seen to be inten-
sifying in three areas. First, in the increasing consumption, at a personal
level, of global or branded products (see **Advertising** and **Branding**). Second
is the increased volume and variety of financial instruments that have become
channels for accumulation in their own right, rather than simply furthering
capitalist production in agriculture or manufacturing. And, finally, in the
last few years there have been new forms of commodification, as the content
that passes through electronic processing systems, whether data, ideas,
messages or images, is also commodified. Indeed, in the 21st century **information and communication technologies** are moving to the core of capitalism,
as accumulation processes spread to intangibles, such as finance, communications and information, rather than tangible merchandise.

Commodities

The term commodity encompasses any object that has a value in relation to
other goods, and can therefore be the object of economic exchange. In its
original and simplified sense, commodities are things of value, of uniform
quality, produced in large quantities by several different producers such that
items from different producers might be considered equivalent and comparable. Commodities are given a non-standard form when they are branded, when they become unique in some sense, and distinguishable from other,
similar commodities. Branded products also tend to be priced differently,
usually higher than similar but non-branded commodities (see **Advertising**
and **Branding**).

In business parlance, a commodity is an undifferentiated product whose
market value resides not so much in something inherent in it or its use, but
in the owner's right to sell it. Thus, for instance, any product traded on a
commodity exchange is a commodity. Examples include agricultural products, foreign currencies, metals, oil and financial instruments.

In Marxist political economy, a commodity is simply any good or service
offered as a product for sale on the market. This also includes items treated
like commodities, such as human labour, or even works of art, or natural
resources, that might be traded in the market (see **Commodification**).

The production and distribution of commodities is the central defining
feature of **capitalism**, structuring the entire society. Under capitalism, everything becomes a commodity, in that everything can be bought or sold. In
this respect, capitalism is different from preceding forms of society. The

principal focus of production here is no longer the production of use value, but the production of exchange value, to generate profit. Indeed, use value is subordinate to exchange value.

Commodity Chains

Commodity chains might be considered a tool to analyse the hierarchies of production in the global economy. The concept of global commodity chains helps to explain how marketing and consumption patterns in core areas shape production patterns in peripheral and semi-peripheral regions (see **Comparative Advantage** and **World Systems Theory**).

Commodity chains link, at the global level, networks of labour and production processes, whose end result is a finished commodity. Production and distribution of goods today take place in complex global networks that tie together groups, organizations and regions, with backward and forward linkages. Design, distribution and marketing constitute important nodes from which innovative strategies are developed that allow enterprises to capture a greater share of wealth within a chain. Indeed, a firm's growth and success is often based on its ability to capture a succession of nodes along the commodity chain, increasing its expertise and control over the critical areas of design, distribution, marketing and **advertising**, often leading to a complete reshaping of both production and consumption.

This is not, however, to say that all production is governed by large transnational enterprises determining where to locate what kind of production. Nation states still exercise some control in determining the kind of production undertaken within their boundaries.

The outsourced or transnational linkages are critical. There exists a division of labour between the core or post-industrial societies specializing in certain services, and managing the command and control operations, and the non-core societies at various levels of industrialization (largely agriculture- or manufacturing-based). The chains formed between these sites with varying levels of expertise may be producer- or buyer-driven. Producer-driven commodity chains operate in high-tech and specialized industries, able to exercise control over both raw materials and components as well as retailing. As such, core firms control these commodity chains at the point of production, and they operate from within established areas of accumulation. Buyer-driven commodity chains, on the other hand, are controlled at the point of consumption. They tend to be more mobile and most of the labour-intensive production is likely to take place in cheaper, developing country locations.

Economic globalization does not imply that the costs and benefits of economic activity are globalized or more equally distributed. Instead, the extension of the value-creation chain to different locations around the world has also brought about a new allocation of advantages and disadvantages. The unequal nature of the different points in the chain becomes evident, for instance, when examining the ecological division of labour between countries of the South (or East) and the North. As supply chains lengthen, there is a tendency to separate costs and benefits by redistributing them up and down the chain, with the environmental repercussions and other competitive pressures being shifted to the periphery, while profits and control are concentrated at the core.

Common Market

A common market is a form of economic integration between nation states. According to the stage approach to integration, a common market is an intermediate stage between a **free trade area** and full economic integration. At the heart of a common market is usually a **customs union** providing for the free flow of goods across national borders. According to some theoretical approaches to integration and **regionalism**, in particular the functionalist/neo-functionalist tradition, once a customs union has been created, pressure for further integration will result in a common market, which would allow for the free flow of labour, capital and goods. Such a move would lead to even further integration. For, in order that a common market can function efficiently, harmonization of different fiscal policies, competition rules, sales taxation and social policies, for instance, may be necessary.

Like the customs union, a common market may lead to trade creation and trade diversion. As such, customs unions provisions are of concern for the **World Trade Organization**. Economic integration in the form of a customs union or a common market is inconsistent with the **General Agreement on Tariffs and Trade's (GATT)** non-discrimination principle. Thus, GATT includes provisions for the existence of both customs unions and free trade areas. In general, according to GATT, neither the creation of a **free trade** area nor a customs union should raise the barriers to trade with third countries.

The goal of a common market was adopted by the Treaty of Rome, which created the European Economic Community. However, even today this has only partially been achieved. Rather than common market, the term single market is more broadly accepted when talking about European integration. This single market is the outcome of a long historical process of integration, culminating in the Single European Act of 1986 and the Maastricht Treaty of 1992 (see **European Union**).

Communitarianism

A school of thought in political philosophy that places the origin of values in the community such that the individual derives meaning by virtue of membership of that community. Though one can trace the origins of this philosophy to the Greeks, the approach underwent something of a renaissance in the post-Enlightenment era with the publication of a number of key texts that shared an antipathy to many of the premises underpinning **liberalism**. Chief among these is a particular view of the individual, or 'self'.

According to the communitarian stance, it is incorrect to consider the individual in the abstract or atomistically. Instead, the communitarian position stresses the embedded nature of the self, pointing out that one's sense of right and wrong and one's very identity, can only be realized through membership of a community. This leads to a renewed interest in the rights of the community (as opposed to the liberal's interest in the rights of the individual). In the communitarian view, then, the state should be guided by a republican concern to promote the common good, and ought not to see itself as a neutral body, indifferent to the competing versions of the good life articulated by each member of society.

The communitarian position also raises key questions concerning the standing of rationality and the possibility of a universal (as opposed to a particularist) morality. Difficulties with respect to formulating a guide to (moral) action beyond the state or society are thereby raised, with some equating this position with cultural relativism. The question they ask is, do we, indeed can we, talk of moral obligations to other humans outside of our community, raising questions about the desirability of such a view in an increasingly interconnected world? (See also **Cosmopolitanism**.)

Comparative Advantage

The theory of comparative advantage describes the benefits of the **international division of labour**. The theory is usually attributed to David Ricardo who articulated the case for **free trade**. Ricardo's model discussed two countries and two products. It displayed how, under given costs of production, **international trade** would be beneficial for both countries. If each country specializes in the production of the goods and services in which it is most efficient, both countries will eventually benefit from international trade since it would enable them to consume more than they would have been able to otherwise.

This is the foundation of modern neo-liberal economic theory (see **Neo-liberalism**). It suggests that the economy will prosper and economic growth and living standards will improve if a free trade system is adopted. The neo-liberal trading order is based on the premise that trade ought to be undertaken by countries according to their comparative advantage. Many multilateral **international organizations**, such as the **International Monetary Fund (IMF)**, follow this logic. The **structural adjustment** programmes prescribed by the IMF, for instance, urge **developing countries** to open their economies, to drop any protectionist barriers inhibiting the free movement of international trade (see **Protectionism**) and to follow export-oriented industrialization strategies. Another example is the **World Trade Organization**, which was established to encourage states to decrease tariff and **non-tariff barriers** and to facilitate the specialized international division of labour.

Modern trade theory in the form of the Hekscher-Ohlin model takes the notion of comparative advantage a step further. The assumptions of Ricardo's theory were too narrow as they concentrated on differences in labour productivity as the sole reason for the existence of a comparative advantage. The Hekscher-Ohlin theory focuses on factor endowments (capital and labour) and argues that a comparative advantage arises from the relative differences in factor endowments between countries.

Concentration of Capital

This term refers to the gradual ownership of capital by fewer and fewer capitalists, as competition leads to smaller capitalists being done out of their businesses or taken over by larger outfits. Larger units of capital are often better placed to survive crises through waging price wars, swamping the markets, and/or monopolizing supplies. (For examples, see **Naomi Klein**'s *No Logo*.) Thus, large **multinational companies** are able to corner entire markets, ousting smaller players. For Karl Marx, economic laws brought about an increasing concentration of capital. Every accumulation becomes the means of new accumulation. As the mass of wealth which functions as capital increases, wealth begins to concentrate in the hands of individual capitalists. This concentration then brings about the historical crisis of **capitalism**, as society becomes increasingly polarized between the bourgeoisie and the proletariat, with the middle classes becoming impoverished and joining the ranks of the proletariat.

One of the arguments for the failure of **development** has been the increasing concentration of capital in a few hands, as the gap between the rich and the poor increases—whether it is between industrialized and industrializing nations or between the richest and poorest within these nations—and the numbers of the poor continue to swell. Current discourses tend to talk about the exacerbation of **inequality**, connoting not just inequalities in economic terms, rather than use this Marxist term. (See also **Capitalism**.)

Conservatism

This might be defined as a political doctrine or philosophy that places a high value on tradition, organic society, property and authority and stresses the superiority of common sense and experience over more abstract guides to action that derive from rational thought or utopian thinking. Suspicious of the perfectibility of human nature and sceptical of utopian visions, be they Communism, Socialism, equality or world peace, conservatism operates less as an ideology and more as an attitude of mind, favouring continuity over radical change. Society is seen as an organic unit or, in Edmund Burke's terms, a partnership between 'those who are living, those who are dead and those who are still to be born'. Existing institutions, where they have stood the test of time, are generally thought of favourably. So is paternalistic behaviour, a requirement for a functioning hierarchal society, itself in turn a reflection of the natural abilities and differences between individuals.

Institutions and values are seen to have evolved out of necessity, and ought, therefore, to be preserved. Conservative politics are essentially adaptable, however, and do not simply derive their programme in terms of resisting change. Recent conservative philosophy, for example, has drawn heavily on liberal thinking, particularly with respect to the value of the free market. This has none the less highlighted a number of inner tensions in the approach as the permanent revolution associated with the market has been seen by some as antithetical to other values traditionally associated with conservatism, such as the centrality of the family, the community, and national **sovereignty**.

Globalization captures modern conservatism nicely—on the one hand it is good and to be encouraged, spreading market values across the globe. On the other, it is to be resisted where it undermines and challenges the nation. Age-old concerns about just how much change is desirable in order to conserve remain valid.

Consumer Culture

A culture in which **consumerism** has become a way of life. Under consumer culture, signifiers of health, happiness and beauty, for instance, are commodified and chained by association to products, particularly branded products that, **advertising** assures, will automatically endow the user with the desired attributes (see **Branding**).

Since consumer culture is symbolically mediated, it also has a certain liberatory potential. It frees values and preferences from particular geographies or social spaces, and can even invalidate the social and political structures of modernity, delegitimizing standards once set by the élite. A dominant class's claim to special knowledge of cultural standards in art, morality and justice, for instance, becomes merely one of a range of opinions that can be accepted or rejected. Such delegitimization of standards can often lead to a more widespread and popular dissemination of what were previously regarded as high or élite cultural products, then marketed by the **mass media** to a huge global audience. Consider, for instance, the three operatic tenors, symbols of 'high' culture, in concert at the opening of the 1992 World Cup, at a sporting event (football) that might be perceived as 'popular' culture.

The transformation of the culture-ideology of consumerism from a sectional preference of the rich to a globalizing phenomenon has been made possible due to two historically unprecedented factors. First, from the second half of the 20th century, the capitalist system had developed sufficiently to provide for the basic needs of all in the First World, and of privileged groups in poorer countries. Second, the rapidly globalizing mass media became the means to sell ideas, values, products and, most importantly, the consumerist world-view that it was the sole route to fulfilment and happiness. The act of buying with credit cards sealed the contract, locking consumers into the financial system of capitalist globalization.

Consumerism

Consumerism is most commonly used in a rather pejorative sense, suggesting the attainment of pleasure through identification with, or the purchase of, material objects or services. It is seen as being oriented to 'experiencing', paying scant attention to facts; it places greater value on sensation than on science, and sees the gratification of desires as more important than solving problems.

Consumerism involves both the generation of desire and its gratification. It describes people frenetically acquiring, and usually just as quickly discarding, a variety of goods that provide the user with some kind of instant but fleeting gratification. The ephemeral nature of consumerism must be stressed—it centres on the satisfaction of passing desires, especially cravings for novelty, fashion, entertainment and fantasy. It rejoices in excess while at the same time it is unable to see that the excess exists.

While an interest in consumption might be said to be historically and cross-societally universal, in a **consumer culture**, or under consumerism, the items consumed take on a symbolic as opposed to a merely material value. A discourse about lifestyle choices is created, shaping desires, and marketing dreams as needs, thereby opening up new spaces for capital accumulation. Consumption begins to appear as the main form of self-expression and the chief source of **identity**. Need creation is effectively managed through design, packaging, **advertising**, and **branding** of products, with the simulatory effects of **mass media** in turn creating new markets for itself.

Consumerism is seen as an outcome of late capitalist restructuring. It has been expanding since the 1950s, with food and beverages, designer clothing, health and fitness aids, recreational drugs, sports and tourism all being channelled to the creation and gratification of desires parading as needs. The core ritual of consumerism is shopping. Its largest consumers are urban, middle-class youth, proportionately greater in the North, though the South and East are quickly being sucked into consumerism through globalization. Marked-up prices and short product lives feed the growth of **capitalism**.

There are two ways in which consumerism is seen to pervade the globe and control the individual. There is the view that capitalism transforms people into consumers by altering their self-images, their structure of wants, in directions that serve capitalist accumulation; and there is the view that consumer culture is an extension of the process of Western rationalization, taking the form of the social technology of **McDonaldization**. In the latter sense, the spread of Western-style consumerism the world over is seen to be a hallmark of contemporary globalization, whereby local cultural difference is attacked and eroded by mass-produced Western goods. (See also **Americanization**; **Cultural Imperialism** and **Westernization**).

Convergence Theory

This theory is built on two strands. A first suggests that industrial societies are more similar to each other than any non-industrial society. And second, driven by the logic of industrialization, industrial societies will, over time, become increasingly similar to one another, or converge. This is despite the fact that processes for industrialization might be generated in different ways in different societies. But since societies will seek the most effective technology of production, their social systems will adapt to that technology, leading to convergence.

Core-Periphery – *see* World Systems Theory

Corporate Farming – *see* Agribusiness

Corporate Social Responsibility (CSR)

The relationship between private profitability and public responsibility lies at the heart of the corporate social responsibility agenda. Public opinion, particularly public interest **non-governmental organizations (NGOs)**, is largely believed to have shaped the drive to ensure that privately-owned businesses, particularly **multinational companies (MNCs)**, embrace the idea of corporate **citizenship** and are made responsible for achieving shared public policy objectives. In pursuit of the goal of **sustainable development**, they are to run their businesses in close conjunction with different stakeholders, with particular focus on the economic, environmental and social repercussions of their businesses, rather than a limited focus on profitability and shareholder value. Performance of companies should be measured on these three effects, with independent audits to measure performance. With reputation becoming a key factor in firms' success, it is believed that they would try to act in socially responsible ways in order to ensure a good name. It might be seen as the human face of modern **capitalism**.

The concept and practice of corporate social responsibility (CSR) has been endorsed by a growing number of business ventures, particularly the larger MNCs that have been taken to task by hostile public campaigns for not showing socially responsible behaviour. Evidence of CSR's increasing take-up is in the growing membership of business organizations committed to it, e.g. World Business Council for Sustainable Development, the Prince of Wales Business Forum and CSR Europe. A number of governments are also wedded to the idea, including the British government, which has a minister charged with the duty of advancing CSR, and the European Commission, which has responded to pressure from member governments to establish a fully-fledged CSR policy. The CSR framework has been applauded for forcing a number of MNCs to provide better conditions—environmental, social and economic—particularly in **developing countries**, a classic recent instance of which has been the case of Shell in Nigeria.

Critics see the concept of CSR as oversimplifying the issues involved, particularly with respect to the meaning of sustainable development, and how it might be achieved. It further assumes that societal expectations are fully articulated by those who are leading critics of business interests, such as NGOs. There is consensus, however, that businesses have legal and moral obligations to conduct themselves in socially responsible ways, though whether adopting the CSR badge is the most effective way to do this is deemed questionable. (See also **Civil Society**.)

Corporatism

Corporatism is a theoretical and political concept that describes how business interests are incorporated in the process of governance. Two versions of corporatism stand out: authoritarian or state corporatism and liberal corporatism. Authoritarian or state corporatism is an ideology that found its political expression in the institutions of fascism in the 1930s and 1940s. In particular, Mussolini's Italy and Franco's Spain included serious corporatist elements, making them the quintessential examples of corporatist states. State corporatism suggests that people engaged in a particular trade, be they employers or workers, have by far more in common with one another than with people working in other trades. Society was subsequently organized around trade corporations, rather like the guild system of medieval times, instead of geographical constituencies. State corporatism tries to bypass class conflict and democratic elections.

Liberal corporatism is a concept closely connected to liberal **democracy**: organized interests are granted institutionalized access to policy-making processes. Liberal corporatism became significant in the post-1945 period. It is closely related to Keynesian economics, or the idea of economic management by governments (see **Keynesianism**). As a social phenomenon driven by particular economic and social developments, corporatism is manifest in all industrialized countries. It reflects a set of relationships between group interests and government. Groups may, for instance, seek to promote their interests by gaining insider status in policy-making processes. Governments, on the other hand, rely on the information and co-operation provided by various interest groups to make their policies workable. Subsequently, major industrial institutions, such as trade unions and **multinational companies (MNCs)**, have created close alliances with governments, with the result that economic policies are being jointly worked out between these industrial institutions and governmental agencies.

Since the 1970s, however, the drift towards corporatism in the industrialized world has suffered a reverse. There are various factors at work here. First, concerns were raised regarding the rather narrow basis of general representation that leaves non-organized interests out of the policy-making process and restricts access to governmental institutions. This may weaken democratic decision-making processes. Neo-liberal arguments contend that corporatism fuels government interventionism and contravenes free market principles since it stifles competition (see **Neo-liberalism**). And, second, globalization has helped to undermine corporatist arrangements. For instance, the global mobility of capital has increased the incentive to escape the comparably lower profit margins associated with corporatism. Corporatist arrangements rely on a compromise between business, organized labour and the government as outlined by the Keynesian **welfare state** model. This includes progressive taxation, wide-ranging workers' rights and substantial contributions to a relatively generous social insurance system from employees and employers, thus restricting the playing field for companies and investors. Globalization has placed the advantage firmly on the side of business since capital possesses a certain supraterritorial mobility lacked by labour and beyond the control of the state (see **Deterritorialization** and Multinational Companies). Hence, capital finds itself in a substantially improved bargaining position, able to drive down wages, corporate taxation and governmental regulation (see **Race to the Bottom**).

Cosmopolitanism

This might be described as a body of philosophical thought that has emerged as a set of diverse arguments in political, social and international theory. At the core is the notion of a community of humankind that transcends local particularities, political and cultural norms and has a moral status of its own. Cosmopolitan thought can be traced to the Natural Law theorizing of Stoic and Christian philosophy. These schools converge around the idea of the existence of a divine and natural law governing everything, including human conduct. This natural law must be understood as a morality binding all human beings regardless of their affiliation with particular cultural and political communities. At the centre lies the Stoic idea that all humans belong to a universal community, a universal city (cosmopolis) whose law is natural law. Examples for contemporary cosmopolitan ideas are **human rights** norms.

The idea of cosmopolitanism is best contrasted with **communitarianism**, which has an equally long historical and intellectual heritage, but emphasizes the moral value and the moral status of particular political and cultural communities of which individuals are members, and which create a sense of belonging and are the ultimate locus of rights, duties, obligations and moral norms. Elements of such thinking are at the heart of **nationalism** and notions of **sovereignty**.

In the contemporary globalization debate, the conflict between cosmopolitan and communitarian ideas occupies a central position. One expression is the discourse between a developing global ethic (for instance with regard to human rights or environmental protection) versus the norms of sovereignty and national interests (see **Cosmopolitan Democracy**).

The term cosmopolitanism has several related usages today. At its most basic level, it refers to a sociocultural condition, as in references to a cosmopolitan world. It might be described as an aspect of day-to-day life in a globalized world as diverse and remote cultures become accessible, both as signs and as **commodities**. Indeed, the movements of people and capital, which have created a deterritorialized world, are said to have engendered a 'new cosmopolitanism' uniting the cultural, financial and political flows within and between Western and non-Western countries into a single conceptual whole. While movement and the resources to consume music, food, fashion and art from different parts of the world might be available to only a privileged few, a much larger number of people are able to consider alternative lives based on a range of experiences brought to them through the international **mass media**.

Cosmopolitanism is not just an attribute, but might also be conceptualized as a kind of competence, both general and specialized. In a general sense, it is the readiness to make one's way into other cultures through looking, listening, intuiting and reflecting. At a more specialized level it is the skill or ability to navigate particular systems of meanings and meaningful forms. It is a competence that allows for immersion in and distancing from people and objects at will, and has often been described as a characteristic of the lifestyle of middle classes the world over. However, this propensity is at once selective and exclusionary, ordering distinctions of taste in which others' relations to objects are viewed negatively. And in this sense, global cosmopolitanism contributes to the formation of new hierarchies.

Cosmopolitan Democracy

Globalization is often viewed as a stimulus to developing new and more effective forms of **citizenship**. The globalized world is characterized by a **deterritorialization** of social **identity**, posing a challenge to claims of exclusive citizenship by hegemonizing nation states. In its place have emerged overlapping, permeable and multiple forms of identification.

The idea of a cosmopolitan **democracy** is based on the notion that if **democracy** is to play a progressive role globally, new ways must be created for citizens to participate in the different levels and dimensions that constitute their lives (see **Civil Society**). Thus has emerged the notion of global citizenship, resisting and opposing attempts to be contained by states or supranational entities. While individuals might vary in capacities and resources, they have the same basic rights and duties. Transworld institutions, including a global parliament, are seen as facilitating the institutionalization of a global cosmopolitan democracy.

There has been an increase in cosmopolitan attachments to a universal human community. For instance, there is a sense of a global 'we', faced with common ecological and other global problems. It might be argued that there is cosmopolitan solidarity regarding the basic economic, political and ecological standards underlying the notion of **development**. The notion of a strongly egalitarian global citizenship codified in the Universal Declaration of Human Rights depicts a global citizen whose rights transcend national boundaries. Human beings, however, need to turn to nation states for protection of these rights, though increasingly they need not be national citizens to claim them.

Despite these steps towards a notion of universal citizenship, particularist group affiliations are far from having been supplanted, and a liberal, internationalist vision of a single community of humankind underpinned by a world state is nowhere in evidence yet.

Credit Rating Agencies

A credit rating agency is a firm that provides its opinion on the creditworthiness of an entity, and also the worthiness of financial obligations, such as bonds, preferred stock, and commercial paper, issued by an entity. There are some agencies whose ratings are used under the US Security and Exchange Commission's regulations, known as Nationally Recognized Statistical Rating Organizations or NRSROs. The five current NRSROs include A. M. Best Company Inc., Dominion Bond Rating Service Ltd, Fitch Inc., Moody's Investors Service and the Standard and Poor's Division of the McGraw Hill Companies Inc.

Credit ratings tend to distinguish between investment grade and non-investment grade. For example, a credit rating agency may assign a 'Triple A' rating as its top investment grade rating for corporate bonds and a 'Double B' rating or below for non-investment grade or high-yield corporate bonds.

Credit rating agencies have wielded enormous quasi-governmental power in recent years. However, they are not infallible, and were the target of Congressional ire over the Enron debacle in the USA, as they were blamed for failing to uncover the extent of Enron's weakening financial condition. Despite growing questions about Enron's ties to some private partnerships that were to prove its undoing, credit rating agencies kept it at an investment-grade rating until just four days before it filed for bankruptcy on 2 December 2001.

Creolization

The concept, evoking a sense of a mixture between core and peripheral cultures, is based on the notion of flows of culture in a globalized world, leading to diversity, but based on interconnections rather than autonomy between different cultures. There is a sense here of culture as a network of perspectives, an ongoing debate that is open-ended. A Creole culture could stabilize and congeal in a certain form, or the interplay between centre and periphery could go on and on, never settling into a fixed form because of the openness of the global whole. The Creolist view is seen as a positive outcome of globalization, sensitizing the world to the very 'general' nature of culture. (See also **Hybridity** and **Cosmopolitanism**.)

Crime (Transnational)

The globalization of capital through the electronic transfer of credit, or transactions of wealth such as the exchange of property or infotechnology, the apparently limitless expanse of immediate and instantaneous global markets, have enabled the transformation of crime beyond people, places and even identifiable victims. Crime today is as much a feature of the emergent globalized culture as is every other aspect of its **consumerism**.

The jurisdictional boundaries of crime can only be explained in terms of legal convenience and legislative limits for, through history, crime has existed beyond the limits of kingdoms or nation states, whether it took the form of piracy, smuggling, abduction, gun-running, **trafficking** or counterfeiting. Transnational crime is new only in so far as law enforcement and international agencies have identified it as a priority. For instance, as governments realize the potential for criminal activity to endanger world market structures, capital transfer, national security, and international transport and communications, crime targets are selected for collaborative action. Strategies have been developed to prevent and prosecute commodity futures fraud and abuses, but an international approach to crimes against the environment is yet to be convincingly settled.

Transborder criminal networks, such as the Sicily-based Cosa Nostra or the Colombia-based Cali cartel, are some of the more well-known players in the field. Organized crime syndicates, like the Colombia-based Medellín cartel or the China-based Triads, might be seen as adding to the volume of transworld 'business'.

The current discourse on the globalization of crime has emerged from a process of interpretation in which the context-specific nature of crime has been subsumed within claims to uniform materialistic (read free market capitalist) and political aspirations, outstripping the roles generally ascribed to culture and diversity. Thus, for instance, the global 'market' and its influences over crime relationships and crime choices are expressed as if the market is a homogeneous entity, and its aspirations are uniform.

With drugs-trafficking, for instance, global crime control obligations and initiatives are predicated on a developed globalized political agenda regarding drugs marketing and trade, as well as the recognition that co-operative crime control is essential to minimize harm at a local and transnational level.

Globalization and its associated technologies, particularly the internet, have rendered possible crime without any real spatial reference. The crime situation here is rendered 'virtual' and the site for its commission is potentially the entire globe.

Cultural Homogenization – *see* Homogenization; Americanization; and Cultural Imperialism

Cultural Imperialism

This term reflects the twin concerns that, first, globalization brings uniformity, and drives a process of cultural, economic and even political **homogenization**, and, second and related, that the **deterritorialization** of culture is not a benign matter. It believes that the values and beliefs of powerful or core societies are imposed on weak, peripheral societies in an exploitative fashion. The world is seen as being made over in the image of the West. The power of transnational capital, mostly American-dominated and mass-mediated, is seen to distribute cultural goods around the globe. Furthermore, the ways of seeing and knowing of the West, or its epistemological and ontological theories, its values and norms, are all seen as being imposed on the rest of the world such that globalization, in this view, becomes coterminous with **Westernization** or **Americanization**.

The fear of cultural imperialism, in its most extreme form, suggests that local cultures will be overwhelmed by a uniform and invasive Western culture, with its rapacious individualism and its confident belief in progress. It has been perceived as originating primarily from the economic and political domination of the USA, spreading **modernity** and consumerist values. In the face of this onslaught, local cultures, it is feared, will only survive in museums and heritage centres. The term suggests the eventual triumph of a shallow and 'inauthentic' homogenizing culture, subsuming local and national cultures (or ethnies). It is effected widely (and cheaply) by global media (like **Cable News Network (CNN)** and Time-Warner), information systems and huge multinational organizations. 'Authentic' local goods, meanwhile, are under attack by the careful glocal marketing of global products (see, for instance, **Coca Colonization**).

The discourse of cultural imperialism is seen as a heterogeneous ensemble of complicated, ambiguous and contradictory ideas. At one level, it is seen as beginning from shaky foundations—the idea that pristine cultures exist. Some argue that already hybrid cultures simply become more hybridized with the continued acceleration of globalization. Indeed, often globalizing influences might stimulate a revival of local culture, and a desire to cling on to it. At another level, there are those who argue that this view of cultural imperialism is too simplistic in that it constructs **Third World** subjects as passive consumers of imported cultural goods, instead of actors who engage in a creative encounter with these cultural forms, interpreting, translating and appropriating them to suit local conditions. While there is substantial asymmetry in the flow from West to the rest, the rest talks back as well. Thus, it is a mutual, if uneven, imbrication. And it is not simply a homogenizing affair; it is also about differentiation, and heterogenization. The consequence is that there is no longer a neatly distinguishable 'here' and 'there'; the core simply becomes 'peripheralized', with the reverse traffic in people and culture setting itself up at the heart of the West.

Cultural imperialism theories also fail to consider the circuits of culture that circumvent the West, be it the movement of capital (e.g. flows into China from Taiwan, Hong Kong and south-east Asia); or people (the movements from India to South Africa, Fiji, Guyana, etc.), or indeed **mass media**, such as the hold of Bollywood on large parts of Asia and even Africa. (See also **Global Culture**; **World Systems Theory**.)

Customs Union

A customs union can be defined as a preferential trading agreement under which two or more countries agree to eliminate all tariffs between themselves while continuing to maintain a common tariff regime against the rest of the world. A customs union is, therefore, a form of economic integration that includes a **free trade** element among the participants and discriminatory characteristics against third parties. The emergence of customs union agreements is usually the outcome of a lengthy harmonization process, going through several key stages, reflecting the complexity of economic integration processes (these stages have been amended in various ways since first conceptualized). The five stages include a **free trade area**, a customs union, a **common market**, an economic union and total economic integration.

The opinion on economic integration in general and customs unions in particular is divided. On the one hand, a customs union fosters free trade by abolishing tariff barriers among member countries. It thus creates a larger market for products and services and enhances productivity and efficiency by supporting internal competition and trade creation. On the other hand, a customs union can create inefficiency and **protectionism** through the establishment of external tariff barriers and trade diversion. For instance, the notion of 'Fortress Europe', coined in the 1990s following the Single European Act and the Maastricht Treaty, captures this side of the argument (see **European Union—EU**). The most important customs union was established with the Treaty of Rome in 1958 that created the European Economic Community and committed member states to create a customs union by 1969. The customs union remains at the heart of the EU and more than a third of world trade takes place within the EU without any tariffs or explicit quotas. It is important, however, to point out that customs unions are not an exclusively European phenomenon. Examples, albeit on a somewhat smaller scale, exist world-wide.

Cyberspace

A term coined by William Gibson in his novel *Neuromancer* (1984), cyberspace is used to refer to a placeless sense of the real, based on simulation. It refers to the environments created by computers and online networks—a host of artificial spaces, developed through streams of data, audio and video. Spawned by globalization, some see it as an invisible space that simulates urban space and urban experience. It describes the world of connected computers and the society that gathers around them. The **internet** and the **world wide web** are examples of new cyberspaces.

The capacity of this space is limited only by the power of the computers being used. A highly simplified and finite version of this space is screened by many computer games, such as flight simulator games. However, in its more sophisticated form, it is a site with scope for innumerable regions of action, with its own agendas, interests and values, thus making for innumerable regions that are potentially beyond the containment of the **nation state**.

Cyberspace, however, is accessible to only a small fraction of people outside the West, as about 80% of the world's population still lacks telecommunications infrastructure. Thus, while cyber-discourse imagines an interconnected world, this is only partly true.

D

Davos – *see* **World Economic Forum (WEF)**

Debt Crisis

Debt has been a serious problem for **developing countries**, including the newly industrializing economies (NIEs), particularly since the late 1970s, as overseas borrowing has financed much of their industrial growth.

Following the Iranian Revolution of 1979 and the second oil shock (the first occurred just a few years earlier, in 1973), the US Federal Reserve adopted a tough anti-inflationary monetary policy by raising interest rates. That move was to contribute to pushing the international economy into recession, with serious consequences for the developing world. The resulting debt crisis of the 1980s is still considered something of a landmark event for developing countries.

Several factors were to play a part in moving countries to the brink of financial disaster. First, the onset of the world-wide recession in the late 1970s resulted in a plummeting of demand for manufactured goods and materials in the older industrialized countries. Protective barriers, largely in the form of **non-tariff barriers**, were erected, thus slackening developing countries' exports, with devastating consequences for them. Second, the governments of industrialized countries also began to pursue very tight financial and fiscal policies that, while reducing price inflation in their economies, raised interest rates. As a consequence, the floating interest rate debts that the NIEs had incurred began to cost far more to service than when they were initially incurred. For instance, the value of the US dollar appreciated *vis-à-vis* other currencies, so that interest rates of loans denominated in US dollars rose sharply. Thus, since most loans were denominated in US dollars, the debt of many developing countries increased in real terms.

Crisis point was reached when Mexico spectacularly collapsed in August 1982 after the Mexican government announced that the country was no longer able to service its interest payments, let alone hope to repay its foreign debt. Mexico's announcement ushered in the debt crisis of the **Third World**. Before long other countries in Latin America (for instance, Brazil, Venezuela and Argentina) and Africa found themselves in equally difficult financial situations. It became clear then that a number of developing countries, particularly the middle-income group of developing countries, were in financial difficulty. These were the countries that had come to depend most heavily on commercial lending. The very poor countries were less affected as commercial banks have generally been unwilling to lend to these countries, so that their borrowing has mostly been in the form of public-sector **aid** borrowing.

The debt crisis had a devastating impact and wiped out decades of progress in the affected countries. The 1980s subsequently came to be known as the 'lost decade' for the developing world. There was little money to be spent on social programmes and **development** as servicing interest payments of foreign loans alone accounted for a substantial chunk of government expenditure. By the early 1990s, many developing countries had emerged poorer and with smaller economies compared to the beginning of the 1980s, severely undermining **poverty** alleviation measures in these countries.

Debtor nations had to turn to international financial institutions like the **International Monetary Fund (IMF)** to reschedule their debts. But while total breakdown was averted, the severe conditions placed by these institutions created huge social and political problems for the countries involved. Indeed, the debt crisis enhanced the power of the IMF and the **World Bank** (see **Structural Adjustment**). It was, in many ways, to contribute to the triumph of **neo-liberalism** (see **Washington Consensus**).

Such financial crises have hardly been limited to the 1980s. The threat of catastrophe still looms, as the collapse of the Mexican peso in December 1994, the repercussions following the fall of the Thai baht in 1997, the economic crisis in Russia in 1998, and the Argentinian crisis in the early part of this century illustrate. (See also **Debt Trap**; **Capital Flows**.)

Debt Trap

As a result of the **debt crisis** of the 1980s, many **developing countries** are caught in a debt trap where they are committed to spend a large proportion of their gross domestic product on servicing external debts rather than on domestic economic and social development. Indeed, between 1980 and 1994, most of the US $1,300,000m. in developing country debts consisted of an accumulation of unpaid interest rates rather than new credit. Notwithstanding various initiatives to reduce the debt burden of developing nations, the net South-North transfers of official and commercial global loans have exceeded previous flows, including those in colonial times.

While the debt crisis was managed, it was never resolved. Indeed, the gap between the industrialized North and the underdeveloped South has sharply increased over the last two decades. According to the **World Bank**, developing countries are forced to pay more to creditors in debt payments than they receive in loans and grants. The Jubilee 2000 campaign highlighted that the developing world is spending $13 on debt repayment for every $1 it receives in grants. Some countries are forced to dedicate 20%–25% of their export earnings to debt repayment.

The burden of debt and repayment commitment severely limits the capacity of the **Third World** to tackle issues such as **poverty** reduction. In fact, the ongoing debt crisis has resulted in a humanitarian disaster. Over the last 20 years, Africa, for instance, has experienced falling incomes, falling investment rates, a rise in poverty, disease and infant mortality and a decrease in life expectancy. The economic, political, social and environmental implications are immense and could have transnational repercussions. Relatively poor countries are forced to accept rising poverty levels while, at the same time, exporting scarce resources abroad. Rising poverty and unemployment only further increase the pressure on the environment and social stability, resulting in political unrest.

There have been several attempts to address the issue of Third World debt traps. While the arguments in favour of debt relief are overwhelming, some commentators argue that it would create a moral hazard. Countries would fail to adhere to the stringent budgetary constraints imposed by, for instance, the **International Monetary Fund (IMF)**, and continue to borrow in the expectation that they would not have to repay their debt. It might also stifle much-needed inward investment, as investors become increasingly wary of investing in these countries. However, over-borrowing is only one side of the coin. On the other side is over-lending. Consequently, it might be argued that creditors ought to share responsibility and write off at least part of the unsustainably high debt levels. Debt traps are the result not only of local failures; creditors and the workings of the global financial system in general also bear responsibility (see **Capital Flows**). However, hardly any supraterritorial democratic frameworks have been available to the affected countries (see **Democracy**).

Since the 1990s there have been several initiatives to bring the pressing issue of debt traps to the attention of the international community. Some governments concluded so-called Brady Deals to convert part of their bank debts into bonds at lower interest rates. Similarly, the Paris Club of official creditors developed a series of measures to help low-income countries. In 1996, the IMF and the **World Bank** formulated a Highly Indebted Poor Countries Initiative (HIPC), offering relief from unsustainable debt. HIPC was extended in 1999 with larger funds, less stringent eligibility criteria and faster delivery of relief. **Non-governmental organizations (NGOs)** and direct action campaigns have also helped to publicize the issue of debt traps and debt relief. Examples are the **World Social Forum**, the Live Aid campaign and grassroots action, such as that under the aegis of the Jubilee 2000 Coalition spanning more than 60 countries that helped generate increased debt relief for the South.

Decentralization

The socio-spatial dialectic provoked by globalization encourages both opposition to concentrations of power, information and knowledge, and the increasing centralization of command and control functions. It is in this context that the term 'decentralization' needs to be broadly understood. In relation to globalization at the political level, it generally describes the distribution of decision-making power and governance away from the centre, here typically conceived as the **nation state**. Decision-making power can either be transferred to or subsumed by institutions at the international level or devolved to the sub-national level (see **Devolution**; and **Regionalism**).

Contemporary globalization has penetrated previously exclusively sovereign spaces and generated new modes of governance, challenging traditional notions of the nation state and **sovereignty**. However, it would be premature to consider the nation state obsolete. Indeed, as argued with some justification by proponents of the neo-realist school of thought, the last decade has witnessed a resurgence of **nationalism** and a renewed interest in national sovereignty around the world. Although there is much evidence that the nation state survives, it has lost its claim to supreme and exclusive rule. Other public and private actors have joined the nation state at the international level. A multi-layered system of governance is emerging where decision-making and regulatory power is increasingly shared between national and sub-national authorities, **international organizations** and private agencies (see **Multilayered Governance**). Decentralization, therefore, could equally describe the processes of increased international collaboration between national and sub-national authorities, the establishment and expanding role of global and regional multilateral regimes, devolution of decision-making power to sub-national authorities and the widespread privatization of governance.

Decentralization has also been a key term in organizational theory in relation to governance issues of both **civil society** organizations (transborder women's associations) and large **multinational companies (MNCs)**. Conventional bureaucratic arrangements in civil society organizations are moving towards more horizontal networks with a decentralization of responsibility. Similarly, several large corporations have undergone significant decentralization, adopting 'federal' structures so that lower or local levels of management have greater autonomy in decision-making. However, it is far from clear whether such practices are significantly departing from the way large organizations work, rather than simply tweaking arrangements to present a better front to the world (see **Corporate Social Responsibility**).

Thus, it is far from clear whether the diffusion of regulatory activity, as encouraged by globalizing forces, can actually decentralize power and thereby enhance **democracy**. Devolution to sub-state authorities, for instance, is not automatically democratizing, and suprastate structures have rather weak credentials where transparency and **accountability** are concerned.

Decolonization

Decolonization is a political process by which a former colony gains independence from its colonial power (see **Colonialism**). The academic discourse usually distinguishes between two major waves of decolonization. The first wave occurred in the late 18th and 19th centuries in the Americas, beginning with the revolt against British rule in North America and followed by several wars of independence in Central and South America. The second and more recent wave occurred in the mid-20th century, following the end of the Second World War and the break-up of the European colonial empires, most notably the British **Empire**. This wave of decolonization resulted in the independence of overseas territories and peoples in Africa and Asia from European control. In some of the academic literature, these newly independent states are often collectively described as the **Third World**.

The particularly active period of decolonization through the 1950s and 1960s saw a dramatic increase in the number of sovereign nation states in the international system. More than 130 colonies or dependencies gained independence in the 20th century, a number of them too small and weak to defend themselves, indicating that state **sovereignty** had itself become a central feature of global society. Thus, the period witnessed the transformation of the Western European state system into a truly global state system, with the state becoming established as the most desirable, viable and legitimate way of structuring political life.

Decolonization has occurred in various forms, depending on the idiosyncrasies of colony and colonial power and on geopolitical circumstances. It did not always involve violent means such as revolutions or wars of independence. The standard example for a country achieving decolonization with relatively little violence is India. At the other end of the spectrum are Algeria and Viet Nam, which achieved independence only after prolonged and bitter struggles with the colonizer, France.

Decolonization did not necessarily imply the end of influence from external powers or even from the former colonial power. This was reflected in the Bandung Conference in 1955, which included participants from many newly independent states from Africa and Asia which expressed strong sentiments against new forms of dependency in the form of **neo-colonialism**. The Non-Aligned Movement in 1961 arose largely as an outcome of this conference.

Critics of the globalization process, in particular of the neo-liberal version of economic globalization (see **Neo-liberalism**), have repeatedly argued that globalization is nothing but colonialism in a new guise, reflected in the widening gap between former colonies in Africa, Asia and Latin America and their colonial oppressors in the West. Globalization, it is argued, has led to the continuous exploitation of the South by the North, undermining the hopes of poor countries that they would ultimately be granted true self-determination and equal opportunity in the global political economy. (See also **Anti-globalization (Movement)**; **Global Justice Movement**; **World Systems Theory**.)

Deep Ecology – *see* Ecocentrism

Deglobalization

This is a radical vision seeking to actually reverse the process of globalization and return to a pre-global status quo. Typically, this state would be achieved through the re-empowerment of the local and national levels over the international and global level.

Deglobalizers see globalization as being largely responsible for the loss or devaluation of traditional ways of life, leading to the destruction of the social and moral framework of society and the ecological balance. Nothing short of a complete reversal, they argue, would be required to regain economic health, ecological balance, cultural integrity and **democracy**. As such, the deglobalizing is often also referred to as **traditionalism**.

The call for deglobalization has often been associated with the more radical elements of the **anti-globalization movement**, including proponents of economic **nationalism**, ethnocentrism or religious revivalism. Despite the diversity of their particular arguments, they all share a rejection of contemporary globalization. Economic nationalists (see **Protectionism**), for instance, tend to emphasize the continuing importance of the **nation state** as the only legitimate centre of authority in the international political economy, and espouse the view that states must delink from global economic networks. Such views stand in direct contradiction to the more neo-liberal vision advocating the retreat of the nation state in favour of the free market (see **Neo-liberalism**).

Deglobalizers also view negatively the impact the globalization process has had on cultural, moral and social values. The resurgence of **identity** politics might be read as a direct defensive response to this. To a certain extent, the rise of right-wing populist parties propagating more extreme forms of nationalism in many Western countries and forms of religious revivalism and **fundamentalism** amongst Christians, Jews, Muslims, Hindus and Buddhists might all be deemed manifestations of this defensive reaction (also sometimes referred to as particularist protectionism).

Radical environmentalists see globalization leading to **environmental degradation** and ecological disaster. They have, in turn, repeatedly called for a return to self-sufficiency and a society with more respect for nature and the environment, in contrast to the more moderate reformist pitch for **sustainable development**.

On the whole, deglobalizers tend to romanticize a pre-global past and, indeed, posit the local as the comforting, unchanging locus of tradition and life. In dismissing globalization outright, they tend also to throw the baby out with the bath water, as they themselves often use the technologies of globalization to enlist support, e.g. the **internet**, email, or other **information and communication technologies**.

The critics of globalization are many, but the following for a radical deglobalizing alternative has so far been limited. Those with a more reformist or proactive agenda, arguing for a change in the emphasis of the globalization process, in particular away from the current free market doctrine towards global justice and social equality, seem to have much greater appeal (see **Global Justice Movement**).

Democracy

Democracy literally means rule by the people, or rule by the *demos*. It describes a form of government in which decision-making processes are characterized by the preferences of a majority of its citizens (see **Citizenship**). In modern times, democracy emerged in tandem with the growth of a middle class in Europe as **capitalism** took a hold there. This class promoted a role for **civil society**, and argued for state power to be based on the sovereign will of the people rather than on natural or divine rights. While often used in the context of the state, participative democratic principles are equally applicable to any form of governance, state or non-state.

There are several different models of democracy. An important distinction is often made between *direct democracy* and *representative democracy*. Direct democracy is characterized by direct, unmediated participation in the governmental decision-making process. Representative democracy is indirect in that political mandate is transferred to governmental decision-makers elected by the people. This is the most widespread form of democracy today. Important preconditions for representative democracy are **accountability**, participation, openness and transparency.

Globalization challenges traditional modes of governance and has thus presented risks and opportunities for the spread of democratic principles to all aspects of life. In relation to the state, globalization has entailed a shift away from the pre-eminence of the Westphalian conception of territorial **sovereignty** to more decentralized and multilayered forms of governance (see **Decentralization** and **Multilevel Governance**). Some see the erosion of the state's power as positive. Communitarian anarchists, for instance, see the centralization of power in the hands of the **nation state** as contradictory to democracy.

Insofar as the nation state has been the locus of democratic rule and the basis for popular sovereignty, neo-liberal globalization might be seen to represent a direct challenge to democracy. For **neo-liberalism**'s advocacy of the retreat of the state in favour of the market has the potential to undermine democratic rule, leading to the 'tyranny of the market'.

On the other hand, the space of both the nation state and the power of its citizens are potentially undermined or at least redefined under globalization, with a new role for information and media technologies, supranational political and financial institutions, and the penetration of national and regional boundaries by a profusion of products, services and images. As such, politics and democracy themselves are being re-envisioned. The technologies of globalization are seen to be facilitating an increase in the possibilities for political participation. Through new and ever-faster means of communication, people have access to unprecedented amounts of information and are able to exchange views across transnational borders, set up civic associations and organize campaigns (see, for instance, **Global Civil Society**). Some see globalization as resulting in the extension of democratic norms and principles from the national to the international arena (see **Cosmopolitan Democracy**). Yet others see the future of democracy in the ability and capacity of the state to operate both upwards, promoting international regulation, and downwards, promoting social cohesion as well as appropriate forms of regional, local and private government.

The number of electoral democracies increased steadily following the end of **colonialism** and the opening up of Eastern Europe, and democracy gained strength as a global model for organizing nation states. However, there are few states that might be described as truly dynamic, functioning democracies. Often, in the confrontation between global commerce and parochial ethnic interests, the instrumentalities, the principles, and thence the practice of democracy itself, are put at risk. There are real tensions between attempts to promote democracy and the increasingly global rather than local dynamics of capitalism. George Soros, for instance, has pointed out that international businesses often prefer to work in highly ordered autocracies than in activist, less-regimented democracies.

Many analysts have commented on the spread of democratic values over the last two decades as global governance institutions actively promote **human rights**, accountability and liberal democracy as good governance. However, this has not always been the case. For instance, the exercise of power by international or supraterritorial institutions, such as the **European**

Union, the **World Bank** and the **International Monetary Fund**, has demonstrated a democratic deficit, with none of them completely and adequately fulfilling the requirements of accountability, participation and transparency.

And while democracy cannot be grafted on to any society that does not have the political will and institutional basis for it, there have been attempts to promote, or indeed impose, democracy and **liberalism** as universal values, exemplified recently in the **Bush Doctrine**.

Dependency Theory

Dependency theory arose in the 1960s and 1970s as a direct critique of **modernization theories**, which focused on factors internal to countries in the **Third World** to account for their low levels of **development**. Instead, dependency theory analysed underdevelopment as integral to the power asymmetries or the broader relations of domination and dependency between the First World and the Third World, the former colonizers and colonized, or core and peripheral countries (see **World Systems Theory**). Underdevelopment, they argued, was the result of structural inequalities operating at the level of world **capitalism**.

There was increasing acknowledgement of the issues of underdevelopment and global inequality with the institutionalization of economic **aid** programmes set up individually by most rich capitalist societies in the 1950s and 1960s. Aid began to form part of a spectrum of relationships between rich and poor states, including trade and debt, which appeared to reinforce global **inequality** rather than leading to development and 'catching up'.

Two social theories emerged in the 1970s to explain underdevelopment and delegitimize any claims to morality in the way in which rich states treated poor ones. These were the Singer-Prebisch or structuralist argument, and dependency theory. The structuralist argument posited that rich states have dynamic economies committed to technological advancement, with monopoly corporations and effective labour unions that can hold up the prices of manufactured goods. Poor states have feeble investment patterns and a disorganized labour force. As such, there is constant downward pressure on commodity prices. There is no incentive for industrial diversification, thereby leading to increasing disparities between the prices of manufactured goods and raw materials, and thence between developed and developing nations. Dependency theory focused on the allocation of capital, and argued that international capitalists deliberately use capital allocation to control the pattern of development in **developing countries**. In fact, **capitalism** could not flourish even in middle-income countries unless there was a deliberate suppression of indigenous development. Among the foremost proponents of dependency theory were André Gunder Frank, Fernando Cardoso and Theotonio Dos Santos.

Thus, dependency theory argued that underdevelopment and **poverty** are not so much the result of a lack of modern values and the absence of modern economic and social structures in developing countries, but are directly related to the organization of the international political economy. Like **world systems theory**, it suggested that the politically and economically crucial relations in the modern world are not between classes within a society, but between societies of the core and societies of the periphery (see **Wallerstein, Immanuel**).

For dependency theorists, then, underdevelopment in the Third World was unquestionably linked to the economic development of the First World. The international political economy of dependency was historically created with industrialization and the spread of Western values, norms and structures around the world through European and American **colonialism** and **imperialism**. Indeed, the industrial revolution and successful economic development of some countries could only be achieved through the extraction of economic surplus from other countries.

Today, it is often argued that developed and industrialized countries actively secure dependent relations through various policies at the national and international levels, effected through, for instance, the control of **international organizations** (such as the **International Monetary Fund**), and by setting the rules for international governance, **international trade** and international finance. However, unlike modernization theorists, dependency theorists are less optimistic regarding the successful transition of developing countries through the adaptation of certain practices and norms, so long as they are working within the confines of the current structure of the international political economy. They would go so far as to argue that developing countries have no meaningful choices.

In the course of time, the rise of the newly industrializing countries seemed to discredit dependency theorists. Marxists attacked them for confusing a mode of production (capitalism) with a mode of exchange (the market). Other critics pointed out that dependency theorists were not only overly pessimistic regarding the prospects of development in the Third World, but also tended to overlook the impact of domestic forces within developing countries, or the way external influences are always mediated through internal structures.

Deregulation

Deregulation refers to the removal of regulatory mechanisms in favour of market forces and the retreat of the government from markets in general. It is based on the idea that market forces and not governmental policies ought to determine economic policies, and goes back to 18th century **liberalism** and thinkers such as Adam Smith, David Ricardo and Richard Cobden. Today, it forms part and parcel of the economic **neo-liberalism** and privatization package.

Deregulation signified a reversal of the economic management strategies involving tight regulations that were hallmarks of economic policies in the industrialized world in the post-1945 period. The Keynesian policies in place then had been motivated by fears that unregulated competition could have serious political, social and economic consequences, threatening the very fabric of the state (see **Keynesianism**). Support for regulation came not only from governmental agencies and organized labour, but also from the corporate sector itself. Companies within a regulated market found themselves in a somewhat favourable position as regulations represented entry restrictions for potential competitors from abroad. Entry restrictions ranged from licences and state monopolies to a restriction on the number of competitors allowed in any particular sector. Examples of typical heavily regulated industries included, for instance, the transport and communications sector.

From the 1970s, however, pressure grew on governments to remove regulations and restrictive legislation. This was a reflection of the neo-liberal agenda gaining ground, and its tenet that the market would most efficiently allocate resources to achieve an overall increase in prosperity. States were no longer to intervene and hinder market forces either by heavy regulation or by restricted market access through tariff and **non-tariff barriers** (see **Protectionism**). A retreat of official market regulations, especially with regard to cross-border flows of capital, goods, finance and services, was advocated. Government agencies were to restrict themselves to harmonizing different international standards and implementing the neo-liberal agenda in order to further promote globalization.

The reason for deregulation is often couched in terms of the need to become globally competitive or retain the competitive edge. The USA in particular has been at the forefront of deregulation, not only within its own borders, but also in undermining international regulatory bodies like, for instance, the International Telecommunitions Union and INTELSAT. Most **G8** countries and **international organizations** such as the **International Monetary Fund**, the **World Bank**, the **World Trade Organization** and the **Organization for Economic Co-operation and Development** have linked globalization with deregulation and **liberalization** of market activities. This coalition provides a strong political basis for neo-liberalism and makes its policies almost 'common sense' rather than an ideology and an orthodoxy in respect to globalization (see **Globalism**).

Liberalization, together with deregulation, has had far-reaching impacts on wages, prices, **exchange rates**, welfare, health care and the social insurance sector. The mantra of 'global competitiveness' and the measures taken to secure it have often meant states attenuating or terminating many redistributive wage and price policies, with cut-backs and compromises on spending on state-provided education, health, housing and social security benefits. As a consequence, inequalities within societies have only been exacerbated, whether in the global North or the global South.

Deregulation has led to rapid market changes, together with the emergence of new mega corporations, as well as a new global class of purveyors of cultural commodities, entertainments and information technology, and a new class of professionals, including lawyers, management consultants and financial advisers. The deregulation of the financial markets, for instance, has led to a shift in the centre of gravity of the financial industry away from large transnational banks towards **global cities**. Indeed, some of the technologies of globalization have been made possible due to deregulation. Global electronic networks, for instance, have been facilitated by the privatization of public telecommunications services, the liberalization of electronic markets, and the deregulation of tariff structures which, in turn, have led both to the creation of global communications giants and increasing convergence between sectors.

Deterritorialization

This term suggests far-reaching changes in the nature of social space, whereby territory, though it still matters, becomes less completely constitutive of our geography. Social space can no longer be wholly mapped in terms of territorial places, distances or boundaries; instead, there is a transformation in the spatial organization of relations and transactions. Since the spatial and other aspects of social relations are deeply interconnected and mutually constitutive, changes are affected in all dimensions of social relations, including in the nature of production, governance, and notions of **identity** and community.

In international relations, the term attempts to delineate a key facet of globalization—its supraterritorial quality (also referred to as its 'transworld' or 'transborder' qualities). People, capital, goods, businesses and services increasingly operate in markets beyond national borders, and as such they are delinked from territory. The **deregulation** and **liberalization** of markets has immensely contributed to this process of deterritorialization. However, the spread of supraterritoriality has not meant an end to an era of **nationalism**, and it is far too early to write off the state.

More culture-oriented studies argue that with deterritorialization, any 'natural' relation of a culture or process with a geographical and social territory is sundered, and the connections between cultural structures, relationships, settings and representations are torn apart. Multiple grids replace physical location or territory, which had so long been the only grid on which cultural difference could be mapped. The fixity of distinctions between here and there or ourselves and others becomes destabilized, and cultural certainties are upset in the core as much as in the peripheries (see **Cosmopolitanism**; **Glocalization**; **Hybridity**; and **World Systems Theory**). Even people remaining in the same familiar place might find the nature of their relationship with the place changed, and the illusion of a natural or essential connectedness broken.

But deterritorialization is only part of the story, it is argued, as culture is inserted and reinscribed in new time-space contexts. The possibility for ethnic pluralism increases, but in such a way that ethnicity is not tied exclusively to any particular territory or polity. Indeed, **diaspora**, transnational culture flows and mass movements of populations make it almost impossible to map the globe as a set of 'culture regions' or homelands. Deterritorialization brings labouring populations, often migrants from the periphery, into lower-class sectors and spaces of relatively wealthy societies (see, for instance, **Global Cities**). In a world of movement, identities themselves become, if not deterritorialized, at least differently territorialized.

Deterritorialization can also create exaggerated and intensified senses of criticism or attachment to politics in the home country and, as such, might be at the core of global fundamentalisms, be they Islamic, Hindu, Palestinian or Ukrainian. Indeed, **David Harvey** has suggested that place-bound identities might actually have become more important in a world of diminishing territorial barriers. On the more positive side, deterritorialization creates new markets for businesses that thrive on the need of the deterritorialized population to keep in touch with home. Thus, both greater connectedness and deterritorialization are consequences of globalization.

Developing Countries

This term is often used interchangeably with the global South, or **Third World**. The term developing countries encompasses a range of different levels of **development**, with some countries, or regions within countries, mired in **poverty**. Thus, the countries of sub-Saharan Africa are amongst the worst off even among developing countries, and rural areas tend to perform much worse than urban areas, with limited amenities and access to basic services. The majority of the world's population, more than 80%, live in developing countries, which together have a share of less than 22% of global wealth. Globalization is said to be skewing this balance even further, with the wealthier countries and richer people able to capitalize on opportunities presented by globalization, while more than three-quarters of the world remain on the peripheries of the world economy, becoming increasingly marginalized (see **World Systems Theory**).

The weighted averages of three development indicators, income per caput, life expectancy and infant mortality, are often used to measure levels of development. Poverty, together with a lack of employment opportunities (both unemployment and underemployment), are considered key features of countries designated as developing countries. A large proportion of the workforce in these countries is still to be found in the agricultural sector. And where some form of employment is available, it is largely confined to the disorganized informal sector.

The three key concerns for developing countries today seem to be to build and sustain economic growth, to ensure that such growth is equitable, and to pay off all foreign debts. Their remaining marginal in both investment and trade, except for a small minority of newly industrializing countries, means that they have remained largely receivers of globalizing processes with limited or no positive fall-outs. (See also **Debt Crisis** and **Dependency Theory**.)

Development

From the mid-20th century, this term has referred to an economic process, generally understood to involve the expansion of production and consumption and/or rising standards of living, especially in the poor countries of the **Third World**. In the period immediately following **decolonization**, this emerged as the new universal prescription for **poverty** and inequalities, with its promises of economic growth and socio-cultural modernization. As such, it is associated with the international projects of planned social change set in motion in the years after the Second World War that gave birth to development agencies and development projects.

The development narrative was framed in terms of moving along a predetermined track, out of backwardness and into **modernity**. The mid-20th century thus saw a revival of a 'stage' theory of development, linked to the problem of contemporary economic transitions (see **Modernization Theories**). The world was divided into the developed and the underdeveloped, suggesting a continuum, movement along which brought one to the pinnacle of 'development', which most Western societies were seen to be at.

The first challenge to the idea that individual societies were moving along different routes/stages into modernization came from neo-Marxists, particularly in the form of **dependency theory**, neo-Marxist modes of production theory, and **world systems theory**, all of which insisted that differences between societies had to be related to a common history of conquest, **imperialism** and economic exploitation that systematically linked them. The proponent of world systems theory, **Immanuel Wallerstein**, for instance, argued that underdevelopment did not denote an earlier stage in the transition to industrialization; rather, it was the result of countries, largely those that had been colonized, being involved in the world economy as peripheral, raw material-producing areas. Thus, instead of being undeveloped (with its suggestion that poverty was an original condition, and which sought non-systemic explanations such as the nature of the state or culture), the Third World now appeared as actively 'underdeveloped' by a First World that had 'underdeveloped' it. Thus, in various ways, the promise of development was critiqued for having been no more than a set of conceptual and organizational tools for managing, legitimizing, and sometimes contesting and negotiating over what was a pre-existing set of geopolitical inequalities.

Neo-Marxists also brought into question the assumed identity of development with a process of moral and economic progress. They insisted that what was called development was really the global expansion of the capitalist mode of production at the expense of existing pre-capitalist ones. However, here neo-Marxists fell into the same evolutionary categorization of progress as the earlier developmentalists, seeing the march of the capitalist mode of production in a linear, teleological progression towards a future culminating in socialism.

By the 1970s, the wider institutional context for development had begun to change quite dramatically as mainstream development agencies began to place a new emphasis on the basic needs of the poor, and on the distinction between mere economic growth and 'real' development, understood in terms of human welfare measures such as infant mortality rates, nutrition and literacy.

Today, however, there is increasing acknowledgement that the development project was built on faulty foundations. As it emerged that the path of production and consumption that had been followed by industrialized countries was fraught with disastrous consequences, particularly for the environment and the ecological system itself, the path of development being recommended to the developing world began to be questioned (see, for instance, **Climate Change**; **Club of Rome** and **Global Warming**). The need for models of **sustainable development** was now put forward. Furthermore, the picture of social and cultural modernization sold as part of the development package was now criticized for having been an imposition of Eurocentric values and ideals.

More recently, a number of critical analysts have heralded the end of 'the age of development'. This comes in a context where the state, in its redistributive role, is in retreat, the goal of industrialization has been abandoned, and there is a commitment to market forces and private enterprise, creating greater inequalities and greater deprivation for larger numbers, particularly in large parts of Africa. There is, however, a grave danger in hailing a quick end to development. For, with it the project for equity and justice for the world's less well-off is also likely to be quickly abandoned. (See also **Developing Countries**.)

Devolution

The process of devolution is closely associated with **decentralization**. It can be defined as the transfer of power from a central level of political decision-making to a subordinate level, usually located at the sub-national or regional level. Theorists distinguish between two principal forms of devolution: administrative and legislative. The first involves the transfer of administrative powers to the sub-national level. Thus, while policies continue to be framed at the national or central level, the implementation of these policies is left to sub-national institutions. The second, or legislative, devolution implies the establishment of sub-national regional legislative assemblies with real legislative decision-making powers. For instance, in the case of the United Kingdom, examples of devolved government would include the Scottish Parliament, the Welsh Assembly and the Northern Ireland Assembly. It is believed that the devolution of administrative or legislative authority would potentially provide an outlet for regional identities without directly challenging and subsequently jeopardizing the **sovereignty** of the **nation state** as a whole. Critics, however, have taken the opposite view, pointing to the possibility of devolution fostering and strengthening ethnic and regional divisions, thus undermining national cohesion in the long term.

Globalization has facilitated devolutionary forces in several ways. Technologies of globalization, such as **information and communication technologies**, have facilitated the development and expression of regional and ethnic identities at the sub-national level. Globalization has also challenged traditional notions of national sovereignty and created decentralizing pressures on national governance. Indeed, several authors have heralded the arrival of the post-sovereign state—a system of complex multilayered regulation involving private and public actors at various levels. Indeed, globalization has provided sub-national regional authorities with the means to bypass the national level (see **Multilayered Governance**). Examples include the development of transborder regions and sub-state transborder co-operation. Organizations at the international level have frequently deliberately fostered devolution by providing the necessary financial, legislative and communication infrastructure. Within the **European Union** regional cohesion funds and the principle of subsidiarity enshrined in the treaty framework are good examples of this. And, finally, globalization has also introduced a variety of problems (**air pollution**, transborder **crime**, etc.) that can be more effectively addressed at a devolved, sub-national level.

Diaspora

The term diaspora (in ancient Greek, 'a scattering or sowing of seeds') had a specific historical reference to the exile of Jews, and was used interchangeably to refer to the population itself, historical movements of this dispersed ethnic population of Israel, or the cultural development of that population. With the increasing use of this term in the context of other peoples, references to the particular Jewish diaspora is signalled by capitalizing the 'd' in 'diaspora'.

Today, diaspora embodies a variety of historical and contemporary conditions, characteristics, trajectories and experiences. Indeed, its meaning is interpreted widely by contemporary observers. As a social form, it is characterized by its triadic relationship between globally dispersed yet collectively self-identified ethnic groups, the territorial states and the contexts in which they reside, and the homeland states and contexts they or their forebears came from. With the increased migrations of people, there are large communities outside their land of origin. A large number of these form what are called diasporic attachments, implying the dual affinity that migrants have to localities of origin and domicile, and to their involvement in webs of cultural, political and economic ties that encompass multiple national terrains (see **Deterritorialization**; **Ethnicity**; **Migration** and **Nationalism**).

For analytical purposes, three main types of diaspora are recognized. The first are victim diasporas, such as those of the Jews and Armenians. Then there are the labour diasporas, such as those of Indians who were moved as indentured labour to the Caribbean and parts of south-east Asia during the colonial period, and have continued to move as labour, skilled and unskilled, since. And, third, there are trade diasporas, which consist of groups whose entrepreneurial skills have enabled them to flourish outside their countries of origin. The Chinese and the Lebanese are good examples of trade diasporas. A fourth diasporic community is also sometimes distinguished, namely the imperial diaspora. This consists of groups that established communities overseas as a consequence of the history of **imperialism**, such as the British.

Diasporas have gained in political significance over the years, with governments tapping emigrants' ethnic or other roots in order to raise funds or involve these communities in **development** 'back home'. Diaspora studies have gained currency in academic circles as attempts are made to understand transnational lives, and the dynamics and politics of these communities. (See also **Transnationalism**.)

Division of Labour – *see* Global Division of Labour

Domestic Work

Included under this term are a range of tasks, from cleaning, washing and cooking, caring for children, the elderly and the infirm, to assisting at family celebrations. Of particular interest in the context of globalization are the people who are recruited to perform these tasks in what are now termed global care chains, which have become an integral aspect of the **global division of labour**.

For a long time during the 20th century it was expected that technological progress would increasingly eliminate the need for human inputs in reproducing households. However, at the end of the 20th and in the early 21st century there has been a resurgence in demand for domestic workers. Indeed, the number of domestic workers is predicted to rise considerably in the years to come, particularly in the developed world where there are rapidly ageing populations and an increasing retreat of the state from care provision for children, the elderly and the infirm.

Most of these 'new' domestic workers are migrant women, moving to wealthier centres in order to support and sustain families they leave behind. They migrate across borders to work as live-in nannies, caretakers for the elderly, and house-cleaners. Intersecting here are class, gender and ethnic differences within the context of globalized labour markets and transnational **migration** movements. Reflected here is not only the world-wide feminization of migration and the globalization of the international labour market, but also the shift of **exploitation** and dependence from a national to an international context.

The globalization of domestic service is said to reproduce gendered and racialized divisions of labour in global **capitalism**. House work and care work have become commodified products (see **Commodification**) and these can be 'bought in' from the large reservoirs of female labour in the impoverished and deregularized labour markets of the **Third World**. As such, it highlights the interdependence of women situated at unequal points along social, economic, and national hierarchies, as well as the different effects of global restructuring of care on these women. The globalization of domestic service thus constitutes a form of transnational transfer of reproductive labour, which links women from different nation states in an unequal yet interdependent relationship. Indeed, in some countries of Eastern Europe, Asia, Africa and South America, domestic workers have been lauded as the country's main export products. Striking examples are Sri Lanka and the Philippines.

Agencies operating world-wide offer maids or domestic workers via the **internet**. Commercial agencies compete with religious organizations (mostly Catholic), which operate in places such as Latin America and south-east

Asia, and arrange travel, as well as charitable care, in the host country. And most recruitment is through informal labour markets in the private sector.

While domestic work is increasingly associated with a gendered transnational labour system globally, it is reconstituted anew as a labour regime locally. The state mediates the globalization of domestic service. Indeed, it is argued that the globalization of domestic service is illustrative of the state's appropriation of women's labour and the gendered nature of all national systems of care.

The situation of migrant domestic workers is a particularly stark illustration of the need for transnational governance in an era of globalization. While a globalized labour market exists, it is still highly unregulated. Domestic workers around the world lack basic labour protections that most governments guarantee for other workers. They are typically excluded from standard labour protections such as a minimum wage, regular payment of wages, a weekly day off, and paid leave.

E

Earth Summit – *see* **United Nations Conference on Environment and Development**

Ecocentrism – *see* **Ecologism**

Ecologism

This term is used to describe an ideology challenging the existing social order and providing a model of a more desirable future. It outlines how this future might be achieved, and how change can be brought about. At this ideology's foundation is a view of nature that is non-hierarchical, such that the world works as an interconnected whole. As such it stands in stark contrast with most environmentalist perspectives that tend to be anthropocentric. Ecologism adopts an ecocentric standpoint that accords priority to nature and the planet as a whole, with humans constituting one part of it.

Ecologism rejects the primacy of economic growth and offers a powerful critique of global **capitalism** and neo-liberal ideologies. It fundamentally questions modern economic growth and the institutions that support it. Ecologists argue that the emphasis in the contemporary political economy is not so much on human need as on human desires. Ecologism, therefore, criticizes a materialistically-oriented capitalist society.

This philosophy draws attention to the imbalance between human existence and the natural world and the growing threats to life on earth in the form of global warming, resource depletion and overpopulation. Indeed, some writers believe that ecologism has gone further than any other ideological tradition in questioning and transcending the limited focus of Western political thought. In its concerns with a global situation, it is the nearest thing to a 'world philosophy' that political theory has produced.

The literature identifies two strands of ecologism: deep and shallow ecologism. Deep ecologism rejects anthropocentric beliefs that humans are more important than other species, whereas shallow ecologism might be regarded as being closer to **environmentalism**. It accepts the lessons of ecology but harnesses these to human ends. Ecologism has also marched with other ideologies and given birth to eco-socialism, eco-anarchism, eco-feminism and reactionary ecologism. Deep ecologism, however, rejects all of these hybrid forms and has developed into an independent political creed. It rejects capitalist and socialist modes of production, both of which are driven by a desire for economic growth. Deep ecologism propagates biocentric equality such that human beings, animals and the inanimate world are part of a wider 'community' and are endowed with equal rights.

While ecologism directs much of its critique to neo-liberal understandings of contemporary globalization, globalization itself has supported the spread of ecocentric thinking in at least two ways. First, ecocentrism has certainly benefited from the formation of international and transborder associations and international political activities that characterize the globalization process, aided by the new **information and communication technologies** (see **Transnational Advocacy Networks**). Global conferences, research programmes and advocacy groups have all played their part in creating an ecological sensitivity and a consciousness of the 'global' scale of the problem, while raising awareness of the damage caused by modern economic activity. And, second, global laws and institutions have provided invaluable frameworks for ecological protection and regeneration.

Electronic Commerce (e-Commerce)

Any transaction conducted over an electronic network, where buyer and seller are not at the same physical location, constitutes electronic (or 'e') commerce. With the world-wide accessibility of the **internet**, e-commerce has become a global phenomenon, using the technologies of globalization to sell to customers situated anywhere in the world. It includes any commercial activity that involves buying, selling, leasing, licensing or otherwise providing a good or service online, including marketing as well as soliciting donations and operating contests and clubs. These are activities that generally involve the electronic exchange of information to acquire or provide products or services, to place or receive orders, to provide or obtain information, and to complete financial transactions. Thus, this could be as simple as an order taken over a phone, or a plastic card transaction conducted over the internet. In a globalized world, electronic commerce holds the promise of increasing sales and broadening coverage across the world at a low cost and at very little or no risk.

Commercial exchanges on the internet are only one of several advanced forms of electronic commerce that use different technologies, integrated applications and business processes to link enterprises. For instance, business-to-business (B2B) commerce focuses on transactions and communications, specifically the electronic exchange of information, goods, services and payments. Key business processes include procurement, order entry, transaction processing, payment, inventory, and customer support.

E-commerce is a hot and complex topic today due to privacy rights and fraud as well as the enormous amount of money it can generate for some businesses. The take-up of e-commerce was initially inhibited by fears about the security of transactions conducted over the internet, but advances in the encryption process have largely addressed these. A key element in the continuing success of e-commerce will be the forging of alliances and partnerships between the different operators, internet service providers (ISPs), content providers and vendors.

Empire

A political entity linked to the notion of **imperialism** describing a particular hierarchical relationship of international relations based on dominance and hegemonic control. Traditionally, the term empire referred to a country possessing foreign dependencies over which various levels of direct and indirect control were exercised (see **Colonialism**). Unlike the vertical structure of international order that characterizes an international society of sovereign states based on the principle of sovereign equality, empires establish hierarchical structures of international relations based on authority.

There are many examples of empire in history. Indeed, for the longest period of human history, empire has been the typical order in international relations. Examples include the Babylonian, the Assyrian, the Persian, the Macedonian, the Roman, the Chinese, the Mongolian and the Mogul empires of the pre-modern period. Modern international history conventionally identifies two distinctive periods of empire. The first period, between 1492 and 1763, was characterized by mercantilist forms of imperialism and witnessed the conquest of North and South America and much of East Asia by European powers. The second wave, between 1870 and 1945, often referred to as new imperialism, saw the scramble for the African continent, the creation of Pax Britannica and the subjugation of the so-called Far East.

In contemporary globalization discourse the term empire is associated with Michael Hardt's and Antonio Negri's book *Empire* (2000). Here, Hardt and Negri define empire as a 'new global form of **sovereignty**'. Empire is the new political order of globalization, a universal order that accepts no boundaries. This interpretation is fundamentally different from the traditional meaning of empire. Previous notions of empire and imperialism presupposed the extension of sovereignty of states beyond their own boundaries. Today's empire establishes a decentralized and deterritorialized mode of governance that incorporates the entire global realm (see **Deterritorialization**). This is a new form of sovereignty based on hybrid identities, flexible hierarchies and expanding frontiers.

There is some discussion among political scientists as to whether the global military, economic and political preponderance of the USA, and its predisposition to act unilaterally, qualifies it as a modern empire. There is increasing concern about the direction in which US foreign policy is moving. Recent examples of its exercise of domination and its tendency to unilateralism include its refusal to sign the **Kyoto Protocol**, its withdrawal of support for an **International Criminal Court**, and its decision to proceed with military action against Iraq without authorization from the **United Nations**. (See also **Bush Doctrine**.)

End of History

This term is derived from Francis Fukuyama's *The End of History and the Last Man* published in 1992, which constituted an expanded version of a 1989 essay 'The End of History' published in *The National Interest*. The term sums up Fukuyama's conviction that the end of the Cold War signals the end of the progression of human history. According to Fukuyama, what we are witnessing is not just the end of the Cold War, or the passing of a particular period of post-war history, but the end of history—the end point of mankind's ideological evolution and the universalization of Western liberal democracy as the final form of human government. By the end of history, then, Fukuyama does not mean that war and conflict will no longer continue to occur. Drawing on a particular reading of Hegel, whereby the dialectical process has reached a conclusion, Fukuyama suggests that mankind's ideological evolution has reached an end point in **democracy**, there being no alternative. His primarily normative argument, based on a particular political philosophical perspective, is that humanity has found its preferred form of political, economic and social governance after a long period of experimentation. At the end of the Cold War, **capitalism** and liberal democracy have proved to be superior to any other form of political and economic organization. Indeed, with the demise of Communism, capitalism and liberal democracy lost their last credible challenger.

For his argument Fukuyama draws on a particular interpretation of human nature. Human nature, he argues, is driven by two fundamental desires: the desire for material goods and the maximization of wealth, and the desire for recognition by fellow human beings. This last point is directly drawn from Hegel and accounts for the superiority of liberal democracy and capitalism over rival systems. While capitalism is able to fulfil the first desire driving human nature, or materialism, it is through liberal democracy that the human need for recognition, political freedom and equality is met. If history is regarded as a dialectic struggle between different forces, liberal democracy represents the end point of this struggle. It provides society with political equality and ends the relationship between the superior and the inferior, a relationship that inevitably leads to conflict, as the dominated are never willing to accept their subordinate status.

By drawing on the ideas of another political philosopher, Alexandre Kojève, Fukuyama then goes a step further. With the **welfare state**, he argues, capitalism has managed to overcome its internal contradictions. As such, it provides now not only for material prosperity but also for a **homogenization** of ideas and values. This, in turn, reduces the risk of ideological conflict between big powers and severely reduces the risk of war between those powers.

Fukuyama's view has drawn varied and at times vociferous responses. Samuel Huntington, for example, replaces the clash of ideologies with the **clash of civilizations** as a future source of conflict, thereby dismissing Fukuyama's idea. Marxist criticisms continue to assume historical materialism and thereby question the idea of a capitalist democracy as the end point. Other critiques have drawn attention to the challenge posed by the environment. None the less, it remains an important perspective on the nature of political globalization. More recently, Fukuyama has himself questioned his original position, pointing to the changes brought about by technology and modern science which, he suggests, have the potential to alter human nature itself, potentially rendering the very idea of democracy redundant.

Environmental Degradation

Global environmental degradation encompasses a wide range of issues and problems. They include, for instance, physical changes of the environment (**air pollution**, **acid rain**, ozone depletion), **development** activities (including growth in energy production and use, growth in waste, tourism, and intensified agriculture) and changes in the human condition (population growth and an increasing strain on natural resources). Environmental degradation can be the direct result of human activity (deforestation, desertification, etc.) or an indirect consequence (waste-related issues).

Environmental degradation is today presented as a global concern requiring collective solutions at the international level. A number of reasons are cited for this. First, a number of environmental problems have global consequences, regardless of the actual location of the cause of the problem. Carbon dioxide emissions, for instance, contribute to global **climate change** irrespective of where they come from. Second, there is a marked increase in the exploitation of what might be called the '**global commons**', or resources shared by the world community. Examples include the depletion of the oceans due to overfishing and pollution (see **Public Goods**). Then there are a number of environmental issues that may not be global in reach but whose fall-outs nevertheless might be across boundaries (acid rain, for instance).

There is no denying that the processes leading to the overexploitation of natural resources and environmental degradation are intrinsically linked to wider socio-economic processes and, ultimately, form part of the contemporary global political economy. Environmental degradation is linked to the generation and distribution of wealth. As such, it cannot be addressed without taking into account inequality and the factors underlying world **poverty**. Indeed, there are those who argue that globalization is restructuring the control over resources such that the natural resources of the poor are systematically being taken over by the rich, while the costs of their economic success, the pollution and the environmental degradation, are being passed on to the poor. Several examples are cited to support this argument.

For instance, in the run-up to the Rio conference (see **United Nations Conference on Environment and Development**), the global North was identified as contributing to the destruction of the environment disproportionately, generating 90% of the historic carbon emissions, and most of the waste. Large **multinational corporations** have exploited **Third World** resources to sustain and multiply their global activities. And resource- and pollution-intensive industries are simply being relocated to the global South through the economics of **free trade**.

The late 1960s is identified as the period when there began to be increasing awareness of environmental risks the world over (see **Club of Rome**). Since the 1972 UN Conference on the Human Environment in Stockholm, the **United Nations** has been at the forefront in dealing with issues concerning co-operation over environmental issues. The conference institutionalized the importance of environmental concerns by establishing a number of principles, institutions and programmes to offer a framework for international co-operation. The 1970s and 1980s saw the emergence of many environmental interest groups, **non-governmental organizations**, green movements and international institutions as international actors alongside governmental agencies (see **Transnational Advocacy Networks**).

An important milestone in environmental consciousness at a global level was the publication of the Brundtland Report in 1987, which trained the spotlight on the concept of **sustainable development**, which has gained discursive ground, but remains an aspiration in so far as economic growth remains the primary goal of national economies. The 1992 Rio Conference agreed on three conventions to limit climate change, preserve **biodiversity** and combat desertification. However, international co-operation necessary to make these conventions effective has not always been easy to achieve. This became all too clear during the negotiations to further develop the Climate Change Convention. Although the 1997 **Kyoto Protocol** is critical to creating a legally binding international framework, many challenges still remain.

Environmentalism

Environmentalism is a political attitude concerned with issues such as pollution, **climate change**, etc., which retains human beings at the centre of its analysis. It might be described as a perspective based on the assumed superiority of Western cultural values, and the transformational capacity of **capitalism**. It recognizes the existence of complex linkages between the environment and the global economy. Environmentalism sees **environmental degradation** and pollution as transboundary problems, the management of which requires international co-operation. The future is characterized by uncertainty, and damages once done are likely to be irreversible (see **Risk Society**). However, in playing up the global, this view tends to downplay the importance of power relations in the way problems are structured and solutions devised and advocated.

Environmentalism views degradation merely as a negative side effect of modern economic growth and market activity. Environmental degradation, for instance, is seen to arise from market failure that can be corrected by either putting market-based solutions in place or by command and control measures. In order to mitigate unwanted consequences, therefore, environmental components need to be priced fully and accurately. Examples of market-based solutions include, for instance, pollution trading, whereby pollution comes with a price tag. Command and control measures are another way of referring, for instance, to specific legislation and regulations regarding emission levels.

Two principle forms of environmentalism might be distinguished: light green and dark green forms, where 'green' flags up a supportive attitude towards the protection and preservation of the environment. A light green approach is reformist, accepting the major institutions of capitalist society, while seeking to engender respect for, and preservation of, the environment without disrupting modern economic growth (also sometimes called the technocentric approach). With its managerial outlook, it attempts to achieve **sustainable development** with the help of market incentives and the development of greener technologies. Its central goals are to promote economic growth and **development** and to cater for human needs. The darker approach (also referred to as the ecocentric approach) proposes a more radical vision, and begins with the assumption that today's practices have a consequence for future generations (see **Ecologism**).

Environmentalism manifested itself in the political arena in the form of 'green' politics in the 19th century. It emerged as a reaction against the widespread environmental destruction caused through industrialization. But it was not until the 1960s that environmentalism emerged as a political force to be reckoned with, driven by growing public concern over deforestation, resource depletion, and air and water pollution (see Environmental Degradation). The period saw the formation of green parties in many industrialized countries, offering a legitimate alternative to the more traditional parties. The number of green parties has been growing steadily since then, and some of them have successfully managed to influence government policies. The Green Party in Germany, for instance, transformed itself from a protest party into part of the ruling SPD-Grüne coalition between 1999 and 2005. However, while many mainstream green parties initially adopted a 'dark green' stand, this stance has since been watered down to a lighter approach. At the same time, environmentalism has come to be promoted by national and international **non-governmental organizations** and is today an important constituent of the **anti-globalization movement**.

Ethnicity

The term is derived from the Greek *ethnos*, meaning nation. The foundations of an almost essentialist connection between ethnicity and nation were laid in 18th century Europe. It was a deliberate human construction, as political classes attempted to raise national consciousness in favour of the new and modern form of political organization—the **nation state**.

Ethnicity can assume many forms. It might be defined as an aspect of a relationship rather than the property or essential characteristic of a group; it is the articulation of cultural difference between groups. Its distinction from race is problematic, though ideas of race may or may not form part of ethnic ideologies.

Understandings of the term ethnicity have undergone several changes in a globalizing world. In the late 1960s ethnicity was being treated as a remnant of the pre-industrial social order, to be overcome by the advances of the modern state, and processes of national integration and assimilation. Assimilation was the operative word through this period, exemplified, for instance, in the idea of the USA as a melting pot. (This is, however, not to say that there were no more national movements seeking exclusive territorial expression for ethnicities and sub-ethnicities.)

The concept of ethnicity began to acquire a different kind of strategic significance again from the mid-1970s, partly as a response to post-colonial geopolitics. Ethnicity was now used to define groups which diverged in some way from whatever was considered the mainstream. New disciplines emerged to study these ethnic minorities under the rubric of race relations or minority studies. It was a matter of some controversy as to whether analytical emphasis should be placed on ethnicity, or on **poverty**, or class or culture as ethnically distinct groups often also tended to constitute economically and politically disadvantaged sections of the population. Indeed, theories of ethnicity were now used to explain a whole range of issues, including social and political change, identity formation, social conflict, race relations, nation building and assimilation. This period also saw the rise of what was represented as 'ethnic minority activism' in many states.

There are three key approaches to understanding ethnicity. The first, the primordialist view, ascribes deep primordial or essential attachments of an individual to a group or culture. The instrumentalist view sees ethnicity as largely a political instrument exploited in the pursuit of one's self-interest. Finally, the constructivist view emphasizes the contingency and fluidity of such identities, treating them as created by specific social and historical contexts.

There are said to have been two adaptive responses on the part of ethnic groups to globalizing trends—translation and tradition. Translation is a syncretic response in which groups that inhabit more than one culture seek to develop new forms of expression that are entirely separate from their origins. Tradition is ethnic **fundamentalism**, or an attempt to rediscover the untainted origins of an ethnic group in its history.

Globalization has resulted in more mobile populations such that ethnicities are no longer tied to any specific territory or polity. There is greater 'ethnic pluralism'. However, ethnicity no longer resides in the narrowly local, as is witnessed in the proliferation of ethnic cuisine, ethnic fashion, ethnic holidays and ethnic music. While there has been a **deterritorialization** of identities in terms of ethnicity, globalization has also made scope for greater connectedness. Indeed, some writers argue that rather than the emergence of a homogeneous global culture, the world has seen the birth of a greatly increased global cultural diversity. (See also **Cosmopolitanism**; **Creolization**; **Hybridity**; and **Third Cultures**.)

Euro and Economic and Monetary Union (EMU)

The euro is a supranational currency and is the centrepiece of (European) Economic and Monetary Union (EMU). Its origins can be traced back to the beginnings of the **European Community (EC)** and the desire to create a single market area by removing all obstacles to the flow of goods, services, capital and, later, labour between the member states of the EC. An additional and related motivation was the aspiration to combat the effect of fluctuating **exchange rates** on intra-European trade.

In the 1970s, following the demise of the **Bretton Woods system**, the EC countries began to search actively for greater exchange rate stability. The outcome was the **European Monetary System (EMS)**, based on the proposals of the Werner Plan of October 1970. However, a large inflow of US dollars into some European economies, such as Germany, in 1973 triggered a financial crisis resulting in rising inflation, unemployment, and widening trade deficits. Together with the oil price shock, it became clear that a monetary union any time soon was unrealistic, and by the mid-1970s it had become a non-issue.

By the mid-1980s, however, a favourable political and economic climate helped to launch the European Single Market Programme. In 1988, a committee set up by European Commission President Jacques Delors outlined the path for the Single European Act, which was accepted by the majority of member states' governments as the basis for an Intergovernmental Conference (IGC), launched in Rome, Italy, in 1990.

This, in turn, was to result in the Treaty on European Union (also known as the Maastricht Treaty), which put forward a deadline for monetary union between all member states of the **European Union** except the United Kingdom, Sweden and Denmark. However, these were not the only states to have reservations about a monetary union; several others were also resistant to the idea at this stage, resulting in problems with treaty ratification. Despite this, European monetary union became a reality as **exchange rates** between the participating countries were fixed and on 1 January 1999 the euro was officially launched. At that time it was merely a virtual trading currency, used only for bank transfers and electronic payments. The euro became a physical reality with the circulation of notes and coins in January 2002. Since then it has replaced the national currencies in all participating countries.

Critical to the life and functioning of EMU is the European Central Bank (ECB), which replaced the European Monetary Institute as the core economic organization in Europe. Its primary goal is to ensure price stability, or low inflation. It is vested with powers to manage foreign reserves of participating countries, determine interest rates and exchange rates, produce notes and coins, and determine the value of national currencies of Europe in relation to the euro.

EMU and the euro have enhanced the transparency of prices, and reduced transaction costs and exchange rate risks in the single market. On the other hand, this has involved the transfer of a substantial degree of

sovereignty to the ECB. The stability criteria determine how states use economic and fiscal policies and, thus, place tight controls on public debts and budget deficits. EMU is often regarded as a stepping stone towards further political integration and further co-ordination in fiscal, economic and social matters among the member states.

The euro is the most recent example of a trend in which national currencies have lost their monopoly as means of exchange and repositories of wealth. Single currency systems, such as the euro, are often represented as threatening national economic, tax and social policies. It is an example of the globalization of money that began with the Bretton Woods agreement, which effectively elevated the US dollar to the status of a global currency. While the Bretton Woods system came to an end in the 1970s, there was no return to the territorialization of money. The US dollar was joined by other national currencies (such as the Japanese Yen and the German Mark) as global stores of value and means of exchange, the euro being the latest experiment in this direction.

Eurocurrency

The financial term eurocurrency describes currency deposits held off shore, and, hence, beyond the regulatory reach of the country that issues the currency. Looked at another way, it refers to a wide series of financial transactions that take place in currencies other than the currency of the state in which business is being conducted, so that state authorities cannot regulate them. Thus, motivations for holding deposits of eurocurrency include the wish to escape jurisdiction, particularly domestic regulation and taxation, in the countries that issue them.

The term eurocurrency is a misnomer in that it does not refer to European currencies. The eurocurrency market was initially composed of the exchange of US dollars in London (and hence the interchangeably used term 'eurodollar'). While London dealt in dollars, the eurocurrency market in New York would operate in funds other than US dollars. Banks which accept deposits denominated in eurocurrencies are called eurobanks.

The eurocurrency market began in London after the Second World War when the Soviet Union used London banks to store and exchange US dollars beyond the immediate reach of its Cold War rival, the USA. US corporations, in turn, used investments in Europe to escape restrictive US laws on banking activities. By the 1960s, the large amount of eurocurrencies being moved between markets had even begun to destabilize the management of exchange rates.

The growth of international trade, transnational production, and the spread of globalization increased the amount of offshore banking and trading in eurocurrencies. But in the 1970s and 1980s, the deregulation and the liberalization of capital markets took place, led by the USA. As barriers were dismantled, the mobility of capital increased. With the end of regulation in most countries, national stock exchanges and capital markets have become merely local manifestations of a larger, world-wide market. The creation of credit is beyond the purview of national authorities. Furthermore, with the creation of new financial instruments in the 1980s, virtually any economic and financial activity can be securitized and traded internationally.

European Community (EC)

The European Community (EC) began life as the European Economic Community (EEC) in 1957, being set up by the Treaties of Rome as part of the effort towards building a more integrated Europe.

It is important to distinguish the European Community from the European Communities. The European Communities are part of the three pillar structure of the **European Union (EU)**. The remaining two pillars comprise Common Foreign and Security Policy (CFSP) and Justice and Home Affairs (JHA). Under the Treaty on European Union, also known as the Maastricht Treaty, the *acquis communautaire* of the European Coal and Steel Community (ECSC), the European Atomic Energy Community (Euratom) and the EEC was preserved and extended. Among the revisions was the renaming of the EEC as the EC. Hence, a confusing situation was created whereby the EC is part of the European Communities, which in turn is part of the EU.

European Currency Unit (ECU)

The ECU can be regarded as the predecessor of the **euro**. However, unlike the euro, it was not a real currency but served as a unit of account between the members of the **European Monetary System (EMS)**. The ECU was conceived in 1979 as part of the EMS and was a currency based on a 'basket' of all of the currencies of the EMS participants. It was composed of fractions of all member states' currencies (weighted according to the country's share of the collective gross national product, share of collective exports and size) and served as a means of defining the central parities of **exchange rates** from which all other bilateral exchange rates could be derived. The ECU was the first step in the direction of a genuine European currency. In January 1999, it was replaced by the euro.

European Monetary System (EMS)

The European Monetary System (EMS) is an example of a regional currency regime. It was the brainchild of German Chancellor Helmut Schmidt and French President Valéry Giscard d'Estaing. The breakdown of the **Bretton Woods system** of fixed **exchange rates** in the 1970s created considerable concerns regarding the stability of the global financial system. The EMS was created as a regional response to the volatility of floating exchange rates. The arrangement was approved by the Bremen European Summit in 1978 and was formally established in 1979, with the nine member states of the **European Community (EC)** as its original members. These were Germany, France, Italy, Luxembourg, the Netherlands, Belgium, Denmark, the United Kingdom and the Republic of Ireland.

The objective behind the EMS was to create a zone of monetary stability among the EC member states and to respond to the requirements of closer economic integration. The EMS rested on three main pillars. First, the EMS created a new unit of account, the **European Currency Unit (ECU)**. The ECU was a basket currency determining the central parities or exchange rates from which all bilateral exchange rates between the members could be derived, and might be seen as the first step towards the establishment of a European currency (see **Euro**). Exchange rates were fixed but adjustable by a margin of ± 2.25% around the central parity. The second pillar of the EMS was the **Exchange Rate Mechanism**. And, finally, the EMS also included the European Monetary Co-operation Fund.

The main purpose of the EMS was to prevent intra-EC exchange rates from fluctuating too widely, a goal which was largely achieved. In the 1990s, several speculative attacks on key currencies of the EMS and changing political conditions, such as the reunification of Germany, put a strain on the system. In 1992, the United Kingdom permanently withdrew from the system, leading to the Brussels Compromise, which set a new margin for permissible exchange fluctuations (± 15%).

The successor of EMS was EMS II, which was officially launched in January 1999. The ECU was replaced by the euro, following which the exchange rates of the participating countries were permanently fixed against each other and against the euro.

European Union (EU)

The European Union (EU) is an example of regional political and economic integration (see also **Regionalism**). It is an international organization that came into existence with the ratification of the Maastricht Treaty (Treaty on European Union) in 1993. However, the beginnings of European integration can be traced back to the late 1940s. It was driven by the desire to overcome the century-old plague of intra-European warfare. The Second World War had severely discredited the ability of the **nation state** to guarantee a stable and peaceful European order. Indeed, unrestricted **sovereignty** combined with a virulent form of **nationalism** had turned out to be the root problem. Hence, from the beginning European integration was driven by the imperative of pooling sovereignty and, thereby, limiting the danger of repeating the events that had resulted in two world wars.

There were several milestones along the road to European integration, beginning with the Treaty of Paris in 1951, establishing the European Coal and Steel Community (ECSC), and the Treaties of Rome in 1957, setting up the European Atomic Energy Community (Euratom) and the European Economic Community (EEC). These agreements set Europe on a path of further and deeper integration by pooling sovereignty in well-specified areas and establishing novel institutions with supranational competencies. Only six countries participated in the initial stages of European integration: Belgium, France, Germany, Italy, Luxembourg and the Netherlands. In 1987, the Single European Act confirmed the objective of completing the internal market by 1992. Finally, in 1992, the Maastricht Treaty created a new organization, the EU, based on three pillars: the European Communities, a Common Foreign and Security Policy (CFSP) and co-operation in Justice and Home Affairs (JHA).

The pillar structure indicates the division of institutional competencies. The first pillar, the European Communities, includes the three original communities—the **European Community**, Euratom and the ECSC. Economic policy matters and policy-making remain areas of pooled sovereignty where the community method of decision-making is dominant. The other two pillars of the EU concentrate on intergovernmental co-operation in domestic and foreign policy. The EU is, therefore, a hybrid international organization with supranational and intergovernmental features.

European integration has come a long way since the 1950s. Several waves of enlargement have increased the number of EU member states to 27 in 2007. The key institutions of the EU include the Commission, the Council of Ministers, the European Parliament and the European Court of Justice. The Commission has an external representation role. As such, it maintains offices around the world and acts as the EU's chief negotiator in the **World Trade Organization (WTO)**. More importantly, the Commission is the 'guardian of the treaties'. It possesses a monitoring function and ensures that EU law is being respected. Furthermore, the Commission occupies a key legislative position and it is formally the sole institution with the right to propose legislation, albeit in consultation with other EU institutions and with the advice of private actors, such as various lobby and interest groups, trade unions, etc. The right of sole legislative initiative does not apply to the two intergovernmental pillars of the EU, CFSP and JHA. The Council of Ministers is an intergovernmental body, consisting of the representatives of the EU member states. It makes policy decisions on the basis of either qualified majority voting or, if required, of unanimity, depending on the issue in question. The European Parliament is composed of directly elected representatives from the EU member states. It has consistently tried to assert its authority in the decision-making process of the EU. The Treaty on European Union significantly extended the competencies of the European Parliament with the introduction of the so-called co-decision procedure, which was further extended by the Amsterdam Treaty (1999), virtually making the Parliament a co-decision-maker with the Council of Ministers in respect of the enactment of legislation. The European Parliament also has significant budgetary powers and holds the Commission to account. The European Court of Justice has the task of upholding Community law of investigating possible breaches of the treaties and of interpreting them.

The EU may be viewed, equally, as both a regional expression of globalization, and as a banding together to stand up to globalization's forces. As a regional expression of globalization, the creation of this supranational governance structure is seen as disenfranchising states, encouraging the transfer of decision-making power to a supranational entity, and effecting the dissolution of national boundaries. Thus, elimination of customs barriers, free movement of migrants, transferability of university credits, and the creation of a common currency, among other things, are seen to have attacked the capacity of the state to pursue a distinct, independent policy on employment, education, welfare or military organization. However, the EU is equally seen as a pooling of sovereign authority, to cope with the challenges arising from the globalization process. States are increasingly forced to consider international governance solutions which would help them regain control over markets and shield members, while at the same time enhancing their economic competitiveness and their negotiating power in international forums, such as the WTO, by pooling their resources; and to address transborder issues, such as environmental protection, **migration**, health or **international crime**. (See also **Multilayered Governance**.)

Exchange Rate Mechanism (ERM)

The Exchange Rate Mechanism (ERM) was the fixed exchange rate system at the heart of the **European Monetary System (EMS)**. The intention driving the establishment of the ERM was to prevent exchange rate fluctuations among the members of the **European Community (EC)**. The ERM was based on fixed but adjustable **exchange rates**. Under the EMS, exchange rates of the member states were set against the **European Currency Unit (ECU)**.

The ECU served as a means of defining the central parities of exchange rates from which all other bilateral exchange rates could be derived, and was composed of fractions of all member states' currencies. The complete set of central parities and margins of fluctuation was called parity grid. The parity grid implied a central exchange rate with margins of allowable fluctuations from that rate. In most cases the permissible margin was set at $\pm$ 2.25% from central parity. There were, however, some exceptions where the bands were set at $\pm$ 6%.

In the 1990s, the EMS and the ERM came under intense pressure from currency speculators. In 1992, the United Kingdom was forced to withdraw from the ERM. Crisis began as currency speculators began to gamble that Britain would not be able to maintain the value of the pound sterling relative to the German mark. With no way to stop the decline, the United Kingdom withdrew from the ERM and allowed the pound to float freely, instantly depreciating its value further. The Brussels Compromise of 1993 extended the allowable margin of fluctuation to $\pm$ 15%.

In January 1999 the exchange rates of the eurozone countries were permanently frozen and the **euro** officially replaced the ECU. The ERM was substituted by the ERM II. Currencies in the ERM II are allowed to float by a margin of ± 15% against the euro. **European Union** countries that have not adopted the euro have to participate in ERM II for at least two years before being allowed to join the single European currency.

Exchange Rates

An exchange rate is the denominated price of one currency in terms of another, constituting the international monetary system. Today, national currencies are valued against each other, not against gold or silver. Most exchange rates are expressed in terms of the world's most important currencies—those of the G7 states, including the US dollar, the pound sterling, the **euro**, the Japanese yen, and the Canadian dollar.

Exchange rates affect every international economic transaction, whether made in trade, investment, tourism, etc. Because of their strong influence on **international trade** and other macroeconomic variables, exchange rates are among the most important economic indicators. The exchange rate of any currency is closely tied to expectations of future developments of its issuer's economy, and as such, exchange rates function like asset prices.

Economists distinguish between two dominant forms of exchange rate management: fixed (or pegged) exchange rate regimes and floating (or free) exchange rate regimes. The most notable examples of fixed exchange rate regimes include the Gold Standard and the **Bretton Woods system**. At the beginning of the 20th century many countries adhered to the Gold Standard under which the international value of a currency was determined by its fixed convertibility rate into gold. The First World War signalled the beginning of the demise of the Gold Standard. Many countries were forced to abandon the system in order to finance their substantial military expenditure by printing money, and, as a consequence, experienced inflationary pressures. The Great Depression of the late 1920s and early 1930s finally brought the Gold Standard to an end and exchange rates were allowed to float freely on the currency markets.

The Bretton Woods system represented another attempt to establish a fixed exchange rate system. Exchange rates were fixed against the US dollar, which in turn was fixed to gold at $35 per ounce. This was a revival of the old Gold Standard in some ways, in that gold remained the fundamental standard for exchange rate value, the only difference being that the US dollar now mediated it. All other currencies were fixed (or pegged) against the US dollar and most international transactions were determined in this currency. Provisions were made to allow for occasional adjustments of exchange rates against the US dollar.

The Bretton Woods system came under intense pressure in the 1960s following the recovery of the European and Japanese economies. US dollars flowed out of the USA as part of Marshall Aid, to finance US defence spending and its war efforts in Viet Nam and as payments for foreign imports. Subsequently, a point was reached at which the amount of US dollars outside of the USA exceeded the amount of gold in the USA, making it doubtful whether the US government would be able to honour its gold commitments. However, given the central position of the US dollar in the Bretton Woods system, the outflow was needed to provide the global economy with financial liquidity. This dilemma has become known as Triffin's dilemma, after the economist Robert Triffin, who first noticed the intrinsic problem with the fixed exchange system. Many economists began to argue in favour of abandoning the fixed exchange rate regime, allowing currencies to float freely against each other. In 1971, US President Richard Nixon decided unilaterally to sever the link of the US dollar to gold.

Following this, most major industrialized countries adopted floating exchange rates. In this system, global currency markets, in which private investors and governments alike buy and sell currencies, determine rates. Through short-term speculative trading in international currencies, exchange rates adjust to changes in the longer-term supply and demand for currencies. National governments may periodically intervene in financial markets, buying and selling currencies in order to manipulate their value, though governments are at a disadvantage in this as even acting together they control only a small fraction of the money moving on such markets.

Among the advantages of a floating exchange rate regime is an independent monetary policy. Central banks direct monetary instruments to respond to developments in their respective domestic economies. The fixed exchange rate system had its advantages too, including monetary discipline, avoidance of competitive currency depreciation (**beggar-thy-neighbour policies**) and the prevention of destabilizing currency speculation (see **Financial Crises** and **Casino Capitalism**). In short, international price developments became more predictable.

Floating exchange rates were regarded as a temporary emergency measure in the 1970s. A period of monetary expansion, coupled with the oil shocks of the 1970s, resulted in exceptionally high inflation. Attempts began to try to manage floating exchange rates at the international level. However, it was becoming clear that it would be difficult to put a fixed exchange rate regime back in place in the face of increasing capital mobility. Ad hoc co-operation in the G5 countries (see **G7/G8**) on this issue led to the 1985 Plaza Accords, whereby the USA, Japan, the United Kingdom, Germany and France agreed to take action in order to reduce the value of the US dollar. The West European response to increasing exchange rate volatility was to try to create a new exchange rate arrangement based on the principle of Europe-wide stabilization (see **European Currency Unit**; and **European Monetary System**). **Developing countries**, meanwhile, had clung on to the dollar as the exchange rate peg until, in the late 1980s and 1990s, they too abandoned fixed exchange rates, adopted inflation targets and liberalized exchange controls. However, developing countries continue to be hugely at risk from the volatility of exchange rates. (See also **Capital Controls**; and **Capital Flows**.)

Exploitation

To exploit generally implies to take unfair advantage of. The definition of what 'unfair' conditions entail might be specific to the context. In globalization discourse the concept of exploitation is applied to social, political or economic relationships of uneven power. Exploitation is often used in connection with the structure of the global political economy, **neo-liberalism**, free market policies, the division of the world into a developed global North taking advantage of an underdeveloped South, and **capitalism** in general.

Marxism advances a specific theory of exploitation that is intrinsic to capitalism. All societies are class societies and are prone to class conflict, and in capitalist societies this struggle is between the capitalist class (bourgeoisie) and the working class (proletariat). Class struggle arises through one group in society gaining a monopoly over the economy via the ownership of the means of production, providing this group with the ability to control surplus produce. In capitalist society the capitalist class owns and controls the means of production, while the working class owns nothing but its labour, which it has to sell for a wage. Based on technological innovation, capitalist societies are able to produce a surplus over and above the immediate physical needs of the workers. However, according to Marxism, a particular group or class appropriates this surplus. Thus, in a class society, one class through the exploitation of another appropriates the social surplus. And hence, according to Marxist theory, capitalist relations are built on systematic exploitation. Workers are denied a fair remuneration, and are paid less than their labour is worth.

These power dynamics, characterized by dominance and exploitation, occur both within and between societies. Marxism maintains that free market relations are structurally exploitative. Firms and corporations are the main instruments of exploitation. Many commentators argue that the current structure of the global economy systematically exploits the developing world for the benefit of developed countries, leading to uneven **development**, **poverty** and the North-South divide. **Dependency theories, world systems theory** and modern Marxist thought analyse in great detail the exploitative relations inherent in the world economy and such theories are at the forefront of the **anti-globalization movement**.

Exploitation is not limited to the structural level. It is also inherent at the micro level. The exploitative behaviour of **multinational companies** is cited as an example. Due to their disproportionate size and power, and their transnational nature, they are able to take advantage of less-regulated markets in the developing world, where they have to pay only subsistence wages and can avoid adhering to environmental and labour standards (see **Race to the Bottom**). The most notorious examples in this context are the use of child labour and sweatshops where work is characterized by long hours, low wages and unsafe or harsh conditions. Nike and Gap Inc. are two prominent multinational companies that use **developing countries** for their supply of cheap labour and sell their produce to the developed world.

Export Processing Zones (EPZ)

Export processing zones (EPZ) are special production zones where normal tariff and **non-tariff barriers** do not apply. They are created to attract foreign companies by offering various incentives, such as elimination of tariffs and quotas, the provision of financial incentives (e.g. tax breaks) and/or regulatory exemption or relief from national laws (e.g. those governing the minimum wage, flexibility of working hours and the right to unionize). The term **offshoring** is also used for these territorial and juridical enclaves (though this includes not only production but also the provision of tax havens, such as the Cayman Islands). EPZ are an important focus of the discussions and debates about the **global division of labour**.

The jury is still out on the relative merits and demerits of these zones. While critics see them as exploitative enclaves with few or no linkages to local economies, and bringing few, if any, benefits to the countries concerned, supporters view them as an imperfect but potentially useful mechanism for providing an opening into global markets, and as contributing to employment and income-generation. It is argued that foreign-owned, export-oriented factories offer higher pay and better working conditions than comparable jobs in domestic companies.

EPZ have been used by **developing countries** as an incentive to attract investment. Indeed, countries have often competed for investment, increasingly deregulating in order to maintain their attractiveness and remain globally competitive (see **Race to the Bottom**). **Multinational companies** have found this inviting, since they have been offered cheap labour with minimal external costs. It has also given them a foot in the door, enabling them to break into these growing markets while also locating part or all of their production there. The governments providing these services hoped to reap the benefits of capital investment and foreign currency earnings from exports.

EPZ grew exponentially in the 1980s and 1990s. While they have traditionally been associated with manufactured products, there have been variations in this pattern. For example, some developing countries have agri-export zones (AEZ), specializing in some agricultural or horticultural produce. Women often constitute the bulk of the workforce in these zones.

The benefits accorded by EPZ, however, seem to be directly related to the degree of sophistication of the goods produced. Thus the Asian Tiger economies are considered to have benefited by this strategy, while poorer countries in Africa and South Asia, which sought to attract investment to labour-intensive, export-oriented industries, have not seen any technology transfer, skill enhancement or integration with local industry.

Extraterritoriality

In **international law**, the concept of extraterritoriality refers to a particular aspect of diplomacy where the legal jurisdiction of one state is extended into the sovereign sphere of another. Extraterritoriality is often bound up with diplomatic immunity (immunity from the laws of the host state enjoyed by diplomatic representatives from other states). Such extra-territorial rights are often exchanged on a mutual basis and according to the principle of reciprocity.

However, reciprocity is not a necessary condition. For instance, during the period of European **colonialism**, it was common practice for an imperial power to extend its jurisdiction into the territory of another state, in particular in Africa, Asia, the Middle East and the Pacific. This implied that expatriates of a European state were subject to the legal system of the sending country but not the country of residence. This practice severely undermined and limited the **sovereignty** of the country of residence. Since the Second World War and **decolonization**, this version of extraterritoriality has almost disappeared.

Extraterritoriality is not a concept exclusive to international law. It refers to a general problem of the extended jurisdiction of one state infringing on the sovereignty of another. Such a clash of sovereignty is, for example, inherent in the structure of **multinational companies (MNCs)**. It raises questions, such as, for instance, does a subsidiary obey the decisions of the government of the country in which it is located, or is it subject to decisions made by the government of the country in which it is based? The transnational nature of MNCs generates clashes of sovereignty between governments, as the legal authority of one country has extraterritorial consequences for the sovereignty of another. This creates a set of complex and overlapping authorities and is a driving force behind the trend towards greater standardization of domestic issues at the international level. In many areas of economic policy, transnational activities have severely limited the effectiveness of national sovereignty. Regulatory efforts in these areas have resulted in the creation of a web of bilateral and multilateral agreements at the regional and the global level. (See also **Global Governance**.)

F

Fair Trade

The fair trade movement has grown out of a radical social justice critique of **free trade**. Based on a Marxist perspective, it is possible to identify a number of dissonances with the liberal/neo-liberal school of thought (see **Neo-liberalism**). First, instead of taking the **comparative advantage** concept that underlies free trade theory at face value, some analysts point to the construction of different cost structures, and argue that these have been determined by the histories of nations, some of which are histories of colonial subjugation. Free trade theorists, they argue, not only turn a blind eye to the historical construction of **inequality**, but in doing so also freeze a particular status quo, making it impossible for poorer countries to develop, while economic wealth continues to become concentrated in the hands of wealthier nations, perpetuating relations obtaining in the imperialist past with the colonizers, now the global North, and the colonized, the global South.

By being fundamentally biased against the developing world and perpetuating unequal relations, the prevailing free trade paradigm fails to address issues of labour rights and **human rights** (see **Development**; and **Developing Countries**).

Fair trade campaigners argue that the market confines poor countries to exporting goods whose prices are historically low and vulnerable to fluctuations. Further, the internationalization of production leads to the **exploitation** of workers in the developing world, resulting in lower labour standards and wages below the **poverty** line. **Non-governmental organizations** and **anti-globalization** protesters have made extensive use of **information and communication technologies** to raise awareness globally of the dire working conditions endured by workers in the supply chains of large corporations.

The search for justice in the global economy has taken the form of an international social movement, the Fair Trade movement, promoting equitable labour, production, trade and environmental standards. Its objective is to enable marginalized producers and labourers in the developing world to move from a position of **exploitation** and vulnerability to one of ownership and economic self-sufficiency. Following campaigns by this movement, increasing numbers of people in richer countries are demanding products that are produced in socially and environmentally-friendly conditions. And fair trade has been expanding, becoming almost a brand in itself, with all major retailers and supermarkets in richer countries stocking ethnically produced commodities, and with buyers willing to pay a higher price for these products. An early commodity to come under the fair trade umbrella was coffee, with the setting up of Café Direct in 1991.

Concern about fair trade has led to the establishment of voluntary ethical codes of conduct for people working in supply chains of major corporations. The fair trade movement has promoted better working conditions, with fair trade buyers guaranteeing minimum prices, advancing loans to help producers avoid getting into debt, and ensuring that trade is as direct as possible by bypassing intermediaries, thereby securing for producers a higher share of the final price. The process is also designed to create the development of higher value-added packaging facilities in less-developed countries, and a niche for traditionally made products in the global market. To cite one example, **Oxfam International** has strategies aimed to enable poorer producers working in volatile markets to become viable through trade. However, fairly traded products still constitute only a very small proportion of the overall market.

While these developments have been heralded as being positive on the whole, they can, however, be contradictory. For, although some of the positive aspects of globalization may be realized, it has been argued that these processes, set in motion as they are from the demand side, may preclude alternative, locally autonomous development strategies.

Fordism

Fordism describes a system of mass production and mass consumption named after the American industrialist Henry Ford (1863–1947). Based on a combination of scientific management and the flow line principle, Henry Ford reorganized the space of production into a moving assembly line, thus reducing the time and cost of production, and establishing Fordism as an ideological paradigm for economic organizations. Ford's assembly line was based on semi-skilled labour using specialized equipment to manufacture standardized products.

Fordism is used particularly to refer to the remarkably economically successful post-Second World War era, founded on this new labour process with unprecedented increases in labour productivity. The great advantage of the Fordist production system lay in its economies of scale, achieved through mass production, which reduced costs and increased efficiency through the specialization of the employees. The outcome was standardized products manufactured and sold at lower prices.

Fordism also provided a solution for the demand side. Underlying it was the idea that mass production requires mass consumption. Hence, in order to ensure a steady level of demand, workers on assembly lines had to earn wages high enough to enable them to purchase the products they helped to manufacture. Thus, a constant level of consumer demand was assured for the goods produced. Fordism proved to be an effective means of both, controlling the labour process and satisfying workers' aspirations at a material level.

The Fordist production system was remarkably successful and characterized industrial production in the developed world until the late 1960s. It provided the backbone for the Keynesian compromise (see **Keynesianism**) that dominated industrial relations in the industrialized countries. This compromise rested on an implicit trilateral pact between governments, corporate business and organized labour. States introduced some form of Keynesian demand management and expanded the **welfare state**, creating national systems of economic and social regulation. Corporate business delivered higher wages, benefits and protection to workers. And the trade unions, for their part, delivered acquiescent and more productive workers to business.

During this period, Fordism also characterized the **global division of labour**. **Multinational companies** exported Fordism to the South and East, seeking semi-skilled and cheap labour supplies. Fordism remained a feature of the global economy until the late 1960s. There followed the demise of the **Bretton Woods system** and decades of economic upheaval, with slower and less certain economic growth. Productivity increases could not be sustained, and competition increased as a range of countries industrialized. The Keynesian compromise was slowly replaced by a new emphasis on economic **neo-liberalism**. The revolution of transport and communication and information technologies facilitated the development of new management and new production systems. (See also **Post-Fordism**.)

Foreign Direct Investment (FDI)

Foreign direct investment (FDI) refers to transboundary **capital flows**, where control over the resources transferred and the production process remains with the investor. It is long-term, and entails investments in fixed facilities, assets and also in intermediate goods, including capital, technology, management skills, access to markets and entrepreneurship.

FDI is contrasted with foreign indirect investments, better known as portfolio investments, which refer to the transfers of specific assets and intermediate products between two agents through the market, but where control over the resources is relinquished by the seller in favour of the buyer.

For many poor and transitional states desperately in need of capital to stimulate growth, encouraging FDI is seen as the answer (see **Developing Countries**; and **Export Processing Zones**). Governments have actively tried to lure externally-based business by lowering corporate tax rates, reducing restrictions on the repatriation of profits, relaxing labour and environmental standards, and so on. Some of the countries that had been recipients of FDI in the 1960s and 1970s have now become generators of it (e.g. the newly industrializing countries of East Asia). However, the **European Union**, the USA and Japan together dominate flows of FDI. The firms engaging in transnational production, and thereby making foreign direct investments, are variously referred to as **multinational companies**, or as transnational or global corporations.

Free Trade

The essence of free trade is the absence of any tariff and **non-tariff barriers** inhibiting the flow of goods and products between countries (see **Protectionism**). The theoretical school that has most invested in propagating the virtues of a free trade system is arguably the liberal/ neo-liberal tradition (see **Neo-liberalism**). According to the perspective of the liberal international political economy, free trade has the capacity to enhance overall efficiency and productivity and, potentially, benefits everyone.

The theoretical origins of this line of thought can be traced back to the 19th century and the theory of **comparative advantage**. Until then, mercantilist theories dominated, according to which trade was a zero sum game, with a focus on relative advantage: the gains of trade for one country meant inevitable losses for another. It was the Scottish political economist Adam Smith who developed the concept of absolute advantage: all countries could benefit from trade if they specialized in and traded the goods they produced best. David Ricardo built upon Smith's advancement and established that trade was an absolute sum game. His theory of comparative advantage demonstrated that countries that specialized in the production of goods and services in which they were relatively efficient would ultimately be better off in free trade relations. This theory, later further developed by Eli Hekscher and Bertil Ohlin (the Hekscher-Ohlin theory), forms the basis of much neo-liberal trade theory.

Free trade has been promoted as a means of increasing wealth. For liberals, protectionism diminishes competition and increases monopoly power. It also limits consumer choice and inhibits general **development**. Agricultural subsidies in the **European Union** and in the USA provide a good illustration, as they adversely affect agricultural sectors in **developing countries** and consumers in developed countries, who are forced to pay premium prices for agricultural products to finance protectionist policies.

Another strand of liberal theory connects free trade and international stability. Immanuel Kant and Richard Cobden, for instance, argued that a free trade system would create a more peaceful world order. This idea was formulated in American President Woodrow Wilson's famous Fourteen Points, which outlined a liberal 'reform programme', largely based on Kantian thought, for **international order** after the First World War. Although post-1945 theorists are far more pragmatic, commercial **liberalism** still propagates the spread of a free trade system as a necessary precondition for a more stable international order. It is part of the foreign policy portfolio of all G8 countries.

Free trade theory has been consistently attacked from various sides. Mercantilists and neo-mercantilists, for instance, continue to emphasize the centrality of relative gains in an anarchical international system of sovereign nation states. They support protectionist measures to stabilize national economies by shielding infant industries from international competition (the infant industry argument). Mercantilism also argues that states ought to be self-sufficient in certain sectors for security reasons (national security argument). Other points of critique come from the Marxist tradition, from environmentalists, trade unionists and feminist writers. Marxist theorists often put forward a social justice critique of free trade principles, while environmentalists argue that free trade contributes to **environmental degradation** by lowering national and international standards (see **Race to the Bottom**).

Globalization and free trade are deeply linked, and globalization has contributed to a significant increase in **international trade** flows. Free trade systems are being increasingly promoted as part of a wider neo-liberal agenda. At the same time, however, resistance against the negative implications of neo-liberal globalization and free trade has grown. This comes in the form of protectionism as states struggle to mitigate the negative effects of trade liberalization. In addition, elements of the so-called **anti-globalization movement** are explicitly opposed to trade **liberalization**. Developing countries have repeatedly complained about one-sided trade liberalization and the bias of the free trade system in favour of the developed North. Many industrialized countries, so the argument goes, preach a free trade orthodoxy while, at the same time, regularly employing protectionist measures to shelter sensitive domestic industries.

Free Trade Area

A free trade area constitutes an arrangement between two or more countries among themselves to eliminate all tariff and **non-tariff barriers** on stipulated goods while maintaining tariff and non-tariff barriers *vis-à-vis* the rest of the world. Unlike a **customs union**, there is no common external tariff. The participants in a free trade area maintain their individual tariffs against third parties.

Free trade areas are often regarded as the initial step towards a full customs union. They tend to work best where the participating members agree on a full harmonization of their external tariffs in order to eradicate any differences that might result in a diversion of trade flows in favour of those members of a free trade area with the lowest tariffs. They are examples of economic integration and are covered as such by the **General Agreement on Tariffs and Trade** and its successor, the **World Trade Organization**.

Examples of free-trade areas include the **North American Free Trade Agreement**, **Mercosur**/Mercosul (Argentina, Brazil, Uruguay and Paraguay) and **AFTA/ASEAN** (Cambodia, Laos, Indonesia, Myanmar, Singapore, Viet Nam, Brunei, Malaysia, the Philippines and Thailand).

Fundamentalism

A term that entered the Oxford English Dictionary in the 1960s, fundamentalism might be described as a call for a return to fundamentals, to basic scriptures or texts, to be read in a literal manner. It is thus a doctrine marked by a putative return to basics, giving new vitality and importance to the guardians of a 'beleaguered' tradition. Tradition is defended against what is perceived as an increasingly rational and globalizing world.

Fundamentalism has little to do with the contexts of beliefs, religious or otherwise. What is critical is how the truth of beliefs is defended or asserted. It is a refusal of dialogue; a closing within itself against people who might think or live differently, which it finds difficult and dangerous to deal with.

Fundamentalism raises its head in a world where the familiar begins to crumble. It might therefore be argued that fundamentalism is a condition of globalization. The global condition is both a context and target of fundamentalism, and the chief factor precipitating it. As a reaction against **modernity**, it claims to address a global predicament, with a distinct view of 'the world'. And fundamentalist movements target a global culture, attempting to change both the balance of power and the cultural terms on which global actors are seen to operate.

Fundamentalist elements can be found in all major world religions, including Christianity, Islam, Hinduism and Judaism. Some see religious fundamentalism as an attempt to reaffirm or reconstruct traditions and a collective **identity** confronted by modernity's secularism, social atomization and moral emptiness, or in the face of homogenizing cultural globalization (see **Cultural Homogenization**). Others consider **deterritorialization** to be at the core of many global fundamentalisms.

Fundamentalism has become both a symbol in the global discourse, and part of the global repertoire of collective action available to discontented groups. For liberal Westerners, it represents the global 'other', a potent symbol of resistance. Indeed, it might be argued that fundamentalists constitute the antithesis of cosmopolitans (see **Cosmopolitanism**). While cosmopolitans embrace complexity and difference, fundamentalists find it disturbing and dangerous, and take refuge in 'purified' tradition or violence. For some, the key battle of the 21st century will pitch fundamentalism against cosmopolitan tolerance.

G

G7/G8 (Group of Seven/Eight)

The G8 consists of the governments of the seven most advanced industrial countries (the USA, Japan, Germany, France, Canada, Italy and the United Kingdom) and Russia. This group of countries meets to co-ordinate co-operation on economic issues. As such, these meetings have a substantial impact.

The origins of the G8 can be traced back to the 1973 oil crisis and the subsequent global recession, which led to regular meetings being held between senior financial officials of the USA, Europe and Japan to discuss economic concerns (see **Debt Crisis**). In 1975, the first meeting of the heads of state of the six main industrialized countries took place in Rambouillet, France. The outcome was an agreement to hold regular annual meetings under a rotating presidency. The G6 (Group of Six) was born, consisting of the USA, Germany, Japan, France, Italy and the United Kingdom. Later, Canada joined and the G6 became the G7 (Group of Seven).

The end of the Cold War fundamentally changed the geopolitical landscape. Political necessities meant that Russia began to meet with the G7 countries annually after their main summit. This constellation, Russia plus the G7, became known as the P8 (Political Eight). Despite Russia's economic and political problems, the country was included in most G7 sessions from 1998 onwards on the initiative of the then US President, Bill Clinton. The result was the formation of the G8. The move to incorporate Russia might be interpreted as an appreciation of Russia's economic reform programme, its geostrategic importance and the necessity of ensuring Russian co-operation and goodwill with regard to the **North Atlantic Treaty Organization**'s eastward expansion. However, Russia is more a nominal than a fully-fledged member. Because of its political and economic instabilities, Russia does not participate in some G7 sessions on economic affairs.

The G8 has a rotating presidency. The host country of the annual G8 meetings usually holds the presidency and hosts a series of ministerial-level meetings and the heads of state summit. These meetings cover a range of global issues, including health, economics, environmental issues (such as **climate change**), **HIV/AIDS** and law enforcement.

G7/G8 summits and activities have attracted criticism from various sides, in particular from the **anti-globalization movement**. In many ways, the group is regarded as an unofficial international authority, almost a world government. However, the membership of the G8 no longer reflects the largest economies in the world. Like the Security Council of the **United Nations**, the G8 constellation is a historical accident. However, G8 members continue to control 45% of the votes on the **International Monetary Fund**'s Executive Board (while 43 African governments between them control less than five per cent). Critics point out that these industrialized countries are the source of many global ills, such as carbon dioxide emissions (**global warming**), the **debt crisis** of the developing world, asymmetrical trading practices and unfair property rights. They, however, still make decisions that have world-wide effects. G8 summits thus suffer from an **accountability** problem and the group has been accused of fostering a very one-sided and self-interested agenda, closing its doors upon the majority.

General Agreement on Tariffs and Trade (GATT) – *see* World Trade Organization (WTO)

Giddens, Anthony

Anthony Giddens is a leading British sociologist who has written extensively on **modernity** and globalization. For Giddens, globalization is a direct consequence of modernization. Characteristic of globalization is a profound reorganization of time and space in social and cultural life. Time begins to dominate over space and society. Unlike **David Harvey**, who sees globalization as a speeding up of economic and social processes, Giddens sees social life being stretched across time and space, captured in his oft-quoted phrase **time-space distanciation**.

Modernization implies universalizing tendencies that render social relations ever more inclusive, thus rendering possible networks of relationships spanning the globe. As technologies (paper, wheels, roads and, more recently, the new **information and communication technologies**) speed up communications, they start to connect distant localities, stretching social relations across distances, and reducing their consciousness of their own local status. Indeed, the driving force of the new globalization is the communications revolution, which, beyond its effects on the individual, is fundamentally altering the way public institutions interact.

Locale does not become any less significant with globalization; relationships simply become less dependent on circumstances of co-presence, relying on interactions across distance, through interlocking the local and the global. Indeed, there is a heightened entanglement of the two, with more and more of the world drawn into webs of interconnection.

The significance of **nation state** boundaries and institutions declines as global and local social relations interweave and world-wide social relations intensify. These networks extend the spatial and temporal distance of social relationships such that local activities are linked to relationships established across great distances, making for **time-space distanciation**, disembedding and reflexivity. With time-space distanciation, time and space are organized so as to connect presence and absence. Disembedding concerns the ways in which social relations are lifted out of their local contexts and restructured across indefinite spans of time-space. Thus face-to-face interactions, which are a condition of modernity, give way to relations between 'absent', locally distant, others.

As a result of time-space distanciation, power centres are able to extend their control over geographic margins. Social relations become 'disembedded', or lifted out of their local contexts of interaction, to be restructured across time and space. There are two types of disembedding mechanisms—symbolic, such as money, and expert systems or technical knowledge, both of which have value across a wide range of differing contexts. Both these disembedding mechanisms also involve trust in the value of money, and in the accuracy of expertise provided, and thus both also entail trust's obverse, namely risk.

Globalization, Giddens argues, does not necessarily lead to increasing social **homogenization**, because distanciated relations are frequently engaged in a dialectical transformation. Furthermore, time-space changes are not uniformly experienced across the globe, with some regions, some nation states, some communities or individuals more integrated than others.

The idea of risk is central to Gidden's conceptualization of the globalized, future-oriented world. In a positive sense, risk alone leads to innovations and breakthroughs, but risk also has negative connotations, as for instance with environmental or health risks. The key is finding an appropriate balance between the positive and the negative. It is scientific innovation that explores the edge between the positive and negative sides of risk. (See also **Beck, Ulrich;** and **Risk Society**).

Global Cities

Global cities may be described as concentrated sites of intensified global transactions and interactions. The more globalized economic life becomes, the more concentrated becomes its management in a few key centres. Global cities are not only the loci for strategic and co-ordination functions in the global economy, but are also the key production sites and marketplaces for leading firms in finance and producer services. Such cities are thus seen as a direct consequence of globalization. Cities such as London, New York and Tokyo constitute the nodes that integrate the global financial structures through which world trade is conducted. Indeed, these three global cities are deemed the largest in terms of their financial dominance and connectivity on a global scale.

Global cities have a particularly vital role to play in an age where productivity and competitiveness of regions, nations and cities is determined by their ability to combine informational capacity, quality of life and connectivity to the network of major metropolitan centres. In network terms, they reinforce metropolitan informational hierarchies. They are the main nodal centres, using their informational potential and the new communications technologies to extend and deepen their global reach. As such they are also referred to as 'informational cities'. They encapsulate the direction functions within the larger network of decision-making and information-processing.

Rather than competing with each other, global cities complement each other, while at the same time fulfilling co-ordinating roles and functioning as international marketplaces for the buying and selling of capital and expertise. The three major cities, London, New York and Tokyo, are each seen to be fulfilling distinct functions. Tokyo has emerged as the main centre for the export of capital; London is the centre for processing capital; and New York City is the main receiver of capital.

While being command and control centres, these cities also encapsulate within them the social divisions in the new economy. They are often agglomerations, within the same geographic space, of very different social spaces, with no apparent relationship to one another. Thus, within the same geographic space may be found ethnically and culturally distinct population groups, deeply polarized in terms of income and social status. For the major growth sectors in global cities generate low-wage jobs, directly through the structure of the work process, and indirectly through the structure of high-income lifestyles. The high wages paid to those working in the financial sector is in complete contrast with the informal economy that exists by its side, with services provided by largely casualized, low-paid workers, consisting mostly of those at the margins or poor immigrants, often working anti-social hours to keep the city running. Indeed, to the extent that migrant populations are likely to be in low-paid, contingent labour arrangements, the global city is seen to encompass within it a **Third World** city. The polarized structures thus created explain why global cities are sometimes referred to as 'dual cities'.

Global Civil Society

Global **civil society** includes thousands of transborder agencies, operating simultaneously across many countries, including business lobbies, trade union confederations, ethnic and religious groups, **non-governmental organizations** and other non-official, non-commercial organizations. Transborder civil society networks and coalitions give citizens unprecedented channels of influence. They form complex networks of ties, sharing information about problems, tactics, solutions, and co-ordinated action that can attract global attention to problems affecting all or large parts of the globe. For instance, women's and **human rights** groups in **developing countries** link up with better-experienced and better-funded groups in the North, which in turn work with the media to influence international public opinion, and lobby their governments to pressure leaders in developing countries, leading to a circle of influence that is accelerating change in many parts of the world. Indeed, it has been argued that global civil society networks have bridged North–South differences that in earlier years would have paralysed co-operation among countries.

Global civil society networks typically address issues of transnational significance, such as human rights, or ecological and **environmental degradation**, and work together on the premise of international solidarity. These networks and their activities are often organized transnationally as decentralized networks, thereby lowering the costs of communication, consultation and co-ordination. New computer and telecommunications technologies have played a critical role in creating and sustaining global civil society organizations, changing people's perceptions of community, which is no longer spatially- or territorially-bounded (see **International Non-governmental Organizations**).

The development of a global civil society raises issues as to how far global principles of **identity** are becoming important, and the strength of **globalism** and related transnational identifiers in its construction. However, the legitimating potential of global civil society remains underdeveloped. Substantial parts of the world, including countries in the Middle East and the former USSR, have few inputs from voluntary associations. Furthermore, many global problems are deeply entrenched in global economic and political structures. It remains to be seen whether global activists working to ameliorate some of these intractable problems will be able to sustain their efforts for long enough to make a substantial difference.

Global Commons

Resources not under the jurisdiction of any state, and as such open for use by the international community, such as oceans, the atmosphere, and Antarctica. (See also **Antarctic Treaty System**; and **Public Goods**.)

Global Consciousness

The term is used to suggest the capacity to conceive of the world as a knowable, accessible and finite whole. Global consciousness might be said to have had its origins in the European explorations and colonizations (though some place it earlier, with the conquest of most of Eurasia in the 13th century by the Mongols), when there was a growing conception of the world as a single place that could be explored and was, indeed, available for **exploitation**. By the end of the 18th century, European institutions had been transplanted the world over, and by the end of the 19th, with railroads, industrialization and **migration**, the world had become a knowable, accessible and finite whole.

Global consciousness implies that when people attribute a supraterritorial or macrocosmic dimension to the world, they think of it or are aware of it as a single place, where distances and borders are, at some level, irrelevant. This goes together with a sense of a common global destiny, best highlighted in environmental concerns, where actions in any part of the globe are seen to have implications for everyone and everything on it (see, for instance, **Risk Society**).

Today, media events packaged by transnational networks like the **Cable News Network**, the BBC, Star TV, MTV and the **internet** have furthered this global consciousness, both through fact (environmental disasters or wars) and fiction (for instance, the repurcussions of alien invasions on the planet, or stories about viruses and human cloning). Awareness of the world as a single place is also evidenced through global sports competitions, such as the Olympic Games, or through social solidarities conceived in non-territorial terms, such as the women's rights movement. (See also **Global Village**.)

Global Culture

New cultural possibilities become available to the world as the flow of images, knowledge, ideas, information, goods, services and people continues to grow. A global culture is believed to be taking shape, riding the tele-communications revolution, as people tune in to the same news, music or sports programmes. Paradoxically, even as the world seems to become cul-turally more singular, it also becomes a more diverse place (see **American-ization** and **Cultural Imperialism**).

The notion of a 'global' culture is often posited in opposition to 'local' culture. What differentiates global culture from local culture is that while the latter is tied to place and time, the former is 'memory-less', dis-connected, disembedded or deterritorialized. Discourses on global culture tend to be interested in the form(s) it takes, and the processes that drive and shape it.

Even at its most simplistic level, global culture is inclusive of processes of both 'disintegration' and 'reintegration' at both the state and global levels. Cultural flows here are seen to produce degrees of both cultural homo-geneity and heterogeneity. Some of the unifying commodity and consumer cultures brought into being and sustained by the media and entertainment industries include Coca-Cola, the Big Mac or Dallas. Indeed, very often global culture is dismissed as bereft of roots, changeable, shallow, and inauthentic, and nothing more than a creation of the media and big business.

Processes of differentiation might begin with the way these items are received and consumed, and include forms of resistance, including ethnic resilience, fragmentation and the re-emergence of powerful nationalist myths, memories and symbols that evoke local places rather than global spaces.

Global culture is often defined as being characterized by diversity rather than a replication of uniformity, with a large number of people involved with more than one culture. It seems to be a product of interculturalism, rather than **multiculturalism**, often producing ambivalence rather than coherence of **identity**, spawning multiple identities, and thus providing opportunities to push at boundaries to create hybridized '**third cultures**' which cannot be understood merely as the product of a simple coming together of two cultures (see **Creolization** and **Hybridity**).

For many commentators, the emergence of global culture is the direct outcome of late capitalist restructuring. It is perceived as an ideological tool in the service of a revitalized and accelerated phase of **capitalism**, shaping desires and creating needs, thus opening up new arenas for capital accumulation (see **Advertising** and **Branding**).

The notion of 'a' global culture, however, is not without its critics. The critics' arguments are premised on the conception of culture as a particular, time-bound phenomenon, expressive of identities which historical circumstances have helped form over long periods. Thus, if by culture is meant a collective mode of life or a repertoire of beliefs, styles, values and symbols, then there is necessarily more than one culture in the world. Furthermore, given the diversity in the reception of these flows and signs, and their use by local audiences, critics argue that the notion of 'a' global culture can only be an impossibility.

There is, however, no denying the potential in the idea of 'global culture' in so far as it permits forms of social interaction not tied to place or limited by time, making them apt frames or contexts in which new identities may be formed, and new understandings of the world fashioned. (See also **Robertson, Roland**.)

Global Division of Labour

The idea of the division of labour lies at the heart of liberal economic theory (see **Liberalism** and **Neo-liberalism**). In his classic work, *The Wealth of Nations*, Adam Smith argued that the greatest improvement in the productive powers of labour comes with the division of labour. Practice increases dexterity and specialization, and these in turn increase speed of production and quality. The global division of labour describes a particular form of organization of labour that potentially encompasses the whole globe. Smith's concept of the division of labour went through several intermediary stages of evolution before assuming a global form. The idea itself was fine-tuned by Henry Ford, who used this fundamental principle and added machinery and an assembly line system to it (see **Fordism**). David Ricardo applied the concept of the division of labour to the international level to develop his theory of **comparative advantage**.

It was **colonialism**, and the expansion and deepening of capitalist relations of production, which created an international division of labour. Industrialization in the imperial powers created a demand for primary commodities from other countries. But industrialization also undermined traditional manufacturing in the colonies, through both colonial trade restrictions, and because of the competitive superiority (lower costs) of goods produced in the industrialized world. As such, this division of labour reflected the unequal and skewed power relations between imperial powers and colonies.

By the late 19th and early 20th centuries, in addition to processed goods, capital was also beginning to be exported from the core, industrialized countries, partly to increase the production and export of primary commodities from the colonies, and partly to develop new markets. However, this did not change the fundamentally unequal nature of the relationship. The industrialized core continued to perform capital-intensive, high value-adding production while the colonies were confined to the labour-intensive, low value-adding production.

The system did not evidence much change as the colonies began to gain freedom from about the mid-20th century. There were gloomy predictions for the newly independent **developing countries**, as the international division of labour was seen to be perpetuating a relationship of domination and mutual dependency, a relation between head office and branch plant (see **Dependency Theory** and **World Systems Theory**).

By the 1960s, the internal division of labour within the firm, deepened by the introduction of scientific management and Fordism, was being exported across state boundaries, leading to the fragmentation and internationalization of production. A new international division of labour was said to be emerging as command and control continued to vest with the core, while the labour-intensive parts of manufacturing were exported to developing countries, which provided proximity to raw material-producing areas, and/or taking advantage of different time and wage cost zones. Trade increasingly consisted of the flow of components between plants of the same multinational company (MNC), made by people in different countries. Meanwhile, some least-developed countries managed to cartelize and improve returns from primary production.

But this international division of labour began to change in the 1970s, to move towards a more global division of labour. As developing and newly industrialized countries that had been recipients of **foreign direct investment (FDI)**, such as Taiwan (Republic of China), Singapore, Malaysia, Thailand, Brazil and Mexico, began to export manufactured goods to the industrialized West, it became evident that the old **core-periphery** relations were neither absolutely clear-cut nor terminal. Indeed, by the 1990s these countries had become generators of FDI.

The hierarchical division of labour is far from having disappeared. However, it is no longer possible to map these divisions neatly on to particular spaces—countries or regions. Sweatshops abound not just in the developing world, but also in pockets of the industrialized world. While India might be exporting raw materials, and hosting call centres, the country is also producing high-quality software for the global information technology industry. Social and spatial divisions continue to exist, but they have taken on much more complex forms.

The global division of labour has entailed a decline in the share of manufacturing employment in total employment in the industrialized world. Meanwhile, management of the highly fragmented production process has become far more efficient with the **internet** and other **information and communication technologies** as it has become possible to track the progress of components through various stages, thereby allowing firms to make adjustments at an early stage to match fluctuations in global demand. (See also **Commodity Chains;** and **Post-Fordism**.)

Global Financial Crises

Financial crisis is endemic to the current global financial system. This is attributed to several reasons, including the breakdown of the **Bretton Woods system** of fixed exchange rates, the innovation of new financial products, the introduction and development of new communication technologies, the **deregulation** of financial markets and the triumph of neo-liberal financial management actively promoted by international organizations such as the **International Monetary Fund (IMF)** and major industrialized countries. The result has been a gradual increase in short-term transactions in commodity futures, stock options and the manipulation of currency markets. A global financial web of institutional speculators has been created, comprising investment banks, stock brokerage firms, insurance companies and currency dealers. Large financial capital transits take place through the global financial web at ever-increasing speed and frequency via electronic transfers. These transactions take place outside the real economy, producing no commodities. They are difficult to regulate and lead to destabilizing speculation and currency market disturbances.

Thus, while **liberalization** has facilitated financial deepening and development, with positive effects on growth, financial markets can also be volatile, with extreme instances leading to crises that result in costly output losses (see **Casino Capitalism**). Crises in Asia and Latin America have threatened the economies and the stability of all **developing countries**. There has also been a noticeable increase in the frequency of crises, with many more in the 1970s, 1980s and 1990s than during the previous decades of the 20th century. The **World Bank** has estimated that there were 112 systemic banking crises in 93 countries between the late 1970s and the end of the 20th century. Particularly worrying has been the increase in the incidence of twin crises—currency and banking crises coinciding and reinforcing one another. The countries most affected have not been the poorest countries, which often have relatively rudimentary financial markets, but the next tier of developing countries and emerging markets, where the costs of financial instability are also the greatest (see **Capital Flows**; **Debt Crisis** and **Exchange Rates**).

In the mid-1990s, Mexico plunged into a financial crisis, having only just overcome the effects of the debt crisis of the 1980s. After the negotiation and signing of the **North American Free Trade Agreement**, short-term capital flowed into the country. By 1994, however, a series of events, including higher interest rates in the USA and the **Zapatista** rebellion in Chiapas, caused a rapid outflow of capital and forced Mexico to abandon its currency's link with the US dollar. The result was a rapid devaluation of the Mexican currency, causing savings to diminish, interest rates to rocket and living standards to fall. The crisis quickly spilt over into other Latin American countries in what has been termed the 'tequila effect'.

The Asian financial crisis in July 1997 is viewed as something of a pivotal event. It was completely unforeseen, very costly, and had repercussions throughout the world, on Russia and Brazil, and also on a giant US hedge fund, Long-Term Capital Management. Until the outbreak of the crisis, the

East Asian economies attracted almost 50% of all investment directed towards developing countries. Like Mexico, Thailand, Indonesia and the Republic of Korea (South Korea), the countries most affected by the ensuing crisis, had currencies pegged to the US dollar and had liberalized their financial markets, causing a massive inflow of short-term speculative capital. In 1997, investors began to doubt whether Thailand could maintain the value of its currency against the US dollar and began to withdraw from the country. Thailand subsequently had to devalue its currency, triggering a contagion effect. The financial turmoil that was occurring in Thailand spread quickly through the region, causing capital flight on a massive scale. The crisis resulted in dramatic falls in GDP per caput. What started as an exchange rate disaster threatened to cause the collapse of the region's banks, stock markets and even entire economies.

The IMF came in for severe criticism for both its role in precipitating the crisis, and its response to it. Excessively rapid financial and capital market liberalization was cited as a critical (though not perhaps the only) cause of the crisis. And the IMF's remedies came with a host of conditionalities that compromised economic **sovereignty**, with critics arguing that it did not actually restore the economies' health.

The Asian financial crisis was followed by a financial crisis in Russia. What all three examples had in common was that they were caused by hot speculative capital attracted by the deregulation of financial markets. The crises highlighted the potential vulnerability of all countries to massive inflows and outflows of capital (see **Capital Controls**). Investors, alarmed by crisis in one part of the world, have the tendency to withdraw money from other parts of the world, spreading panic.

The devastating implications of financial crises have triggered discussions about regulations to slow down capital mobility and new forms of governance. One suggestion has been the imposition of a tax (sometimes referred to as a Tobin tax) on short-term foreign exchange dealings. Such a tax would control speculative short-term investments but would not hinder medium-term or long-term direct investments, tourism or imports. Given the obstacles posed by powerful institutional speculators to maintaining the structure of the financial system, such a tax would be difficult to implement.

Concerted thinking about new forms of governance in international finance led to the emergence of two institutional innovations: the Financial Stability Forum (FSF) and the Group of Twenty (G20) (see **Global Governance**). The FSF concentrates on offshore financial centres, cross-border capital flows and highly leveraged institutions, such as hedge funds. The G20 is more of a political body, comprised of the finance ministers and bank governors of the **G7** states plus Argentina, Australia, Brazil, China, India, Indonesia, South Korea, Mexico, Russia, Saudi Arabia, South Africa and Turkey, and representatives of the **European Union**, the IMF and the World Bank. As a group they account for more than 85% of the world's gross domestic product, and 65% of the world's population. This wider participation in decision-making is seen as an attempt to bolster the legitimacy of financial reforms. It is doubtful, however, whether these institutions have the resources or the political will to effectively deal with the recurrent problem of financial crisis.

Global Governance

Global governance is not a synonym for a global or world government. Rather than the existence of a formal authority above state level, global governance refers to a loose framework of global regulation, both institutional and normative. Governance is, therefore, a much wider term, incorporating activities that do not necessarily need the backing of sovereign power.

The issue of governance is central to debates on globalization. Discussions revolve around the most appropriate locus of authority and power in the context of a world experiencing both integration and fragmentation. A hotly contested issue is the role of the state, with arguments that globalization has deprived the state of **sovereignty** countered by the assertion that states remain the final arbiters of governance in national and international relations. A less polarized view is to see globalization as a move away from the Westphalian system with its emphasis on sovereignty and non-intervention. National governments remain in an important position, but governance is increasingly multi-layered, with authority becoming diffused between sub-national, national and international levels (see **Multi-layered Governance**). Thus, regulatory state structures are enmeshed with various forms of regional and global governance.

The mechanisms and rules of global governance are created by the actions and agreements of the key actors in the international system, namely nation states and their respective national governments. However, global governance incorporates non-governmental actors as well, such as capital markets, **non-governmental organizations**, **multinational companies** and civic associations. Indeed, global governance has many elements and includes within its range **international organizations**, international law, transnational regulatory frameworks, elements of **global civil society** and shared normative principles. In many ways, global governance creates an overarching system regulating international affairs, thereby creating a link to the concept of **international order**. It is global governance that provides structure and order in an anarchical international system, according to liberal and neo-liberal theories in international relations.

Global governance institutions create 'regimes', which entail implicit or explicit principles, norms, rules and decision-making procedures regarding the behaviour of international actors. Most national governments participate in the creation and maintenance of such regimes because they find regular co-operative behaviour beneficial. Indeed, it might prove costly to remain outside such regimes.

Regimes influence international behaviour in several ways: by providing legal frameworks which compel participants to obey rules by the threat of sanctions (**World Trade Organization**); by distributing money and providing credit based on certain conditions (**International Monetary Fund**; **World Bank**); by appealing to moral standards (International Labour Organization); and by defining the structure of the global system itself. As a result, a new international **multilateralism** has developed, with international organizations developing into global governance agencies with some degree of autonomy from nation states. At the same time, non-governmental actors have become instrumental in some regulatory processes.

Global governance, therefore, is a move towards a more co-operative international system based increasingly on norms and principles such as support for **democracy**, free market principles and **human rights**. The **United Nations** system is perhaps the most vivid expression of global governance.

The system does suffer many limitations, including the privileging of some issues at the cost of others, double standards, limited enforcement, poor co-ordination between institutions, widespread understaffing and underfunding, and fragile legitimacy, but these do not detract from the importance of transworld regulation in a globalizing world. (See also **Accountability**; and **Democracy**.)

Global Justice Movement

The Global Justice Movement constitutes an umbrella movement for protests against supranational institutions and the neo-liberal project, which took concrete and a somewhat concerted shape with the protests against the world trade meeting in Seattle, USA, in 1999, when a powerful alliance of consumer protection groups, trade unions, labour activists, environmentalists, debt relief campaigners, **human rights** activists, **Third World** farmer associations, animal rights activists and feminists protested against the policies of the **World Trade Organization (WTO)**. Between 40,000–50,000 people are thought to have taken part in the demonstrations in Seattle, which became known as the 'Battle for Seattle'. The protests saw an eclectic alliance where right-wing protectionists concerned about the decline of living standards in the global North marched side by side with left-wing groups from the global South. Yet despite these differences, the vast majority of the demonstrators focused their criticism on free market **capitalism** and the policies of the WTO.

The Seattle protests brought together several angles and lines of critique against globalization, largely in opposition to neo-liberal globalization, **free trade** and laissez-faire **capitalism**. Neo-liberal globalization, instead of fostering economic and social **development** in the global South, has brought **poverty** to the developing world. In addition, the unrestrained and unsupervised market has wreaked negative effects on the environment and society at large. Unrestricted free trade is benefiting countries with more financial leverage at the expense of poor, **developing countries**. Further, laissez-faire capitalism has entailed the accumulation of power in the hands of a few very large **multinational companies** which have the strength to directly and indirectly influence national and international agenda-setting. Finally, the lack of transparency and **accountability** of international multilateral organizations such as the WTO or the **World Bank** means there are no counter points or checks on unbridled capitalism.

While protectionists, such as US Senator Pat Buchanan's supporters, may have joined the protests in Seattle, the Global Justice Movement has no intention of returning to narrowly defined **nationalism**. In fact, the movement propagates a form of bottom-up globalization in which democratic norms, labour rights and environmental standards are emphasized and promoted on a global scale. It aims to regulate capital, while being respectful of local cultures and building on a shared vision of how best to meet global societal needs. It addresses transnational problems, particularly the global imbalance of power advanced by the neo-liberal model of globalization, and envisions a new role for **civil society** (see **World Social Forum**).

While the term **'anti-globalization movement'** is used interchangeably with the Global Justice Movement, the term 'anti-globalization' is misleading in that the movement represented the globalization of protest. Activists associated with the anti-globalization movement over the last 30 years have employed the same technologies of globalization, such as innovations in information and communication technology, to organize protests and to associate with each other. Mobile phones, laptop computers, the **internet** and fax machines have allowed activists to create international networks, maintain close contacts and to arrange and co-ordinate activities without the need for a clear organizational structure.

Today, the Global Justice Movement brings together a very broad coalition of church groups, national liberation factions, left-wing parties, environmentalists, unionists and others from different national backgrounds, guided by the ideals of equality and social justice for all people in the world. (Website: http://www.globaljusticemovement.org/.)

Global-Local Links

While the terms 'global' and 'local' are used extensively in the literature on globalization, the relationship between the terms is far from clear. Both are relational, and relative, concepts. There is often a tendency to see the local as the stopping point of global circulations, where global flows fragment and are transformed into something place-bound and particular. The local is where the global is consumed, incorporated or resisted. However, flows themselves create terrains, and so there can be no territorial distinctions between the 'global' transcending of place, or the 'local' making of place.

Furthermore, while terms like 'the global' seem to suggest a world-wide universalism, this is far from the case as the processes of globalization are quite uneven. Different locales seem to react differently to different experiences of the global. Nevertheless, it might be argued that globalization penetrates every aspect of people's lives, including the most routine and intimate. Indeed, in the global arena, economies and cultures seem to be thrown into intense and immediate contact with each other. What is critical here, however, is that the 'other' is not simply something 'out there' but also within.

Contacts between the local and the global produce ambivalent identities, with national and local identities often incorporating 'foreign' concepts into their culture, stripped of their origins and their local meanings, in order to fill perceived needs or gaps in local knowledge. Indeed, the proximity of foreign cultures to dominant national ones does not necessarily produce cultural homogeneity. When one culture borrows from another, often a decontextualization of the borrowed culture takes place (e.g. the deracination of Chinese and Indian restaurants in the United Kingdom to become part of mainstream 'British' culture—see **Cultural Homogenization**).

The global-local link needs to be treated with care. It suggests a buying-in to globalized consumption patterns while translating that consumption in a very particular local context as a local practice. However, it is by no means a one-way influence of power, with cultural products travelling from the West to everywhere else, or from the core to the periphery. There is cultural exchange and **reciprocity**. The equation might still remain largely unequal, but through the relativizing of core and periphery under globalizing influences, local identities may be confirmed and even intensified by global processes. (See also **Glocalization**; and **Hybridity**.)

Global Village

This term was coined by Marshall McLuhan in his 1960 publication *Explorations in Communication* to explore the sense of 'compression' or shrinking through the shared simultaneity of audiovisual media experiences. The idea took root in the 'expressive' 1960s, and is evocative of a new level of neighbourliness as transport and communication technologies appear to have compressed the world and brought everyone in it closer together.

The idea of the global village, however, tends to be treated with some caution, as its communitarian aspects might have been grossly exaggerated. While the technologies of globalization, particularly different forms of media, are key players in producing the global village, or a sense of community, the idea of 'one world' is far from having been achieved. For one, the notion tends to gloss over some of the deep-seated inequalities in access to the technologies of globalization. Furthermore, these technologies are unable to create, in any real way, a sense of place. Instead, the world today seems increasingly characterized by rootlessness, alienation, and indeed, dispossession. (See also **Glocalization**.)

Global Warming

A slow, long-term rise in the average world temperature, thought to be caused by gas (particularly carbon dioxide and chlorofluorocarbon) emissions creating a greenhouse effect, an issue that has dominated the environmental agenda since the mid-1980s. The consequences are predicted to be **climate change** and a rise in sea levels, which could make whole islands in the Pacific disappear, and flood populated coastlines in Bangladesh and China. The costs of controlling global warming are high since they entail curbing economic growth or shifting on to new technological paths. There is a collective goods dilemma attached to combating global warming: the benefits would be shared globally but the costs need to be extracted from each state individually, further complicated by the potential for conflict over who would pay the bills given the North–South divide (see **Public Goods**). (See also **Environmental Degradation;** and **United Nations Conference on Environment and Development**).

Globalism

For globalists, globalization is the most important dynamic in contemporary history. They argue that contemporary social relations have become thoroughly globalized, so much so that the values informing daily behaviour relate to real or imagined material states of the globe and its inhabitants.

Globalists endow globalization with particular neo-liberal values and meanings (see **Neo-liberalism**). The view accords primacy to the market; it believes that the world market is now powerful enough to supplant local and national political action. Globalists include hyperglobalizers such as Kenichi Ohmae and John Naisbitt, who promote the view of a 'borderless world', and a number of corporate managers and executives, powerful business lobbies, journalists, government officials and politicians. They see globalization as an inevitable and irreversible process, reflecting the spread of market forces aided by technological innovation. Implicit here is the idea that nobody is in charge of the globalization project. As such, there is no alternative but to adapt to the discipline of the market.

Furthermore, market **liberalization, free trade** and the integration of markets are presented as 'natural' processes, imputed a positive value. Supporters of free trade, for instance, point out that the principles of **comparative advantage** present a more efficient resource-allocation strategy for all countries, which could benefit from lower prices and lower unemployment. Neo-liberal laissez-faire **capitalism** is believed to emancipate society and individuals from restrictive government control. Thus, neo-liberal globalization, globalists contend, leads to greater liberty, **democracy**, progress and wealth. Market liberalization would bring higher global living standards, individual freedom and technological progress. Embracing neo-liberal policies is the way forward; the consequence of not doing so is failure. An example is made of the 1997–98 Asian financial crisis to attribute blame to government intervention in the economy (see **Global Financial Crises**).

The globalist discourse on globalization is ideological to the extent that it is politically motivated. It supports the construction and preservation of a particular asymmetrical power structure in the international political economy. Anti-globalist arguments (see **Global Justice Movement**) take issue with most globalist arguments, premising their case on the argument that another world is possible.

Glocal(ization)

Roland Robertson coined the term 'glocal', combining global and local. According to Robertson, rather than the local and the global constituting analytical opposites, locality can be regarded, with certain reservations, as an aspect of globalization. Through global compression, localities are brought together and invented, he posits, and 'home', 'community' and 'locality' are produced. While globalization is useful as an analytical concept referring to the simultaneity and the interpenetration of what are conventionally called the global and the local, or the universal and the particular, for Robertson glocalization represents a more accurate term to describe the global-local relationship. Glocalization refers, in the subjective and personal sphere, to the construction and invention of diverse localities through global flows of ideas and information. (See also **Global-Local Links**.)

Greenpeace

Greenpeace is an international non-governmental organization (INGO) working on environmental issues (see **Environmental Degradation** and **Environmentalism**). It was founded in 1971 in Vancouver, Canada, and has played a significant role in shaping the emerging principles of **global governance**, with staffed offices in more than 30 countries today. Greenpeace is part of **global civil society**, a space where civic actors meet to engage in political activity to influence the shape and direction of international society.

Greenpeace began with a focus on nuclear weapons testing, but has since been concerned with all threats to the planet's ecosystem, including, broadly, toxic substances, energy and atmosphere, nuclear issues and ocean and terrestrial ecology, and sub-issues within these. Greenpeace also campaigns for safe and sustainable trade.

The transnational character of environmental problems such as pollution and **climate change** requires concerted international and global responses, and as such, Greenpeace's campaigns and projects are organized on an international scale. Greenpeace uses a wide range of tactics in order to raise awareness, abandon non-ecological practices and infuse environmental sensitivities. These include non-violent direct action and concerted advertisement campaigns in the global media. Examples include the obstruction of whaling ships, the blockading of offshore oil rigs and the climbing of nuclear power stations. These spectacular actions have generated widespread media attention and helped to disseminate Greenpeace's message on a global scale. One of the most noteworthy of these campaigns was to prevent Shell from abandoning the Brent Spar oil platform in the North Sea in 1995. However, the group was criticized for stretching facts a bit too far in order to create a greater media impact. Greenpeace overestimated, by a factor of 37, the amount of hydrocarbons in the rig that might have leaked into the sea.

Apart from direct action, Greenpeace also engages in the lobbying of governments, gathering information, organizing protests and boycotts, and educating and undertaking research aimed at changing general environmental attitudes and the behaviour of governments and the general public. (See also **Transnational Advocacy Networks**). (Website: http://www.greenpeace.org.)

H

Harvey, David

David Harvey's *The Condition of Postmodernity*, published in 1989, was to become a bestseller, and has since achieved the status of a classic. For Harvey, a geographer, building on Marx's explanations of globalization, **capitalism** is the main driving engine of globalization. His 1989 publication was a materialist interpretation of **post-modernity** as born of the inconsistencies and contradictions within capitalism. It advanced a theory of **time-space compression** through the increasing speed with which commodities circulate through the market system. Harvey shows that over a period, time and space have been contracted in the interest of greater profits. He identifies the economic depression that swept Britain and Europe in 1846–47 as a turning point in that, thereafter, throughout the latter half of the 19th century, there was a radical readjustment in the sense of time-space in economic, political and cultural life.

Harvey saw the development of modernism as a response to the crisis experienced in the changed relationship between time and space. Thus, the spate of inventions in the late 19th/early 20th centuries, such as the steam engine, aviation, the telegraph, telephone and wireless, all effected a reorganization of space to reduce time and a reorganization of time to reduce space. These spurred the growth of **globalism**, and the speeding up of capital circulation.

Time-space compression manifests itself in various forms today. For instance, with the proliferation of various forms of media, space has been technologically eliminated as 'real time' coverage implies that audiences can be both 'here' and 'there'. And there is an increasing convergence of technologies.

Harvey characterizes the present era as moving from **Fordism** to one of 'flexible accumulation', while recognizing that more traditional production systems continue to obtain in many parts of the world. This has political implications, since it changes the nature and composition of the global working class, with unionization and left-wing politics becoming increasingly hard to sustain, and thus changes the nature of opposition to capitalism. Other forms of ideologies, however, are on the rise, including those of entrepreneurialism, paternalism and privatism.

Despite the seeming depoliticization of globalization within the theoretical discourse, Harvey argues that it is still very much a political project, put on the agenda by capitalist class interests operating through the agency of USA's foreign, military, and commercial policies. In a recent book Harvey explores the new incarnation of **imperialism** against the background of the production of space by capital accumulation. Neo-liberalization, he argues, has involved a very distinct kind of imperial project. It is an imperialism that does not involve occupation; instead, it uses economic leverage, such as the power of its economy and the power of international institutions like the **World Bank** or the **International Monetary Fund**. Or, in some instances, it uses covert power to place in power someone who the USA prefers, e.g. Pinochet in Chile or the Shah of Iran.

Harvey has been criticized for underestimating the ways in which culture shapes material forces and the effects of political economy on culture, though another view has it that Harvey does not present a case entirely of economic determinism. The experience of time and space mediates between culture and the economy, though the meaning of 'experience' is never substantiated or explained.

Held, David

David Held is a political scientist who sees globalization in terms of its transformation of the world into a single social space, aided by the new real-time communications infrastructure. Of key concern to Held is **democracy** in a globalizing world; globalization presents both a threat and an opportunity for democracy. He sees value in democracy per se as a public good. But for the survival of democracy in a globalizing world, the **nation state** is inadequate, and an extension of democracy into the international arena is required.

Held borrows from the intellectual traditions of both **liberalism** and **Marxism**, attempting to reconcile the one's scepticism about political power and the other's scepticism about economic power through a radical democracy at the level of **civil society** and the state, with each becoming the condition and guarantor for the other's democratization. With the end of the Cold War, Held began to focus his attention on economic globalization and the opportunities and limitations this created for democracy. He is at odds here with Francis Fukuyama, whose **end of history** thesis he critiques on the grounds that Fukuyama fails to see that liberalism and democracy are not single unitary structures but take different forms, that there are tensions between liberalism and democracy, and that Fukuyama fails to question whether liberal democracy can flourish in the face of globalization.

Held associates globalization with what he calls a double democratic deficit. For one, globalization has compounded the tension between democracy, tied to territory or the nation state, and the operation of global markets or transnational networks of corporate power (see **Multinational Companies— MNCs**). States have limited capacity and ability to influence decisions taken by MNCs that have a direct bearing on currency values, employment prospects or other areas within the state's jurisdiction. For another, globalization is associated with the emergence of skewed global politics that exacerbates differences and inequalities by furthering the interests of the global élites at the expense of the wider global community, again making for weak democratic credentials. Thus, globalization is producing an **international order** structured by agencies and forces over which citizens have minimal, if any, control. Nor are there mechanisms available to citizens to signal their disagreement.

For Held then, the greatest political and ethical challenge of globalization lies in redressing these democratic deficits. The answer to these problems lies in **cosmopolitanism**. This entails the democratization of **global governance** and the pursuit of global social justice. The core values of social democracy, identified as the rule of law, political equality, social justice and solidarity, and democratic governance, need to be institutionalized within global power systems.

Held advocates a **cosmopolitan democracy** on the grounds that democracy may not survive in any meaningful form if it remains tied to the **nation state**. The only way of reinvigorating democracy within states would be to extend democracy to relations between and across states. Thus, there would be a double democratization to address the double democratic deficit. Instead of the nation state as the locus of power and democratic regimes, Held argues for democratizing international organizations like the **World Trade Organization**, and ensuring that MNCs are held accountable for decisions that may harm the more vulnerable sections of society. He argues for a cosmopolitan community, made up of members of different societies coming together as cosmopolitan citizens to influence decisions that affect the whole world.

Held's ideas of cosmopolitanism and cosmopolitan democracy have been criticized for being utopian visions. Democracy, critics argue, is unlikely to flourish at a global level, as there is no counterpart to the nation that can engage moral and political emotions, or build the level of trust and commitment to the public good.

HIV – *see* Acquired Immune Deficiency Syndrome (AIDS)

Homogenization

Homogenization means the 'diminishing of difference'. With regard to globalization, it relates to the question of whether the globalization process creates a more uniform, undifferentiated world. Some commentators have argued that the process of globalization is bringing about world-wide political, social, economic and cultural synchronization. They assert that if activities, institutions and values take on global characteristics, they must necessarily replace certain local activities, institutions and values, making the world more homogeneous, with more and more people having more and more in common.

Homogenization, it is argued, can be observed in many different areas of life. **International trade** rules are enforced and negotiated by **international organizations** such as the **World Trade Organization**; the highest form of political community world-wide is the **nation state**, a concept originating in Western Europe; **neo-liberalism** has been adopted by the **Washington Consensus** as the best path to economic growth and **development**; the English language has become the global lingua franca; and the entertainment industry controlled by Western corporations like **Cable News Network** and Time Warner is seen to be shaping global values.

It is on account of these perceived 'Western' homogenizing factors that critics of globalization (see **Anti-globalization (Movement)**) associate globalization with **cultural imperialism, Americanization** or **Westernization**, describing the emergence of a world culture based on Enlightenment principles such as individualism, the Western state system, **capitalism, consumerism**, American popular culture and the English language.

However, while there is certainly an element of truth in such an analysis, it is also possible to link globalization with continuing and even increasing diversity (see **Global-Local Links; Glocalization;** and **Hybridity**). While certain rules and practices have been exported throughout the world, they are often interpreted and adopted in a modified manner to fit local particularities. Market rules and economic principles are often shaped to suit diverse local contexts. **Multinational companies** with a global reach have found it necessary to address specific local preferences in the markets they wish to penetrate. The European interpretation of capitalism differs from the American version and both differ from Chinese- or Japanese-style economic management. States have leeway to structure their own policies. Global media and communication flows have different impacts on different recipients. Nor are media flows always in one direction. If Hollywood has been supported in its spread by the technologies driving globalization, the very same information flows and technologies have also enhanced the global reach of Bollywood cinema from India, or Chinese and Japanese cinema, which have penetrated Western mainstream cinema.

Globalization has not prevented people from asserting their cultural, political and social identities. If anything, the perceived threat of homogenization has resulted in increased awareness and **protectionism** of national differences and heritages. Thus, while there might be a ubiquity of Western cultural forms, this cannot in and of itself be deemed evidence of homogenization. There is some convergence, but customization, it might be argued, is still keeping homogenization at bay.

Human Development Index (HDI)

Pioneered by the Pakistani economist Mahbub ul Haq in 1990, the Human Development Index (HDI) has been developed as a critique of the measurement of **development** that looked exclusively at economic variables such as economic growth. The index, adopted by the United Nations Development Programme (UNDP), comes from a vision of development that sees it as being about expanding the choices people have.

The HDI goes beyond output or income to also take into account social factors in measuring development. It classifies countries according to the HDI value, which is a composite measure based on life expectancy, education (adult literacy and mean years of schooling) and income (as gross domestic product or GDP per caput). Thus, countries with similar amounts of wealth, measured by GDP per caput, could still have different levels of development measured by the HDI, reflecting different degrees of internal **inequality** and **poverty**, and the continuing significance of state policies at the national level. The Human Development Report, published annually by the UNDP, establishes minimum and maximum HDI values and ranks countries according to their relative distance between these two values. Thus the Human Development Report distinguishes between countries with a high human development index (0.800 and above), medium human development (HDI between 0.500 and 0.799) and countries with low human development (HDI below 0.500). But though the HDI is more broadly based and provides a broader conceptualization of well-being, it is still a rather summary calculation, subject to measurement errors.

Over time, more new measures have been introduced to make this measure of development more sophisticated, including the Gender-related Development Index, the Gender Empowerment Measure and Poverty Human Development Index, as well as measures of the quality of governance and the extent of **democracy**.

Human Rights

Human rights are conceived as universal rights that people possess simply by being human, regardless of their association with particular political, social or cultural communities. This notion is deeply rooted in the cosmopolitan (see **Cosmopolitanism**) beliefs of Stoic and Medieval-Christian philosophy and the natural law and natural rights tradition as represented in the writings of Hugo Grotius. The Enlightenment broadened the so-called 'rights of man' and prepared the ground for the post-1945 era.

The contemporary world has witnessed a dramatic upsurge in the question of human rights. A number of global and regional treaties and declarations concerning human rights have emerged since 1945, particularly following the Nuremberg trials. Among the most important ones is the Universal Declaration of Human Rights (1948), which does not have the force of **international law** but sets forth international norms regarding the behaviour of governments in relation to both citizens and aliens, and is based on the principle that all human beings are born free and equal, and that violations of human rights upset **international order**. Other important treaties and declarations include the International Covenant on Civil and Political Rights (1976), and the International Covenant on Economic, Social and

Cultural Rights (1976). Together they form the International Bill of Human Rights, providing the basis for international law on human rights issues, though it remains one of the least-developed areas of international law. A range of other **United Nations (UN)** conventions exists, including the Convention on the Prevention and Punishment of the Crime of Genocide (1951), the International Convention on the Elimination of All Forms of Racial Discrimination (1965), the Convention on the Elimination of All Forms of Discrimination against Women (1979), the Convention against Torture and Other Cruel, Inhuman or Degrading Treatment or Punishment (1984), the Convention on the Rights of the Child (1989), and the Rome Statute for the International Criminal Court (2002). On the regional level are treaties such as the European Convention on Human Rights (1953), the American Convention on Human Rights (1978) and the Banjul Charter on Human and People's Rights (1981).

The period has also witnessed the emergence of **international non-governmental organizations**, such as **Amnesty International**, dedicated to human rights issues. The group actively seeks to obtain freedom for prisoners of conscience and monitors human rights abuses world-wide. Other groups, such as Human Rights Watch, work with a more regional or national focus. The UN also operates a Commission on Human Rights with a global focus.

Apart from being universal, human rights are absolute in the sense that they cannot be qualified and they are fundamental in the sense that they are inalienable. Generally, human rights fall into three categories, succeeding each other historically and each new generation representing a further broadening. First-generation rights concentrate on political rights, such as freedom of speech, freedom of assembly, and the right to take part in government. Second-generation rights focus on economic, social and cultural rights. Both first- and second-generation rights focus essentially on individual rights. Third-generation rights, however, such as those expressed in the Banjul Charter, with it emphasis on the rights of 'peoples', are concerned with community rights.

The inclusion of human rights in international law restricts the **sovereignty** of states by placing certain restrictions and responsibilities on state behaviour. In the current globalization discourse, the extension of human rights norms has not remained uncontested. Two criticisms are worth mentioning. The first one focuses on the historical origins of contemporary international human rights. Critics point to the fact that the rights enshrined in international law have been developed in a primarily Western context. Their universal application in non-Western cultural contexts represents a form of **cultural imperialism** that ignores different conceptions of cultural, social and political rights and duties. And, second, the relationship between sovereignty and human rights remains controversial. Both are fundamental norms of international relations. Problems can occur when the principle of sovereignty clashes with human rights norms. Whether sovereignty prevails under such circumstances or whether states lose their right to non-intervention in their domestic affairs has been a difficult question to answer. (See also **Humanitarian Intervention**.)

Humanitarian Intervention

A new, more violent form of rights protection that began in the 1990s, humanitarian intervention involves the invasion of sovereign territory by one or more states using military force, with or without the backing of international bodies, with the supposed intention of alleviating suffering of some or all within that state. While on occasion such an intervention is condoned by the official authorities of a state, more often than not intervention may be specifically aimed against government authorities. It denotes an intrusion into the sovereign affairs of a state. Examples from the 1990s include the creation of 'safe areas' for Kurds in northern Iraq and the NATO intervention in Kosovo.

Interventions on humanitarian grounds challenge the very premises of the Westphalian system, the sanctity of **sovereignty** and non-intervention. These norms are enshrined in the UN Charter (Art. 2). However, as with the right to self-defence, it is argued that humanitarian intervention is a legitimate exception to the general ban on the unilateral recourse to force in the UN Charter.

The emergence of humanitarian intervention is linked to the rise of an emphasis on human security in international relations. Traditionally, **security** concerns focus on the concept of the state, its territorial integrity, its survival as a political community and its sovereignty. Hence, security was more or less linked with the defence of the state and sovereignty against internal and external threats. Much has changed in the post-Cold War world, which has witnessed the rise of alternative approaches to security. The 1994 UN Development Report highlighted that traditional definitions of security focusing on the state are too narrow. Human security, largely defined as the absence of chronic threats to the individual, needs to be taken into consideration as well. This is important in that state security and human security can be in direct contradiction. **Human rights** abuses are often justified by reference to national security. Thus, the contemporary discourse surrounding human rights, human security and humanitarian intervention demonstrates a considerable weakening of the doctrines of sovereignty and non-intervention.

This might be linked to the increasing strength of the human rights regime, particularly its conception of legitimate state sovereignty as flowing from the rights of individuals, thus placing human rights above state rights to sovereignty. States are now being held to new standards of legitimacy based on their observation of human rights laws and norms. It is also an indication that many deadly conflicts nowadays take place within states. There is a realization of the need to balance sovereignty and non-intervention against legitimate ethical concerns about what goes on inside the domestic jurisdiction of individual states.

While this view may have a history dating back well beyond the 1990s, the Cold War kept it at bay for fear of superpower conflict. However, with the end of the Cold War, consensus over the illegality of humanitarian intervention began to crumble in the face of, for example, massive violations of human rights in Yugoslavia and various African states.

A critical part of the debate around humanitarian intervention has revolved around the motives of those intervening, and who the appropriate agents for this might be. Human rights campaigners tend to support a force constituted by a legitimate international authority, like the **United Nations (UN)**. The argument is that individual states would act only if it was in their national interest to do so, though the UN itself might also be seen as no more than a coalition of states and state interests. Thus, questions are raised with regard to the legitimacy of the intervening authority, command and control structures, and the level of force required.

It has become evident, as in the case of the intervention in Somalia in 1993, that the international community does not have the necessary commitment, military co-ordination, strategy, intelligence, or experience at nation-building to complete these interventions successfully. Indeed, this lack of success was to result in inaction on the part of the international community *vis-à-vis* the genocide in Rwanda barely a year later.

Intervention needs to be considered in terms of power. Thus, questions of humanitarian intervention go beyond issues of legitimacy and authority. The US-led interventions in Afghanistan and Iraq have been repeatedly justified by attaching a 'humanitarian' label to them. This underlines the continuing controversy surrounding questions as to what qualifies for an intervention on humanitarian grounds and about who is actually intervening. Finally, while the concept of humanitarian intervention is imbued with benign cosmopolitan (see **Cosmopolitanism**) objectives to protect against violations of human rights, it might be argued that human rights themselves are a cultural construct. As such, there are no shortcuts to political and diplomatic efforts to bring about a lasting peace. What the concept of humanitarian intervention highlights, however, is a continuing dispute between the cosmopolitan human rights tradition and the communitarian (see **Communitarianism**) concept of sovereignty.

Hybridity

With globalization, intercultural relations are said to have intensified, blurring distinctions between nations, and encouraging cosmopolitan attachments and new forms of identities. As Asian, African, European and American cultures collide and mix, **global culture** emerges as a *mélange*, setting up a dialectic between the local and the global out of which are born increased cultural options. These cultural developments create the need for alternative forms and ethics of community, away from the old dualistic 'us-them' oppositions between neatly defined groups. From this is born the notion of hybridity, whereby no single marker holds clear and consistent primacy over the others. With this more fluid and fragmented self, **identity** is less easily taken for granted, which, in turn, also challenges notions of community, and what it means for the community. The potential, therefore, is for the emergence not of global **cultural homogenization**, but for a plethora of new local, hybrid forms and identities.

Two forms of hybridity are distinguished in the literature. First, it is seen as a long-term cultural process involving materials, language, and difficult choices of discourse, where practice leads to virtuosity learned against the risk of extinction in colonized cultures. Hybridity is seen as a historical effect of **colonialism** that is used as a discursive device to decode the condition of **post-colonialism**. In its second meaning, hybridity is described in terms of the quick ingenuity required to ride current market demands, here coming closer to the meanings ascribed to **cosmopolitanism**.

While there are increased opportunities for the movement of people, goods, businesses and services in markets beyond national borders, transnational **diaspora** are producing conditions for new hybridized cultures and identities (see **Transnationalism**). However, cultural hybridization is far from weakening existing relations of power or in any way threatening Western cultural hegemony. Indeed, being modern (wealthy and powerful) is still largely synonymous with being Western.

Hyperglobalization – *see* Globalism

I

Identity

In simplest terms, identity is the understanding of the self in relation to an 'other'. Thus, the term refers to properties of uniqueness and individuality that make a person distinct from others. At the same time, it also connotes the qualities of sameness or commonalities associated with groups or categories. In the latter sense, it is a classificatory usage. It is based on a conception of the social and cultural world as composed of segments, membership in terms of which individuals must define themselves or, equally importantly, be defined by others. But unlike concepts such as 'status' and 'role', the usage of this term is less prescriptive and mechanical, allowing for individuals' own conscious self-classification.

Being a social construction, the sense of identity, or the predominant or defining identity, has been time- and place-specific. For instance, during industrialization and the rise of **capitalism**, territorial identities, especially those linked to state and nation, tended to sweep aside all other constructions of community. In contrast, it is argued that in a globalized world, there is no stable sense of identity. Identities are increasingly deterritorialized, or at least differently territorialized, with refugees, migrants, displaced and stateless people constituting those who are living out these realities in their most complete form (see **Deterritorialization**).

New forms of non-territorial, collective solidarities, sometimes global in scope, are also developing on the basis of class, gender, profession, sexual orientation, race and religion. Indeed, the development of a **global civil society** raises the issue of how far global principles of identity are becoming important. Many parts of global society are beginning to see membership of this society as a key identifier, alongside nationality and other affiliations. In some parts of the world, other forms of transnational identity are becoming important, e.g. Europeanism.

This is not, however, to say that more locally-based or territorially-based identities are no longer relevant. Indeed, globalization in many instances may be said to have reinvigorated more localized solidarities, with individuals turning inwards to particularist group affiliations. Contemporary globalization has sometimes undermined security of identity through cultural destruction (see **Americanization** and **Homogenization**). However, while global forces can erode cultural traditions and identities, they also have emancipatory potential; they can provide new material to rework identities and empower people to revolt against oppressive traditional forms.

While some view this alleged post-modern heterogeneity positively, others see here the putty that culture industries can model into consumer identities (see **Coca-Colonization** and **Consumerism**). Indeed, consumption forms the basis for multiple identity construction, particularly in relation to youth and popular culture, where the purchase and consumption of certain goods reflects particular tastes and preferences. It is argued that the identities thus created are based on looks and attitudes rather than more fundamental commitments, choices or action.

Imperialism

Imperialism generally describes a particular power structure based on dominance and hegemonic control. An imperial state tends to project power beyond its own territorial borders with the aim of gaining direct or indirect control over other territories, resources or people. This can lead to the complete integration of the acquired territory into the imperial state. It is also possible that a centre-periphery relationship based on systematic subordination remains. **Colonialism** overlaps considerably with imperialism.

The reasons for the pursuit of imperial policies vary and include displays of power, the quest for prestige, economic necessity or economic gain, access to overseas markets, access to cheap labour or natural resources, or strategic considerations. This can be achieved with the application of military force, but political, economic and cultural domination are also important tools in establishing and maintaining imperial relations.

Imperial expansion and the notion of **empire** have a long history. In more recent times, imperialism has manifested itself in the scramble for the African continent, the creation of the Pax Britannica and the subjugation of the 'Far East'. This phase ended with the Second World War.

Several theories on imperialism have been put forward. Perhaps the most famous is Lenin's theory that imperialism represents the most advanced form of **capitalism**. Driven by intrinsic competition and the need to generate profits, monopoly capitalism ultimately leads to overseas expansion in search for markets. This, however, will inevitably result in conflict between competing imperialist powers and the consequent wars would eventually destroy capitalism.

Lenin's theory has been challenged and disputed from a variety of angles. Social-psychological theories inspired by Joseph Schumpeter, for instance, point out that imperial policies predate the advent of industrial capitalism. Other theorists argue with Lenin's theory, pointing to the expansionist behaviour of Communist states like the USSR and China, while some advanced capitalist societies, such as the Scandinavian countries, lack imperial foreign policies.

According to Hans Morgenthau and other realist writers, imperialism represents balance-of-power politics. It is a form of hegemonic control whereby one state seeks to reduce its political and strategic vulnerability by dominating and assuming direct or indirect control of the anarchical international system.

Despite the demise of the European colonial empires after the Second World War, the concept of imperialism has survived and is currently undergoing a renaissance in connection with the globalization process and the hegemonic position of the USA following the end of the Cold War. Some commentators go so far as to associate globalization with post-colonial imperialism based on the systematic **exploitation** and dependency of the global South (see **Dependency Theories**). Western imperialism, in this context, manifests itself through the self-interested control by Western countries of **capital flows**, rules of trade and international organizations, such as the **World Bank**, the **International Monetary Fund** or the **World Trade Organization**, managing the global political economy (see **Americanization** and **Cultural Imperialism**). **Neo-colonialism**, neo-imperialism, cultural and economic imperialism are frequently used terms in connection with these processes.

Inequality

The issue of the distribution of economic gains and losses from globalization has been central to discussions of this phenomenon. There is extensive evidence that globalization has brought prosperity to many parts of the world in stark contrast to the pervasive **poverty** that characterized the world a few centuries ago, with poverty defined here not just in terms of income, but also health, life expectancy, nourishment and education. However, the absolute and proportionate gaps in living standards between the world's richest and poorest countries are rising. Indeed, the starkest divergence has been within **developing countries** with, for example, growing inequalities between the coastal regions and hinterlands of China. There are also growing income differentials within developed countries, due to rising inequality in labour earnings, crystallizing in **global cities**, where the world's highest earners are serviced by janitors, cleaners and cooks on minimum wages or less. Globalization is seen to have given disproportionate opportunities to the already wealthy to increase their wealth, utilizing, for instance, the latest technologies to move money around the world efficiently, while there is little or no impact on two-thirds of the global population.

Thus, the principle issue in a globalized or globalizing world is one of distributive justice in a landscape ridden with inequalities, including not only disparities in wealth, but also gross asymmetries in access to political, social and economic opportunities and power. As such, the question today is how the economic and technological benefits of globalization might be made accessible to the poor, the forgotten and the underdogs, thereby also making possible access to political and social opportunities.

Globalists argue that there is strong correlation between increased participation in **international trade** and investment and faster growth (see **Globalism**). For them, inequality stems not from processes of globalization, but from domestic policies on education, taxes and social policies. They believe that markets, by themselves, are efficient, and that the best way to help the poor is to simply let the economy grow. Indeed, equity is secondary to growth in the globalist view, so that an increase in inequality might be ignored if there is a concurrent reduction in poverty.

Information and Communication Technologies (ICTs)

Globalization is widely associated with technological revolutions in transport, communications and data processing, so much so that these, particularly information and communication technologies (ICTs), are often referred to as technologies of globalization. Transport and communication technologies are seen to have shrunk the world. Indeed, today the global economy is often described in terms of the central role played by information and communications technologies. Thus, it is termed informational, knowledge-based, or post-industrial. With the **internet**, for instance, the cost of global communication is now close to zero, proving particularly important for the global delivery of services and the organization of intra-company trade.

The very nature of work and working arrangements has undergone changes thanks to the ubiquity of ICTs. New information technologies allow for the decentralization of work tasks and for their co-ordination in an interactive network of communication in real time, whether it is between continents or between the floors of the same building. Lean production techniques have emerged together with the widespread business practices of subcontracting, outsourcing, **offshoring**, consulting, downsizing and customization.

ICTs, while being important to **capitalism** as facilitators of other processes of accumulation, have also offered vast potentials for accumulation in their own right. They have extended the reach of **commodification** to hardware, software, servicing and content. So much so that some critics fear that information that is not amenable to commercial exploitation will become increasingly scarce. The term 'information capitalism' is often used to connote the fact that telecommunications, media and information technology have moved to the core of capitalism, having become high-value sectors, also displaying some of the fastest growth rates in the global economy.

While the spread of ICTs has been uneven, with some countries or regions with the connectivity and the infrastructure to make it possible, the growth of ICTs is said to be liberating. They are believed to have democratizing potential as knowledge becomes more accessible, in turn making processes of governance more transparent and accountable.

Intellectual Property Rights (IPRs)

Intellectual property rights (IPRs) are legal entitlements of intellectual property that grant the owner exclusive rights on copying and distribution. They commonly take the form of copyrights, patents, trademarks and trade secrets. A *copyright* grants the holder exclusive right to control the reproduction of books, music and software. *Patents* grant the patent holder exclusive rights to prevent third parties from commercially exploiting a particular invention. *Trademarks* are distinctive and legally protected names, which are used to identify particular products. *Trade secrets* imply that corporations can keep certain information regarding the composition, special ingredients, etc., of their products secret. These rights can be granted, sold or licensed like any other form of property.

Intellectual property rights are a major issue in contemporary international economic relations as they constitute a very contentious area in trade negotiations. The distribution and accessibility of new technologies means that it is increasingly easy and cheap to manufacture products and sell them in violation of copyrights, patents or trademarks. The People's Republic of China is among the countries reported to violate intellectual property rights. Others include Taiwan, India, Thailand and the former Soviet Union. These countries have been identified as being the source of large amounts of pirated software, music, movies, branded textiles and other entertainment products. In fact, the infringement of intellectual property rights is widespread, in particular in the developing world.

Since pressuring foreign governments to prevent and punish such violations has not resulted in the enforcement of national laws for the protection of intellectual property rights abroad, efforts have been initiated to address the problem at the international level. In recent years there has been a steady increase in international instruments to secure intellectual property rights. The World Intellectual Property Organization, an international governmental organization which tries to regularize patent and copyright law across borders, has witnessed a dramatic increase in annual applications for global patents. Until the Uruguay Round, intellectual property rights were not treated as issues related to **international trade**. However, US **multinational companies** lobbied successfully to bring intellectual property rights into the Uruguay Round since counterfeit products, especially from southeast Asia, had resulted in an enormous loss of revenue. Other complaints came from pharmaceutical companies which perceived their products and research and development activities to have been harmed by the local manufacturing of their products in **developing countries** without licensing agreements or fees. The result was the Agreement of Trade Related Aspects of Intellectual Property, which enhanced the guarantees of intellectual property rights through the **World Trade Organization (WTO)**. It gives increased influence to foreign investors and provides increased patent protection to a range of products previously exempt from such protection.

Intellectual property rights are subject to WTO dispute settlement and enforcement procedures, posing a particular set of problems for developing countries. These are most clearly visible in the pharmaceutical sector where large drug companies hold patents for drugs, enabling them to dictate prices and prevent producers in developing countries from offering essential medicines at lower costs. Thus, the poor have been repeatedly excluded from the provision of life-saving drugs. One of the most controversial cases has been that of life-saving drugs for patients affected by **HIV/AIDS**. Another area of controversy has been the applications for patents by large pharmaceutical companies on local knowledge. This can be detrimental for developing countries and local producers who are unable to bear the intellectual property registration costs, and thus lose rights to access what is currently freely available.

Interdependence

The concept of interdependence is closely associated with the globalization process, **international trade**, neo-liberal institutionalism (see **Neo-liberalism**), the activities of **multinational companies (MNCs)**, **foreign direct investment** and transnational **capital flows**. Interdependence is a condition where the decisions and actions of one actor affect other actors. It might be measured in terms of sensitivity and vulnerability. This sensitivity may leave some actors in a more vulnerable and dependent position than others. For example, while two states might be equally sensitive to exchange rate fluctuations, a developing country may find it much harder to compensate for the loss of exports than a developed state. Thus, while being equally sensitive, states do not have to be equally vulnerable. Interdependence can therefore be symmetric, where both states are equally affected, or it can be asymmetric, where one state is more or less indifferent to changes while the other state is significantly affected.

The concept of interdependence gained ground in the 1970s for a variety of reasons. States were becoming increasingly interdependent in areas ranging from economics to **security** issues. Increasing transnational economic flows, technological innovation, the activities of MNCs and **international organizations** resulted in states becoming increasingly sensitive and vulnerable to changes in the international systems.

Some writers posit that the architecture of the global economy features an asymmetrically interdependent world, organized around three major economic regions—Europe, North America and the Asia Pacific—and increasingly polarized between productive, information-rich and affluent areas, and impoverished, economically devalued and socially excluded ones. While the Asia Pacific region appears the most dynamic, it is also the most vulnerable on account of its dependence on the openness of the markets of the other regions. However, the intertwining economic processes between the three inextricably link their fates.

Different theories have interpreted the concept of interdependence in different ways. Neo-liberal international relations theory argues that interdependence paves the road towards international co-operation. Interdependence is, therefore, closely related to international security and stability. Critics of realism stated that 'complex interdependence' had altered the nature of state power, with military power and so-called high politics no longer necessarily occupying a dominant position over low politics such as economic issues. The sensitivities and vulnerabilities generated by complex interdependence have created new power relations between international actors and military force has become a less effective instrument of foreign policy. Greater interdependence requires more collective action, such that global **public goods**, the benefits of which accrue to all within the global community, whether this be related to health or the environment, become more important.

Proponents of neo-realism, on the other hand, perceive interdependence as problematic. States will aim to decrease their respective vulnerabilities by seeking to directly control that on which they depend. Accordingly, interdependence significantly increases the risk of conflict and instability in international relations. For dependency theorists, interdependence is synonymous with dependency, systematic **exploitation** and neo-**imperialism**.

Intergovernmental Organizations (IGOs)

Intergovernmental organizations (IGOs) are an example of **international organizations**. IGOs are organizations formed by nation states and their agencies, transcending national boundaries, possessing formal institutional structures and created by voluntary multilateral agreements (see **Multilateralism**). Their main purpose is to foster international co-operation on matters such as law enforcement, **security** issues, economic and social affairs and diplomacy. Examples include the **United Nations (UN)** and its agencies, including, for instance, the International Labour Organization (ILO), promoting its agenda of adequate working conditions around the world, and the World Health Organization, concerned primarily with improving health conditions in the developing world. Some IGOs were founded as **international non-governmental organizations (INGOs)** and were later co-opted by states, including such bodies as the ILO, the World Meteorological Organization and the World Tourism Organization. Institutions co-ordinating the world's economy, such as the **World Bank** and the **International Monetary Fund**, military alliances such as NATO and political groupings like the Organization of African Unity are also IGOs. There are believed to be about 300 global IGOs and more than 1,000 regional or sub-regional IGOs in the world today, far outnumbering the total number of states and mostly concerned with economic, technical or political issues.

IGOs are established by international treaty arrangements, providing them with legal recognition and, thus, are subject to **international law**. They are legal personalities capable of entering into agreements with other states, international organizations or groupings on behalf of their member states. They often develop their own policies and agendas distinct from those of their respective member states, making them different from associations of nation states such as the G8. IGOs must also be distinguished from international treaties: not all treaties have established IGOs, but all IGOs are established by treaties.

IGOs come in different forms. Membership in some can be open to all states that recognize certain principles (e.g. the UN and the ILO). In other instances, membership might be more restricted, such as the **European Union** and the **Association of South East Asian Nations**, which are dependent on regional criteria.

IGOs are a powerful means of co-operative international action and promote international norms and rules. Their competencies are, however, limited to the areas specified in the founding treaties, though there is the possibility for task expansions in order to respond to changes in the international political economy. Indeed, IGOs are a key element in the emerging prototype for **global governance**, characterized by complex, highly decentralized co-operation involving INGOs, IGOs and states.

International Court of Justice (ICJ)

The International Court of Justice (ICJ) represents a concerted attempt to bring the rule of law to the settlement of international disputes. Also known as the World Court, it was established by the **United Nations (UN)** in 1945 as its principal judicial organ. All members of the UN are automatically members of the ICJ. The jurisdiction of the ICJ includes the settling of international disputes between states and offering advisory opinions to the

General Assembly, the Security Council and other UN agencies upon request. While almost all states have signed the treaty creating the Court, only about one-third have signed the optional clause in the treaty agreeing to give the Court jurisdiction in certain cases, and even here they have reserved their rights and limited the degree to which the Court can infringe on national **sovereignty**. For instance, Iran refused to acknowledge the jurisdiction of the Court when sued by the USA over its seizure of the US embassy in Iran in 1979, an action that violated the **international law** of diplomacy. Notable successes include the settlement of a complex border dispute between El Salvador and Honduras in 1992, and of a dispute about an oil-rich peninsula on the Cameroon-Nigeria border in 2002. The main use of the World Court now is to arbitrate issues that do not involve **security** or sovereignty between countries with friendly relations overall.

The Court consists of 15 judges who are selected by the UN General Assembly and the UN Security Council, both of which have independent voting rights. The Court has its seat in The Hague, Netherlands. (Website: http://www.icj-cij.org/.)

International Criminal Court (ICC)

The International Criminal Court (ICC) was established in The Hague, Netherlands, in 2003, after most of the world's states had signed a treaty in 1998 to create a permanent international tribunal. This permanent tribunal was meant to replace the ad hoc war crimes tribunals of the 1990s. Its aims are to prosecute individuals for severe **human rights** violations, such as genocide, crimes against humanity and war crimes. The ICC is an indicator of the widespread international support for legal doctrines of universal human rights, and aims to hold individuals accountable for human rights abuses. It clashes with the principles of **sovereignty** and non-intervention, since the ICC can prosecute crimes committed on the territory of any **nation state**.

However, as with human rights, there is no consensus at the global level with regard to the establishment of a global legal regime that effectively constrains sovereignty. It is notable that of the five veto powers of the UN Security Council, only two, France and the United Kingdom, have signed up to the ICC. The USA, China and Russia have not signed up, nor has Israel or any major Asian power. (Website: http://www.icc-cpi.int/.)

International Division of Labour – *see* Global Division of Labour

International Law

This constitutes a body of norms, rules and regulations that governs the relations between states and other actors at the international level. There are two principal forms of international law: private and public. Private international law, which is also referred to as 'conflict of laws', is primarily concerned with the rights and duties of individuals when affected by overlapping jurisdictions. It is an adjunct of law within states rather than between them. Public international law refers to the rules, agreements, customs and principles that have been established by states, as legal entities, to govern their relations with each other.

International law has played a critical role in shaping the character of international society, having developed an elaborate system of rules and procedures covering almost every aspect where one state's existence impinges upon another, including land, sea, air, outer space, diplomacy, neutrality, **human rights** and so on.

It is generally accepted that the principles of international law emerged together with the Westphalian state system in the 16th century, though its origins might be traced back to Roman times or even further. The legal scholar Hugo Grotuis (1583–1645) played a vital part in the development of international law, concerned as he was with regulating the occurrence and the conduct of warfare. He provided the foundations for two of the most developed areas of international law: the law in war (*jus in bello*) and the laws of war (*jus ad bello*). The first regulates the conduct of war while the second distinguishes just wars (which are legal) from wars of aggression (which are illegal). The legality of war is defined in the **United Nations (UN)** Charter that stipulates just war as an act of self-defence and a means of last resort.

Unlike national law, international law does not derive from a central authority. It creates principles for governing international relations competing with core realist principles such as **sovereignty** and non-intervention, making its enforcement difficult, depending on **reciprocity**, collective action and international norms.

The principle of reciprocity is very important when it comes to the enforcement of international law. It generates certain expectations and states tend to abide by international law and treaty obligations because they want other states to do the same. States also abide by international law because the long-term costs of disregarding it are generally judged to be too high. For instance, if a state consistently broke treaty commitments, no other state would wish to enter into a treaty arrangement with it in the future. In addition, collective action by a group of states, such as the imposition of sanctions, provides international law enforcement (see **Collective Security**).

International relations scholarship recognizes several sources of international law, international treaties being one of its most important sources. Once signed and ratified, international treaties are binding and must be observed (*pacta sunt servanda*). International law distinguishes between bilateral treaties, concluded between two states, and multilateral treaties, concluded by more than two states. International treaties deal with a broad variety of subjects. The most important and far-reaching treaty is the UN Charter.

Customary practice is another important source of international law. If states behave in certain ways for long enough, these behavioural patterns may become accepted general principles of international law and become legally binding. Reason, general principles of law and the legal scholarship also serve as sources of international law.

In the globalization discourse, the development of international law is linked to the development of new forms of international governance. Since the Second World War, the UN system has emerged as an important reference point for the development of an ever-growing system of international law. Important recent trends include the extension of international law beyond being exclusively the domain of relations between states. The example of war crimes indicated that individuals are increasingly accountable to international law. Human rights issues, one of the newest and least-developed areas of international law, also fall into this category. Furthermore, international law is also being extended beyond the traditional areas of political and geopolitical concerns to the regulation of international economic, communication and environmental matters. There have also been attempts to create a global legal regime, as indicated by the formation of the **International Criminal Court**.

International Monetary Fund (IMF)

The International Monetary Fund (IMF) is an international organization overseeing the global financial system (see **Intergovernmental Organizations**).

The IMF, together with the **Bank for International Settlements** and its sister organization, the **World Bank**, was created as a Bretton Woods institution (see **Bretton Woods System**), to manage the international political economy. The mission of the IMF was to oversee and manage the fixed exchange rate system set up by Bretton Woods. While the World Bank provided long-term loans and technical assistance to help with **development** projects, the IMF was founded to oversee the international currency exchange market. In addition, it was to promote currency convertibility and, thus, encourage **international trade** to supply liquidity to IMF member states in balance-of-payments difficulty. It was not a bank, and as such it provided no loans. Instead it offered rescue packages from a pool of money from which member countries could borrow on a short-term basis if they were in a crisis or needed extra money to stabilize their currencies.

In the 1970s and 1980s, the role of the IMF gradually changed. Important factors contributing to the transformation of the IMF include the end of the Bretton Woods system of fixed **exchange rates** in 1971, the subsequent move to floating exchange rates, the replacement of Keynesian ideology (see **Keynesianism**) by a more neo-liberal outlook (see **Neo-liberalism**) in the USA and the United Kingdom, and the **debt crisis** of the 1980s.

Thereafter, the IMF became part of the increasingly neo-liberal adjunct of the international political economy, assisting debtor nations to meet their balance-of-payments deficits on condition that they implemented a series of economic and institutional reforms (see **Structural Adjustment** and **Washington Consensus**). These *conditionality stipulations* have become part of IMF lending practices and its rescue packages. Loan recipients are also expected to undertake structural adjustments of their economies. Raising rates and cutting public expenditure have become typical IMF policies, all these as clear contraventions of the **sovereignty** of the concerned states.

The IMF has extended its competencies and helped to facilitate the spread of neo-liberal globalization (see **Globalism**). It is part of the multilayered structure of **global governance** (see **Multilayered Governance**), actively setting framework conditions for the international economy and intervening in issues of governance in **developing countries**.

The IMF has attracted scathing criticism for its policies. Integration into the global economy on the back of IMF conditionalities, including demands for the immediate removal of regulations and the **liberalization** of financial and capital markets, have had devastating consequences for a number of countries (see **Global Financial Crises**). Critics from the **anti-globalization**

movement argue that the IMF's policies in the **Third World** have aggravated **poverty** and debt and undermined social stability. It is blamed for having pushed through market-based policies without a broader vision of society or the role of economics within society. Indeed, its policies affect every aspect of life. It forces countries to have tighter monetary and fiscal policies. In evaluating the trade-off between inflation and unemployment, it always places far more weight on inflation than on jobs. As such, the IMF's rules seem to push a particular ideology, with scant regard to its impact in terms of the lack of benefits and the high costs imposed on countries.

There is an increasing tendency to view the IMF as a tool of Western hegemony, through which the West promotes its own economic interests and imposes the economic policies it thinks appropriate on other nations. Such a view is able to gain ground as the IMF largely lacks democratic credentials, such as **accountability** or transparency. (Website: http://www.imf.org/.)

International Non-Governmental Organizations (INGOs)

International Non-Governmental Organizations (INGOs) are **non-governmental organizations (NGOs)** with a significant international dimension, often constituting the regional and national structures underlying global social movements, particularly environmental or **human rights** movements, as individuals band together for a specific cause on a world-wide or regional basis (see **Global Civil Society**). Among the most prominent examples are environmental groups like **Greenpeace** and the World Wildlife Fund, human rights INGOs like **Amnesty International** and Human Rights Watch, and relief and **development** organizations like the Red Cross, the Red Crescent and CARE. Like **intergovernmental organizations**, INGOs are permanent organizations possessing a constitutional structure, including a permanent secretariat and consultative conferences. Like NGOs, INGOs are non-profit organizations that gain most of their funding from private organizations. INGOs tend largely to be drawn from the North, with Southern participation largely through branches of these organizations. Southern NGOs have often lacked the funds, language and organizational capacity to become international players. Many INGOs have consultative status with the **United Nations (UN)** and its agencies, and are key participants in the UN's programmes.

INGOs are extremely prolific in a variety of areas, including humanitarian relief, education, youth and women's movements, science and technology, environmental politics, culture, social, medical, economic and commercial areas. The bigger international NGOs tend to cover three main areas—human rights, development and the environment (see **Civil Society**). A number of INGOs function primarily as advocacy groups (see **Transnational Advocacy Networks**). They raise awareness by lobbying in national and international fora and the media. A second category of INGOs concentrates on operational matters, such as designing and implementing development or relief projects.

The growth of INGOs (and IGOs) has created a complex network of overlapping memberships in international and transnational associations (see **Global Governance** and **Multilayered Governance**). Globalization has fostered the sharp rise in the number of INGOs and their activities in many ways. Most prominently, it introduced many new problems of a fundamentally transnational nature that required international collaboration on a governmental and non-governmental basis. The increase in the number of IGOs, such as the **World Trade Organization (WTO)**, was mirrored and counterbalanced by INGOs emphasizing humanitarian issues, development **aid** and **sustainable development**. The **World Social Forum**, for instance, was born to rival the **World Economic Forum**. The increase in the number of INGOs has thrown open many questions regarding the centrality of the **nation state** as the primary object of analysis in international relations. Many newer approaches consider INGOs, **multinational companies (MNCs)** and IGOs alongside the nation state. However, most INGOs are, strictly speaking, not political actors but single-issue advocacy groups. As such, the continuing diffusion of power away from nation states may well mean more disagreement and conflict, as even the ablest and most passionate of INGOs tend to have a blinkered view, judging every public act by how it affects their particular interest, and polarizing and freezing public debate (see Global Civil Society).

INGOs are especially prominent in the **anti-globalization movement**, with these organizations transnationally accessing experts, activists and paying subscribers. They attempt to focus public attention and stimulate action on new global problems. They also often target states, IGOs and MNCs. A common theme running through INGO proposals is the idea that global justice requires global governance, especially greater regulation of global economic activity. Examples of successful interventions include the Seattle protests which demanded new rules of trade of the WTO; Jubilee 2000, which put pressure on developed country governments to write off the debts of the world's poorest countries; and the sweatshop apparel campaign targeting labour practices by large MNCs such as Gap and Nike.

International Order

A term used to describe a set of arrangements and practices used to regulate the activities of international actors. It might be described as a shared value and condition of stability and predictability in the relations of states. The contemporary international order is the outcome of a long evolutionary process set in motion in the 17th century, with the Peace of Westphalia in 1648. The Treaty of Westphalia ended more than 30 years of warfare, reduced the papacy in Rome and established politically independent territorial units, giving birth to the notion of external **sovereignty**. The foundations of the Westphalian state system were now established and evolved over the next few centuries. A few characteristics of this system deserve highlighting. The first is the principle of sovereignty providing the backbone of the Westphalian state. Sovereignty establishes a double claim. First, the state is the highest authority over a well-specified territory and population. It possesses a legitimate monopoly of violence. And, second, the state (or its government) does not recognize any external superior. There is no legitimate authority above state level. From this follow the doctrines of non-intervention, the legal equality of all states and the main defining feature of international order—anarchy. From Western Europe, the state system was exported to the rest of the world, and with **decolonization** following the Second World War, it became the foundation for a global order. This order is based on an anarchic system insofar as there is no world government, or no sovereign authority above state level.

Opinion is divided on how order might be achieved under such conditions. Writers following the realist/neo-realist school of thought in international relations theory stress the importance of balance-of-power operations, diplomacy and alliances to maintain order between sovereign states. Commentators with a more liberal/neo-liberal theoretical outlook tend to emphasize the importance of international institutions, norms and principles (see **Liberalism** and **Neo-liberalism**). They draw their analogy from the domestic front, arguing that international order is best achieved through a combination of law and institutions. Other theories want to overturn the current system altogether. Critical theory, for instance, argues that current international order is beyond repair since it is characterized by institutional injustice.

Thus, international order is a highly contested concept. Key to the contestation is the underlying tension between the concepts of order and justice.

Some writers argue that order should take priority over justice, making the case for **communitarianism** and the primacy of sovereignty as a cornerstone of contemporary international order. Cosmopolitan writers (see **Cosmopolitanism**) assert that some values and norms transcend particularistic cultural and political communities. Accordingly, international order that enshrines the sanctity of sovereignty and the state should give way to a global order based on individuals and non-state groups. Indeed, cosmopolitan writers have often been suspicious of the centralization of power in the hand of the state. Communitarians, on the other hands, have pointed out that the state as a form of political organization and cultural community has moral value in itself. It is a locus for community living and identity. **Homogenization** is dangerous as it can lead towards **imperialism** (see **Americanization**). It also undermines some of the crucial functions of the state, such as providing welfare to its citizens and assuring some form of legitimate **accountability**.

International order is not static but dynamic. The state and sovereignty are constantly evolving. And so is international order. Currently, globalization and the rise of transnational activities in general pose a challenge to the Westphalian state system. So much so that some commentators have been tempted to characterize the current period as 'post-Westphalian'. While it might be a bit premature to herald the 'withering away of the state', many transboundary issues, such as **terrorism**, **global warming**, international **capital flows**, **migration**, etc., cannot be effectively addressed by individual states. Collective efforts are required (see **Global Governance** and **Multi-layered Governance**). This also has important consequences for the debate surrounding international order and justice, since matters of international and national **security** are becoming increasingly entwined with social justice issues related to **poverty**, **human rights**, hunger and the environment.

International Organizations (IOs)

Following the Second World War, growing political, strategic and economic interdependencies, the increasing connectivity afforded by communication and transport technologies and the increasing **international trade** and investment bringing more countries into the global capitalist system have gone together with the growth of numerous international organizations (IOs), taking on responsibility for addressing issues of common concern. US foreign policy emphasizing **multilateralism** was to further foster this. These organizations have tangible structures with specific functions and missions. IOs consist of both **intergovernmental organizations** and **international non-governmental organizations**. Their number has grown more than fivefold since 1945, weaving together people across national boundaries through specialized groups.

International Trade

International trade refers to the exchange of commodities such as goods and services across national boundaries. Trade itself is an age-old phenomenon, though its scope was limited. Until the industrial revolution, forms of mercantilism limiting international exchange were the rule rather than the exception in Western Europe. Vast empires had been created for the purpose of trade within territories, while trade between territories belonging to different states was actively discouraged. This philosophy was driven by the idea of relative gain: that there was only a limited amount of wealth in the world and that trade would create winners and losers. The Scottish political economist Adam Smith challenged this idea in 1776 with his theory of absolute gains. David Ricardo (1817) took this forward, using the concept of **comparative advantage** to demonstrate how international trade could benefit all parties.

The impact of Smith and Ricardo's views has been substantial. The principle of **free trade** has become a cornerstone of liberal economic thought ever since (see **Liberalism; Neo-liberalism;** and **Trade System**). **Protectionism** is seen to be ineffective as it limits competition, enhances the monopoly power of some domestic industries and reduces the variety of goods available. Free international trade, on the other hand, contributes positively to economic growth and **development**. Furthermore, since international trade creates economic interdependencies between different countries, it helps to reduce the risk of insecurity and the use of military force in international affairs.

Critics of liberal, free trade arguments have pointed to the obfuscation of power politics in these arguments. The trade **liberalization** agenda is seen as having been set by special interests in the global North. While trade negotiations, for instance, open up markets in the developing world for manufactured exports from the North, the latter keeps its doors closed to agricultural goods from poor countries where these countries might have a comparative advantage. Agricultural subsidies to farmers in the North further exacerbate the problem (see **International Monetary Fund**). Thus, trade discussions start from an uneven playing field. It was to these unfair arrangements that the Seattle protesters pointed when they demanded new rules of trade from the **World Trade Organization** (see **Anti-globalization (Movement)** and **Intellectual Property Rights**).

In a globalizing world, there is a proliferation of economic transactions in which territorial distance or borders present little or no constraint. Indeed, the issue is not so much the amount of trade between countries as the fact that much of this commerce forms part of transborder production processes and global marketing networks (see, for instance, **Global Division of Labour** and **Commodity Chains**). Through global sourcing, firms draw materials, components, finances and services from different parts of the world. And with the globalization of production, a large proportion of international transfers of goods and services take the form of intra-firm trade, the share of which in international trade is calculated at more than 40%.

Internet

The internet is a global network that grew out of an experiment at the US Department of Defense involving the construction of a decentralized computer network that could survive a nuclear war. It was born of a combination of military strategy, big science co-operation and counter-cultural innovation looking to democratize information-sharing and dissemination. Communications between dispersed computer networks occurred for the first time in 1969, in the Department of Defense Advanced Research Projects Agency (ARPANET). It was based on packet-switching communication technology, a system that made the network independent of command and control centres, so that message units would find their own routes along the network and could be reassembled in a coherent and meaningful way at any point on the network.

Soon, it became increasingly difficult to separate military-oriented research from scientific communication or indeed personal messaging. Networking began on a large scale as local area networks and regional networks connected to each other. Today, the internet network constitutes the backbone of global computer-mediated communications (CMC). The availability of telephone lines and computers equipped with modems helped them spread widely. Despite efforts to regulate, commercialize and privatize, CMC systems have been characterized by their pervasiveness, decentralization and flexibility, and boast technically and culturally embedded properties of interactivity.

Today, access to the internet is relatively cheap and the internet has become one of the most effective and open media for communication involving an international network of direct links between computers (see **Information and Communication Technologies**). Its low cost and ease of access, however, have thwarted private interests and profit-seekers' efforts to charge for every click of the mouse. But, while global in its reach, the internet is still not total in its coverage, with use largely concentrated in the global North and among more affluent sections of the South. The poorer countries of the world still lack the resources for computers or the infrastructure to ensure connectivity. Some activists, however, hope that the internet can transform poor villages in the global South, partly by letting them produce traditional goods locally and sell them globally. It is also hoped that the internet will empower fringe groups relative to states.

The internet provides an opportunity for the realization of simulated communities that can develop out of transglobal patterns of interaction. It often simulates global space as users need to conceptualize and find other 'places' in order to find information there. Hypermedia software, such as the **world wide web**, act as agents for the user, independently searching the networks, finding items of information in different parts of it, combining them and presenting them back to the user without any reference to space.

Over time, the internet has become a means for communication for and against globalization. The internet has greatly enhanced the effectiveness of **non-governmental organizations** as the collection and communication of large volumes of information is no longer the domain of governments alone, thus advancing a form of global **democracy**. Pressure groups from across the world can link up through the internet for concerted action. It was through the internet that Subcomandante Marcos, leader of the Chiapas' **Zapatistas Movement**, communicated with the world from the depth of the Lacandon forest in February 1995. (See also **Anti-globalization (Movement)**; and **Cyberspace**.)

K

Keynesianism

Keynesian economic theory, or Keynesianism, is based on the ideas of John Maynard Keynes. In his famous work *The General Theory of Employment, Interests and Money*, published in 1936, Keynes provided a response to the Great Depression of the 1930s. Until then, conventional liberal wisdom had believed in the power of market forces to bring the economy back into equilibrium (see **Liberalism** and **Neo-liberalism**). A certain level of unemployment was seen as a normal condition and so were periodical cycles of boom and bust. In the long run, the economy was expected to bounce back into equilibrium between demand and supply. Long-term economic growth and enhanced **international trade** were thought to reduce unemployment levels. Keynes, however, was extremely sceptical of the liberal orthodoxy. Arguing that markets are not self-correcting, he expressed his doubts in the famous statement: 'In the long run we are all dead.' Keynes demonstrated the consequences of market failure on unemployment. In order to be profitable, businesses are forced to keep wages down and to cut costs by developing technology. In the longer term, labour would be replaced by new technologies. Thus, profits would go hand in hand with a certain degree of unemployment. But Keynes went even further by outlining the longer-term consequences for aggregate demand: lower wages and high rates of unemployment would ultimately reduce the number of consumers in an economy. As demand falls, production would decrease too and unemployment would rise even further, creating a treadmill with terrible social consequences. This represents a reversal of *Say's Law*. Keynes argued in essence that demand creates its own supply. Keynes further showed why there was a need for global collective action, because the actions of one country spilled over to others. By putting pressure on countries to maintain their economies at full

198

employment, and by providing liquidity for countries facing downturns, an institution like the **International Monetary Fund (IMF)** could help sustain global aggregate demand.

Keynes developed the radical notion of an interventionist state. Instead of staying away from the economic sector as classical liberal theory had suggested, Keynes argued that the state should actively intervene in the economy. Governments should spend money when business had lost confidence in the market and refused to invest. Where monetary policies were ineffective, governments could rely on fiscal policies, either by increasing spending or cutting taxes. This state spending would be on **public goods** like education, health care and other projects, all of which would rekindle demand and help to stimulate the economy.

Western governments quickly responded to Keynesian ideas. They provided the foundation for the post-Second World War international economic order (see **Bretton Woods System**), which was a far cry from the liberal laissez-faire **capitalism** of the early 20th century. Policy-makers in the main industrialized economies attempted to balance social welfare concerns with a commitment to market principles, leading to the European **welfare state**. The state also assumed some responsibility for managing the economy through Keynesian demand management, in order to ease cyclical crises and enable capitalists to realize profits from their long-term investments.

The Keynesian compromise of the post-Second World War period came to an end with the demise of the Bretton Woods system of fixed **exchange rates**, the **Washington Consensus** and the growing dominance of neo-liberal policies in the industrialized world and in **international organizations** such as the IMF from the late 1970s. The new economic orthodoxy has had implications for developed and **developing countries** alike. For developing countries it signalled a radically different approach to economic **development** and stabilization, with the state increasingly being left out of the equation. Globalization is increasingly associated with economic neo-liberalism (see **Globalism**) where state intervention in the economic sector is criticized for stifling competition, innovation and creativity, ultimately undermining economic growth.

Klein, Naomi

Canadian-born Naomi Klein came into the limelight with her internationally acclaimed bestseller, *No Logo: Taking Aim at the Brand Bullies*. The book, since translated into 25 languages, has become something of a manifesto for anti-globalization, anti-**capitalism** activists, and was called 'a movement bible' by the *New York Times*—see **Anti-globalization (Movement)**. In 2001 *No Logo* won the Canadian National Business Book Award and the French Prix Médiations.

In the book, Klein argues that the growth in the wealth and cultural influence of **multinational companies** might be traced back to their production of brands, as opposed to products (see **Branding**). Klein opined that the global economy of groovy Gaps, Starbucks and Microsofts were not as 'cool' as it was pledged to be. In arguing for the 'tyranny' of brands, she connects the sense of personal inadequacy and guilt of the affluent Western young to the plight of the world's poor. However, a new ethical consciousness was confronting and opposing this world of labels and logos. And brand image, while the source of much wealth, is also the corporate world's Achilles' heel, so that companies cannot cope with bad publicity. As such, she believes that a new world order would emerge, which was neither particularly capitalist nor socialist, but which would lay the foundations for more meaningful politics.

Naomi Klein writes an internationally syndicated column for *The Globe* and *Mail* in Canada, and *The Guardian* in Britain. Her articles have also appeared in a range of other publications, including *The Nation*, *The New Statesman*, *Newsweek International*, the *New York Times*, the *Village Voice* and *Ms.* magazine. Klein has been travelling throughout North America, Asia, Latin America and Europe for several years now, tracking the rise of anticorporate activism. A collection of her work, entitled *Fences and Windows: Dispatches from the Front Lines of the Globalization Debate*, was published in October 2002. (For more information, see: http://www.nologo.org.)

Kyoto Protocol

In 1997, more than 1,500 delegates, lobbyists, and heads of state from over 150 countries gathered in the Japanese city of Kyoto to negotiate a treaty to reduce greenhouse emissions to 1990 levels in the global North over about a decade. Countries in the global South were under no immediate obligation to reduce their emission levels, since their per caput emission levels were much lower, even though China became the world's second largest producer of carbon dioxide after the USA in the 1990s, and India is the sixth largest. However, **developing countries** argued that it would be unfair to make the

South pay for the past sins of the North. Furthermore, they stated that they could not be penalized for trying to pull their citizens out of penury, just as the now industrialized countries had done in the past, with some environmental costs.

The USA saw this as Southern countries having a 'free ride', and refused to ratify the treaty. However, 160 countries decided to proceed without the USA. With Russia's ratification on 22 October 2004, the treaty came into force. As of 16 February 2005, 141 countries, accounting for 55% of greenhouse gas emissions, had ratified the protocol.

The resulting treaty agreement calls for 40 industrialized countries to reduce emissions to five per cent below 1990 levels by 2012, failing which they would face penalties. A trading mechanism was introduced to improve the efficiency of the system, such that states would be able to buy or sell carbon emission credits, and would also receive credits for forests that absorb carbon dioxide. Furthermore, the **European Union** has pledged US $400m. per year to help the developing world reduce its emissions. However, without US participation, and with no clear enforcement mechanism, it is unclear how effective this treaty will be. (See also **Climate Change; Global Warming**; and **United Nations Conference on Environment and Development**.)

L

Liberalization – *see* Deregulation

Liberalism

Liberalism might be described as a theory of economics, and also a political and economic ideology that shapes state policies. Its origins can be traced back to John Locke (1632–1704). At the core of liberalism is the belief that human beings are rational individuals. Individuals should enjoy maximum freedom and the power of the state ought to be restrained to maintain domestic order and personal security.

As an economic theory, liberalism goes back to Adam Smith and his postulations about the efficiency of free markets (see **Comparative Advantage**). It sees the potential for extensive co-operation to realise common gains from economic exchanges. It emphasizes absolute over relative gains, and a commitment to **free trade**. Individual households and firms are the key actors in the economy, with the government acting as facilitator, so that markets can function efficiently. Domestically, the state should be restricted to providing the legal and institutional framework that enables market forces to work. In its outward-looking role, the main function of the state is to provide protection from external threats. Liberalism is thus a theory of both government within states, and good governance between states and people world-wide.

As an international theory, liberalism, having evolved from the ideas of philosophers such as Jean-Jacques Rousseau and Immanuel Kant, can be seen as the main challenger of realism. Whereas realism has a rather pessimistic view of human nature, with rationality defined as narrow self-interest, liberalism is more optimistic, pointing to the capability of human beings to collaborate and partake in long-term collective benefits, secured through capitalizing on common interests.

An underlying and fundamental concern of human life is welfare. This concern for welfare enables the possibility of progress. 'Bad' human behaviour is not so much the result of a flawed human nature, but, rather, is induced by socio-political and cultural structures. Therefore it is the system that has to be changed. And 'the system' in this context refers to the international system of sovereign nations states.

While realism claims that, in an anarchical international system, war is inevitable and almost natural, liberalism argues that war can be avoided and even eradicated. This requires international/collective efforts rather than national or individual ones. Therefore, the international system must be fundamentally reformed—institutions must be in place to replace the anarchy of the international system of sovereign nation states.

Liberalism focuses on three points to improve the international system: the advocacy of **democracy**, the advocacy of free trade and the promotion of international co-operation through international institutions. Liberalism takes the domestic analogy to international relations: that the transfer of the instruments that ensure economic **development** and peaceful relations at the domestic level would serve a similar purpose at the international level. The advocacy of free trade has been central to most variants of international liberalism. In addition to its economic rationale, free trade creates situations of complex interdependence and removes potential sources of conflict (see **Neo-liberalism** and **Interdependence**). According to liberal scholars, economic **nationalism** and the **protectionism** of the 1930s contributed significantly to the outbreak of the Second World War. The post-1945 **international order** witnessed the institutionalization of liberalism with the establishment of the **Bretton Woods system** and the **General Agreement on Tariffs and Trade**, propagating free trade and international co-operation.

The spectrum of international liberal thought is extremely diverse, with economic neo-liberalism and **Keynesianism** forming opposing ends. Contemporary globalization is often associated with neo-liberalism (see **Globalism**), which has become the ruling economic orthodoxy in the **G7/G8** countries and international financial institutions such as the **International Monetary Fund** and the **World Bank**. Liberalism, in the form of neo-liberalism, has emerged as the dominant ideology in the post-Cold War world. This was underlined by Francis Fukuyama's claims about the 'end of history', that with the demise of communism and central planning, the last significant challenge to liberal democracy and economic liberalism had vanished (see **End of History**).

The euphoria with which liberals greeted the end of the Cold War has largely dissipated with 9/11 and the large number of failed states, with conflict and insecurity still ever-present. In this era of globalization, there seem to be emerging two possibilities for liberalism. First, the neo-liberal strain, where institutions would be weak, international rules kept to a minimum, and the status quo maintained, with strong, though unevenly distributed, economic growth. Military action is preventative, to deal with possible chaos. The radical liberal vision would seek to heighten regulation through strengthening international institutions, making them more democratic and accountable.

M

Marxism

With the demise of the Soviet Union and the triumph of **capitalism** and liberal **democracy** (see **End of History**), Marxism's days seem to be numbered. However, Marxism's continuing relevance arises in part from its intrinsic powerful critique of capitalism.

Marxist thought has provided the foundation for a wide array of critical approaches. Examples include **world systems theory**, **dependency theory**, critical theory, Gramscian thought and neo-Marxism. Theorists such as **Immanuel Wallerstein**, **David Held**, **David Harvey** and Robert Cox have been influenced in their writings by Marxism, as has **Noam Chomsky**. More recently, Michael Hardt and Antonio Negri's conceptualization of **empire** draws on Marxist insights, as does Leslie Sklair's definition of the transnational capitalist class. The **anti-globalization movement** (**global justice movement**) puts forward a Marxist critique of contemporary capitalism. Marxism has also inspired various other protest and resistance movements, such as the **Zapatista Movement** in Mexico.

It is incredibly difficult to provide a comprehensive overview of the writings of such a prolific writer as Karl Marx (1818–83). For Marx, economic forces and class conflict make for historical progress. History itself is driven by the clash of dialectic forces. These clashes are generated by tensions at the economic base between the means of production and the relations of production. As the means of production develop, previous relations of production become outmoded.

The prime focus of Marx's interests was class relations. He took issue with the harmony of interest between classes propagated by liberal writers (see **Liberalism**). For Karl Marx and Friedrich Engels, capitalist society is divided between the ones who own the means of production (the capitalists or the bourgeoisie) and the ones who own nothing but their labour, which they have to sell for wages (the workers or the proletariat). The interests of the bourgeoisie and the proletariat are dialectically opposed—they are antagonistic classes. The state is not a neutral facilitator of economic exchange, but a tool of **exploitation** that ultimately fosters the interests of the ruling class by reinforcing a particular power-knowledge structure.

Marxist-informed thought focuses on relations of dominance and subordination between and within societies. Capitalism is regarded as inherently exploitative, denying workers a fair remuneration for their labour by the profit-seeking bourgeoisie. Competition at the marketplace and the search for ever-higher profit margins ultimately leads to the suppression of wages. Thus, capitalism leads to an uneven society. Indeed, Marx was not content with merely analysing economic relations and by pointing to the flaws of the capitalist system. He aimed to overthrow the capitalist system to eventually bring communism in its place.

Marxist thought contains the kernel of many arguments in the contemporary globalization debate. The increasing integration of economic activities and the **global division of labour** are nothing unique, according to Marxists. They merely reflect the exacerbation of a division of the international political economy laid down in the 19th century during industrialization and the age of European **imperialism**. The result was a two-tier structure within and between societies that is still relevant today. Marxism maintains that the **development** of some parts of the world was only possible due to the systematic exploitation of other parts. Hence the industrialization and relative welfare of the global North was achieved through the exploitation of the global South, the so-called **Third World**. This idea is at the core of dependency theories, according to which **developing countries** face major obstacles in their quest for economic progress.

Marx's critique of capitalism also remains relevant. He was among the first writers to flag up the periodic boom and bust cycles that appear to be intrinsic to the capitalist system. Marx also pointed to the social consequences of crisis, a theme all too familiar in the aftermath of major financial upheavals such as the Asian financial crisis of 1997–98 (see **Global Financial Crises**). Furthermore, it was Karl Marx who coined the phrase the 'withering away of the state', a phrase since usurped by hyperglobalizers.

For some contemporary scholars adopting Marxist thought, globalization is nothing but a new form of imperialism. **Neo-liberalism** represents a normative intervention in the international political economy as it prescribes a specific orthodoxy about how best to organize economic relations. As such it has strong ideological undercurrents enshrining the power of the global North and the USA. Accordingly, consent for the neo-liberal system has been established through a hegemony that allows certain ideas and ideologies to be widely dispersed and become generally accepted. Thus, neo-liberalism does not represent a value-free description of the realities of the international political economy under the conditions of globalization, but a biased model, an ideology that aims to preserve a particular power structure.

Mass Media

Modernization and the evolution of **information and communication technologies** have generated media that can permeate and dissolve boundaries between localities and between political entities, thus allowing for the transmission of a variety of images, sounds and messages at an increasingly rapid rate. The early 20th century saw the development of media machines using the complex technology of electricity and the opportunity for a truly symbolized form of globalization. Radio, the first true electronic mass medium, became well established in the 1920s and 1930s. Television began to penetrate mass markets after the Second World War, a medium with greater potential to affect the minds of those consuming its contents. Indeed, radio and TV reach even the poorest areas of the **Third World**.

All this technology originates in advanced capitalist societies, as does much of its content (see **Americanization**; **Cable News Network**; and **Homogenization**). As such, it is said to export the culture ideology of **consumerism** from the centre to the periphery, as most of the news, information, entertainment and advertising flows in that direction (see **World Systems Theory**). However, while mass media are often described as a one-way communication system, there is interaction between the sender and receiver insofar as the message is interpreted upon reception; and the signifying form of the message can be filled with different meanings. Thus, programmes and messages circulate in the global network, but it does not constitute a **global village**, where messages flow in one direction with no scope for interpretation or interaction.

At the same time, mass media communications establish transnational connections, linking collective actors and individuals and potentially subverting state frontiers. Insofar as the mass media can convert human relationships into symbols or tokens, they can connect people across great distances, with the potential to promote greater cultural sympathy and understanding. And since symbols can be transmitted very rapidly, the compression of time eliminates the constraints and therefore the social reality of space. An event happening in one part of the world can be immediately communicated and experienced in any other part of the world. (See also Information and Communication Technologies.)

McDonaldization

The term McDonaldization, coined by G. Ritzer in 1996, connotes **consumer culture** as an extension of the process of Western rationalization and world-wide cultural standardization (see **Homogenization**), such that the principles of the fast food restaurant increasingly dominate more and more sectors not only of American society but also the rest of the world. The principles underline not only their offerings to customers, but also underpin the way McDonald's is organized and run, and its staff treated. These principles are (a) efficiency, whereby McDonaldization compresses the time span and the effort expended between a want and its satisfaction, with organizational rules and regulations also generating efficient ways of working among the staff in this chain; (b) calculability, such that it encourages calculations of costs of money, time and effort as the key principles of value on the part of the consumer, so much so that quantity has become equated with quality— a lot of something, or the quick delivery of it, means it must be good. Some McDonaldized institutions combine emphasis on time and money (e.g. Domino's promised pizza delivery in half an hour or else the pizza is free of charge); (c) predictability, such that it standardizes products over time and in all locations; and (d) control, of consumers by means of queue control barriers, fixed menu displays, limited options, uncomfortable seats, inaccessible toilets and 'drive through' processing, and of staff by the use of material technology involving maximal deskilling of workers.

Thus, it is argued that insofar as the social technology of McDonald's can penetrate the globe, it can convert apparently sovereign consumers into docile conformists. However, the paradox of McDonaldization is that in seeking to control it recognizes that human individuals potentially are autonomous.

While these principles travel with the McDonald's chain, it is a formula that has been adopted by other world-wide chains, such as Burger King, Taco Bell, Kinder Care and Au Bon Pain. McDonaldization is seen as a reordering of consumption as well as production, and a rationalization of previously informal and domestic practices that pushes the world in the direction of greater conformity. Indeed, it has become common practice for opponents of globalization to treat McDonald's, and its ubiquitous golden arches, as the instruments of American **cultural imperialism**. (See also **Anti-globalization (Movement)**; **Bové, José**; and **Branding**.)

Mercosur

Mercosur (Mercado Común del Sur), or the Southern Cone Common Market, is a regional economic international governmental organization in Latin America (see **Regionalism** and **Region**), set up to create a free trade area. Its member states include Argentina, Brazil, Paraguay and Uruguay. It was established by the Treaty of Asunción in 1991, and amended by the Treaty of Ouro Preto in 1994. Other South American countries, such as Bolivia, Chile, Colombia, Ecuador and Peru, have since gained associate status, making Mercosur the fourth largest regional economic bloc after the **European Union (EU)**, the **North American Free Trade Agreement (NAFTA)** and the **Association of South East Asian Nations (ASEAN)**.

Projects to promote economic co-operation in Latin America predate the establishment of Mercosur. Examples include proposals to create a Latin American Free Trade Association and a Central American Common Market in the 1960s. However, the regional and global economic climate of the 1970s following the collapse of the **Bretton Woods system** and political relations among Latin American countries were unfavourable and these early plans for economic integration failed.

In many ways, European integration was to influence the foundation of Mercosur. The revitalization of the European project with the Single European Act in the mid-1980s and the intergovernmental conference leading to the Maastricht Treaty triggered global fears of the creation of a closed European trading bloc, a 'Fortress Europe'. That, in part, motivated a wave of new regional initiatives around the world, resulting in a revival of ASEAN and the foundation of NAFTA and the Asia Pacific Economic Forum.There are certain striking similarities between the EU and Mercosur. At the heart of European integration are France and Germany, states with a history of economic, political and strategic rivalry. Mercosur too has at its core two regional rival powers, in this case Argentina and Brazil. The Iguazú Declaration of 1985 aimed to establish bilateral economic links in order to bind South America's big rivals together. Furthermore, as in the European case, economic co-operation has attracted keen interest from neighbouring countries. Bolivia and Venezuela, for instance, have been invited to become full members. But that is where the similarities end. The aims of Mercosur are not as ambitious as those of the EU, focusing on the abolishment of all tariff barriers between member states and the establishment of a common external tariff against third countries (see **Common Market**; **Customs Union**; and **Free Trade Area**). In contrast to the EU, the institutional framework of Mercosur is very thin, relying exclusively on intergovernmental co-operation. It has, however, been exceptional in representation and **accountability** matters, with a Socioeconomic Advisory Forum through which trade unions and other civic organizations can make representations. In recent years, there has been a substantial increase in economic interaction between Mercosur members, though they still trade twice as much with the USA as with each other. (Website: http://www.mercosur.int.)

Migration

In very general terms, migration refers to the phenomenon of the movement of people, including whole populations. While capital and financial flows have become part and parcel of globalization processes, the movement of people, particularly the movement of labour, remains under the thrall of states and resistant to globalizing effects. This is in rather stark contrast to the earliest stages of global expansion which saw high levels of labour mobility. For instance, between 1500 and 1800, white traders moved slaves from Africa to the Americas, and indentured labour from South Asia to other parts of Asia and Africa (see **Colonialism**). From 1800, free white settler colonization expanded, and as millions of Europeans crossed the Atlantic to settle in the Americas until the Second World War, this came to be called the 'Great Migration'. After a slowing in migration in the years between the two world wars, a number of countries threw open their doors to settler migration in the 1960s, this time to include non-white populations. The USA, Australia, New Zealand and Canada are key examples.

Today, while it is only about 3% of the world's population who have crossed international borders, this still constitutes a significant number in real terms, with a significant proportion of the migration from the global South to the industrialized North, though poorer, Southern countries continue to host a number of refugees and economic migrants.

Early models of migration saw it as economically determined, in which individuals are pushed or pulled by the forces of **capitalism**. More recent work has begun to demonstrate a greater interest in the cultural contexts of migration, examining the ideas and values around which migration is organized, and the changes wreaked in these by migration.

The idea of the free movement of peoples has long been an integral part of the Western conception of **human rights**. Today, global South–North and East–West movements of people are making European and North American societies increasingly multiracial. And while earlier migration streams saw a preponderance of young men, from the last quarter of the 20th century there has been a steady increase in the number of women migrating, either singly or accompanying their families, leading to what has been called the feminization of migration. Today, migrant streams are constituted of roughly equal proportions of men and women.

While historically mass migrations have been associated with the incidence of communal conflict, ethnic cleansing, genocide or economic recession, more recent movements have been facilitated by the technologies of mass communication, and the globalization of markets. State regimes are constantly adjusting to the influx of different kinds of immigrants and to ways of engaging global capitalism that will benefit the country while minimizing the costs. For instance, nation states constantly refine immigration laws to attract capital-bearing and highly skilled subjects, while limiting the entry of unskilled labourers. From the perspective of well-heeled immigrants, such as those originating in Hong Kong, **citizenship** becomes an issue of handling the diverse rules of host societies, where they may be economically correct in terms of human capital, but culturally not in the 'developed', Western club in terms of their **ethnicity**.

Though migrants travel across national borders, they do not necessarily leave their homelands behind. Instead, they often forge economic, cultural and political relations with their countries of origins, linking these countries to their host states. As a result of the increasingly transnational character of cultural networks and socio-political practices as a consequence of migration, discourses on the rights, entitlements and obligations of citizenship have been undergoing dramatic changes in the past couple of decades (see **Transnationalism**). There is also increasing interest in transnational processes and **diaspora** communities, with migration becoming crucial to discussions around **identity** and hybridity.

Indeed, migration is challenging preconceived notions of society and culture, particularly conceptions of bounded, internally homogeneous cultures. Racial heterogeneity, identity politics and resistance to **inequality** more and more mark the institutional landscapes of neighbourhood, workplace, university and political arenas and even kinship and marriage (see **Cosmopolitanism**; **Creolization**; and **Hybridity**). This world of complex mobilities and interlinkages, in turn, has called into question the normative character of the Western **nation state**. Indeed, the nation state might be perceived much less as a self-contained unit now than as a pausing point through which increasing numbers of people shuttle. Furthermore, the technologies of nationhood are finding it increasingly difficult to fashion culturally monolithic national communities in the face of the diversity of their subjects.

Today, the broad areas of concern for policy-makers in relation to migration seem to be the channelling of remittances, engagement with diaspora networks, and instituting temporary mobility schemes to facilitate the movement of labour, particularly skilled labour, given also the demographic transition in most of the industrialized world. Most of these discussions are also increasingly underpinned by the **security** discourse.

Modernity

A condition of the world which, at its most general, serves as a broad synonym for **capitalism** or industrialization or the accumulation of material resources, or whatever institutional and ideological features are held to mark off the modern West from other, traditional societies. As such, it includes institutions such as the world capitalist economy, the **nation state** system, the world military order and the global information system; and features such as rationalist knowledge, or forms of organization like the bureaucratic state.

There have been contradicting views of the role of modernity in relation to globalization. While **Anthony Giddens** sees modernity as inherently globalizing, making globalization a continuation and expansion of modernity, for **Roland Robertson** contemporary globalization cannot be considered simply as an aspect or outcome of the Western project of modernity. Indeed, for Robertson, globalization in many ways predates modernity and the rise of capitalism. Modernization has, however, accelerated the process of globalization, which has now permeated contemporary consciousness.

Phases within modernity are also sometimes distinguished. For instance, Giddens coined the term 'high modernity', which is marked by extreme reflexivity, by a questioning of what we know and how we know it. **Ulrich Beck**'s 'new modernity' comes very close to Giddens' 'high modernity'. The term evokes a new self-limiting and self-critical science.

While forces of modernity are acknowledged to have changed the face of world cultures and altered political-economic relationships, the resulting pervasive globalization is seen more as organization of heterogeneity than as a smothering of difference to produce uniformity. That, however, has not prevented reactions against modernity from taking shape, for instance those of fundamentalist movements seeking to change the balance of power in the world and the cultural terms on which global actors operate. (See also **Fundamentalism**.)

Modernization Theories

Modernization theories are concerned with questions of economic development, and have their origins in sociology and economics. By and large, this body of theorization assumes that different countries are at different points on a trajectory of modernization, on which Western states have a clear lead. It believes that as each non-Western nation becomes modernized, it will move up the hierarchy to duplicate or absorb Western culture to the extent that ultimately every locality would display the cultural ideals, images and material artefacts of the American way of life.

Though adopting an evolutionary perspective, modernization theories also focus on the internal capabilities of developing countries. Proponents work with the assumption that the causes of underdevelopment lie in a failure to harness domestic resources efficiently enough to generate economic growth. By modernizing their respective economic and social structures, developing countries will eventually achieve economic development. For example, in his influential work *The Stages of Economic Growth* (1960), W. W. Rostow laid out five stages of development. In order to achieve modern development, each country has to move through these phases, the move from one stage to the next depending on raising living standards and adopting modern values and structures.

Modernization theories base the answer of how to achieve development on internal, domestic factors. This stands in stark contrast to the body of **dependency theory**, which focuses on external factors. Dependency theorists argue that underdevelopment is not so much the result of a lack of modern values and structures but, rather, is directly linked to the structure of the international political economy (see **Developing Countries** and **Development**). Modernization is not simply a process that occurs in similar fashion across the globe, but, rather, is the result of a deliberate mapping of a global

213

hierarchy by élites which would place their own society at the pinnacle of such a hierarchy. For **Wallerstein**, for instance, this hierarchy was the product of long-term changes in the capitalist world economy, which had brought about not only a **global division of labour** but also a dominant world culture. However, development and economic growth are complex phenomena and are not attributable to forces arising exclusively from a single level of analysis.

The idea of modernization involving a definite trajectory began to be relativized by the 1970s as the criteria for social change themselves increasingly became matters of inter-societal or inter-doctrinal interpretation and debate.

Monbiot, George

George Monbiot is a journalist, academic, environmental campaigner and a prolific writer who has become an activist voice in the **anti-globalization movement**. In his book *Captive State: The Corporate Takeover of Britain* (2000) Monbiot critically analyses the rise of corporate power in the United Kingdom. He puts forward the argument that multinational enterprises (see **Multinational Companies**) have grown and extended their influence to such an extent that they are now threatening the very foundations of democratic governance. A related theme can be found in *The Age of Consent: A Manifesto for a New World Order* (2004). Largely written in support of the **Global Justice Movement**, Monbiot addresses the theme of **global governance** and calls for more democratic forms of governance on a global scale. He has also written about **climate change** and the necessity of generating the political will to effectively combat **global warming**.

Overall, Monbiot is a strong critic of the unrestrained **capitalism** inherent in the neo-liberal globalization project (see **Globalism**). In his newspaper columns he has repeatedly pointed to the adverse effects of policies recommended by international institutions such as the **International Monetary Fund**, the **World Bank** and the **World Trade Organization**. He has also written extensively on topics such as debt (see **Debt Crisis** and **Debt Trap**) and **poverty**. (For more information, see: http://www.monbiot.com/.)

Most Favoured Nation (MFN) Principle

The most favoured nation (MFN) principle establishes equality of treatment and non-discrimination among states engaged in international trade with each other. Under the MFN principle, all parties are obliged to extend to each other the same advantages they establish with other parties. MFN is typically associated with a reduction of tariff and **non-tariff barriers** to international trade. States are not prevented from protecting their own industries, but cannot play favourites among their trading partners.

While the MFN principle is enshrined in the **General Agreement on Tariffs and Trade**, there are several exceptions to this, including trade blocs, free trade areas and common markets. The United Nations Conference on Trade and Development in the 1960s further undermined the MFN principle when **developing countries** demanded a system of positive discrimination in their favour. Trade concessions to **Third World** states led to the Generalized System of Preferences, or a promise by industrialized countries to allow imports from Southern states under lower tariffs than those proposed under MFN. Despite this, the MFN principle remains a cornerstone of the international trade system. (See also **International Trade** and **Trade System**.)

Multiculturalism

Multiculturalism is a concept describing ethnic and cultural diversity. It has been fostered and spread by transnational cultural flows. Globalized culture in itself is an expression of multiculturalism.

The theory and practice of multiculturalism has significant implications for national societies and for issues such as immigration, community cohesion and **citizenship**. Most metropolitan areas and many national societies are nowadays multicultural due to widespread labour **migration**, mostly from the peripheries to the cores of the global economy. This movement has led to the increasing celebration of 'otherness' in official discourse and public policy in receiving societies. Thus, rather than engendering cultural uniformity and homogeneity, multiculturalism entails a celebration of difference and diversity.

The consequences of this multiculturalism are complex. Cultural exchanges may be beneficial for the host society. However, multiculturalism has produced ambivalent multiple identities and anxieties about the stability of national identities. Social policies promoting multiculturalism are often blamed for undermining social integration, the exclusion of minority groups from wider society and the fragmentation (*Balkanization*) of society. This has resulted in a backlash against policies encouraging multiculturalism and encouraged xenophobic reaction from right-wing nationalists in many countries. (See also **Xenophobia**.)

Multilateral Agreement on Investment (MAI)

The Multilateral Agreement on Investment (MAI) is an international agreement negotiated by members of the **Organisation for Economic Co-operation and Development (OECD)** between 1995 and 1998. It was driven by the motivation to enhance international capital mobility by further extending **deregulation** measures and financial **liberalization** (see **Neo-liberalism**). Under the agreement, the signatory states would be compelled to deregulate their economies and allow foreign investment access to virtually every economic sector. Foreign companies would have to be treated in the same way as national ones and would be entitled to compensation for unfair investment conditions. Furthermore, states could be sued in international tribunals by other states and corporations if national health, labour or environmental standards would undermine foreign investment.

The MAI suggested a radical change in the governance of international investment, fostering the denationalization of economic space and the promotion of neo-liberal economic globalization. Critics of the agreement argued that it was unbalanced. To them, the provisions set out in the MAI represented a concerted assault on state **sovereignty** and a transfer of power from national and local governments into the hands of unaccountable multinational enterprises. Growing opposition from various sides finally caused a stalemate in the MAI negotiations and in 1998 the OECD decided to no longer pursue the ratification of the MAI.

Multilateralism

The term multilateralism is used to describe international co-operation between three or more states to achieve particular aims in specific issue areas. Multilateralism is based on the underlying principle of non-discrimination. Furthermore, multilateral co-operation requires diffuse rather than specific **reciprocity** and the outcomes of multilateral co-operation are indivisible.

Multilateral co-operation is closely associated with institutionalization. Many multilateral relations have created a significant institutional overlay to manage and oversee co-operation, to enshrine and enforce codes of conduct, to monitor the behaviour of participants and to sanction rule breaking. However, international governmental organizations do not represent the only forms of multilateralism. The International Gold Standard, for example, was not an international organization but it was a multilateral arrangement that regulated international **capital flows** and **exchange rates** between 1875 and 1914. Other prominent examples include the **Bretton Woods system** of fixed exchange rates and the **General Agreement on Tariffs and Trade**.

The growth of multilateral institutions is linked to increasing international interdependencies (see **Interdependence**) and is often associated with specific issue areas, such as **international trade** and co-operation on economic matters. The **World Trade Organization** is a typical multilateral institution. It is important to remember, though, that increasing interdependencies between states are not only restricted to the economic arena. In **security** matters, for instance, the concept of **collective security** has called into question the old bilateral notion of conventional alliances. The **North Atlantic Treaty Organization** is an example of a multilateral organization that aims to address security matters, while the **United Nations** is a multipurpose organization. Transnational environmental networks ought to be mentioned here as well (see **Transnational Advocacy Networks**).

After the Cold War, integrative forces and the pressures of globalization have enhanced the popularity of multilateralism as an organizational form. In many ways, globalization calls for multilateral regulation and management, and national governments, **multinational companies**, **non-governmental organizations** and other **transnational actors** respond to old and new problems increasingly with multilateral solutions. (See also **Global Governance**.)

Multilayered Governance

The term multilayered governance (or multilevel governance) describes a process and a state of affairs whereby national authorities share more and more governance and regulatory responsibilities with subnational and international institutions. Globalization has helped to foster the creation of dense networks of direct transnational connections between subnational authorities in different countries without going through official national channels, and an increase in international co-operation in the form of **international organizations** and regimes. The increase of regional and global governance arrangements at subnational and international levels alongside national regulatory mechanisms means that governance has become increasingly decentralized and fragmented.

Globalization is fostering the dispersion of centralized national governance to give way to multilayered governance in several ways. First, the growth of supraterritorial space has clearly highlighted the limitations of sovereign governance. Other institutions and agencies have moved in to fill the gap in effective governance (see **Global Governance** and **Regionalism**). Second, globalization has resulted in the increase of problems that need to be addressed co-operatively and where international and subnational actors and agencies may have a comparative advantage over their national counterparts. Examples include transborder environmental issues or transborder communications. And, third, the increase in global communication and information technologies and the structure of global and international organizations and global finance has provided new infrastructures that enable public and private actors to bypass the **nation state** and its authorities. The result is the spread of international and subnational regulatory bodies that have acquired relative autonomy from the state (see **Devolution**). They often operate on their own initiative without being subordinate to the state. This is not to say, however, that a multilayered global governance framework has completely undermined the state, or led to its demise.

Multinational Companies (MNCs)

A multinational company (also multinational corporation, multinational enterprise or transnational corporation) can be defined as a company that controls production facilities in more than one country. The existence of multinational enterprises, therefore, requires **foreign direct investment (FDI)**. MNCs are seen as key to understanding processes of globalization as they are the major institutional form of transnational practices. Their criticality lies in the sheer size and scale of their operations, dominating most of the world's economic system. Their systems of supply, production, marketing, investment, information transfer and management often create the paths along which much of the world's transnational activities flow. The domination by such transnational companies in an increasingly globalized marketplace is seen as a hallmark of 'late **capitalism**'.

The three dominating theoretical approaches to the study of MNCs are the liberal, the structuralist and the radical. For liberal theories, the main motivations for the decision to invest abroad arise from an initial **comparative advantage**, the desire to maintain or to extend market share, or particular ownership and location advantages that increase the desirability of internationalizing production.

Structuralists shift the focus from the decision-making process of companies to major structural changes in the international political economy.

Three major changes, they argue, have accelerated the spread of MNCs: a reduction in the real costs of transport and communication induced by the revolution in **information and communication technologies**, the development of new production technologies, and the creation of new financial instruments. These changes increased the pace of international production, enhanced capital mobility and made international communication and transport cheaper, faster and more reliable. As such, FDI and the activity of MNCs are intrinsically linked to neo-liberal globalization (see **Neo-liberalism**). Radical writers have concentrated on the centralization of capital in their explanations for the development of multinational enterprises and FDI, for example, focusing on oligopolistic business structures.

FDI began to accelerate decisively after the Second World War. The promotion of FDI became part of the USA's foreign policy during the Cold War. Not surprisingly, perhaps, most MNCs were of American origin during those years. In the 1960s American MNCs were joined by European and Japanese enterprises. And joining them in the 1980s were the so-called newly industrialized countries. Indeed, the number of companies operating simultaneously in several countries multiplied sixfold between the late 1960s and the mid-1990s. Along with global organization through direct investment, companies have also formed thousands of transborder strategic alliances, particularly since the 1980s. Today, FDI activities are not only located in the manufacturing sector, but also increasingly in the provision of services, with significant expansions in recent years in retail trade, finance, communications and information technology.

The role of MNCs in international political relations is complex, with some seeing MNCs as agents of their home national governments, while others see them as beholden to no government. They are powerful players in the global arena. The **anti-globalization movement**, for instance, has argued against the large concentration of wealth in these corporations—the largest 100 global companies are said to control up to half of the world's total FDI, and the 15 largest have reached annual sales whose value exceeds the gross domestic product of more than 120 countries.

MNCs invest in a country for perceived advantages of doing business there. These advantages might be the presence of natural resources, cheap labour, geographical location, skill levels, political and financial stability and favourable regulatory environments. As such, very often recipients of FDI are industrialized countries, the largest concentration being in the **G7** countries. However, there has been an increasing outflow of manufacturing operations from Western economies, as companies transferred production to Eastern Europe or Asia in order to take advantage of labour standards and costs, and less stringent environmental standards (see **Exploitation** and **Race to the Bottom**).

FDI has played a critical role in many of the most successful **development** stories, including Singapore, Malaysia and now China. But while the activities of MNCs might have positive contributions for host countries, their role has never been unambiguously good. Among the showcased benefits for the host are an additional stream of tax revenue and the integration of the host country into the global economy, as well as the transfer of technologies, new management styles and the introduction of new and more efficient work practices. However, not all of these benefits are always realized. Conflicts over the distribution of the new wealth generated, for instance, are common. Governments may break the agreed terms on taxation and regulations (see **Export Processing Zones**). Technology transfer may be limited if the control over the production process remains firmly in the hands of the parent company. MNCs often try to avoid taxation altogether through transfer pricing. Further, MNCs want the freedom to assemble goods anywhere from parts made anywhere, whereas governments want to maximize the amount of wealth created on their own territories. Thus, states have been the sites of struggle between territorial and supraterritorial capital.

Conflicts might also arise over trade policies. MNCs are more likely to channel investment to states that restrict imports, as MNCs can avoid import restrictions by producing goods in the host country. Monetary policies could also lead to conflict. For instance, when a state's currency is devalued, imports become expensive, and a foreign MNC selling a product assembled from imported parts may be devastated. As such, MNCs prefer to make long-term investments in countries where the currencies are relatively stable.

More recently, MNCs have also begun to participate in more broadly conceived development projects in the host state, as a means of investing in goodwill (see **Corporate Social Responsibility**).

N

Nationalism

Nationalism is perceived as both a globalized and a globalizing phenomenon. It is one of the components of culture that has been transmitted around the globe. It might be described as the political doctrine which holds that humanity can be divided into separate, discrete units or nations, with each nation constituting a distinct political unit, the state. The claim to nationhood usually invokes the idea of a group of people with a shared culture, often a shared language, sometimes a shared religion, and usually, but not always, a shared history. To this is added the political claim that this group of people should, by right, rule itself or be ruled by people of the same kind (see **Nation State**).

For more than 200 years nationalism has shaped history. It was central to the emergence of the Westphalian system of sovereign nation states and its transformation from a European system into a truly global system of states. The rising tide of nationalism redrew the political map of Europe in the 19th century and the world in the 20th century when the autocratic and colonial empires crumbled in the face of nationalistic pressures.

Nationalism is a highly contested concept as the criteria used to distinguish between insiders and outsiders are often highly subjective. They range from common historical legacies, shared myths, norms and values, shared beliefs and cultural and linguistic similarities to **ethnicity** or religion. Most of these factors are interlinked and reinforce each other. Nationalism is closely linked to notions such as nation, state, national **identity** and self-determination.

Nationalism can be regarded both as a doctrine and an ideology. As a doctrine, nationalism is based on the belief that the nation is the focal point of socio-political organization and that each nation has the right to statehood.

The political realm is seen as composed of several, independent and sovereign nation states, each with the right to self-determination. The principle of self-determination is subordinate only to the principles of **sovereignty** and non-interference. However, current international law does not stipulate the right to change political or state borders in order to unify groups that ostensibly belong to the same nation. Thus, conflict is endemic in cases where nation and state borders do not coincide. Examples include Palestine, India and Pakistan, the former Yugoslavia and Sri Lanka.

Nationalism as an ideology encompasses various forms of cultural, ethnic and political nationalisms. Cultural nationalism places great emphasis on the nation as a particular cultural entity based, for instance, on a distinctive language or religion that must be preserved and defended against external threats, such as **cultural imperialism** and the homogenizing impact of contemporary globalization (see **Homogenization**). Ethnic nationalism places much more emphasis on shared ethnicity (see **Xenophobia**). Political nationalism uses the concept nation to achieve specific political ends, such as the right to self-determination or domestic order and social cohesion.

Nationalism is often enhanced through contact with outsiders. It should come as no surprise therefore that globalization has resulted in nationalistic reactions ranging from the anti-globalist rhetoric (see **Globalism**) of populists such as Pat Buchanan, associated with the right wing of the Republican Party in the USA, who propagates a form of economic nationalism (see **Anti-globalization (Movement)** and **Protectionism**), to reactions against perceived cultural threats, xenophobia and religious **fundamentalism**. Indeed, a steep increase in recent years in the popularity of nationalist parties such as Austria's Freedom Party, the British National Party, the French National Front, or the rise of Hindu nationalists, is indicative of the deep connections between globalization and nationalism. And the re-emergence of powerful nationalistic sentiments associated with myths, memories and symbols of local places rather than global spaces is seen to be leading to cultural disintegration at a global level, while the ubiquity of Coca-Cola or McDonald's represents greater integration.

Nation State

The nation state is currently the highest form of political organization. It is the primary unit of analysis in international relations. The term nation state signifies a conflation of two very different concepts—nation and state. A state can be characterized as a political entity based on a well-delineated territory and a well-defined population. Furthermore, the modern state is a sovereign entity (see **Sovereignty**). Its government possesses a legal monopoly on violence and recognizes no domestic equal, nor any external superior. Thus, the existence of sovereign states creates an international system based on anarchy. Under such conditions, states depend on mutual recognition of each other as sovereign entities. Hence, diplomatic recognition is another feature of statehood.

The concept of the modern state began to take shape with the Peace of Westphalia in 1648. The Treaty of Westphalia brought an end to 30 years of continuous warfare that had ravaged Europe and resulted in the collapse of the Holy Roman Empire and the reduction of the universal authority of the papacy in Rome. Subsequently several independent territorially-based political units emerged. This system evolved over the next few centuries, fostered by the Renaissance, new weapons technologies, the development of new modes of communication (such as print media), new modes of economic organization, etc.

In the 19th century the concept state merged with the concept nation, a group of people sharing a sense of collective **identity**, a common history, a common language, ethnic or racial similarities or common cultural traits. This period saw the rise of **nationalism**, i.e. the idea that each nation is entitled to a state and that the nation is the ultimate source of a state's legitimacy.

It is argued that the objective of early nationalist movements was to invent a coincidence between five reference points—people (ethnic or a common identity); state (a political system); nation (a community); government (an administration); and territory (nationalism sought to establish the exclusive occupation of a territory by the nation). However, not many nation states actually achieve this coincidence between these reference points; rather, they are mostly 'cultural hybrids'. But the nation state is constructed and projected as a territorially compact and culturally homogeneous political space; it is represented as a social, spatial and historical fact that is real, continuous and meaningful. This construction has been achieved through a range of nationalizing technologies and ideological practices, such as stories indicating common experiences of triumph and struggle, assertions about national character (British fair play, Japanese honour, etc.), and inventions of new patterns of ritual, pageantry and symbolism that give collective expression to the nation, such as the granting of

citizenship rights, the development of rules on nationality, the invention of symbols of nationhood, such as flags, ceremonials, the celebration of historical figures, the observance of national holidays, and the building of public works like hospitals, roads, schools and prisons. The establishment of foundational myths and legends helped locate the nation 'outside' history and give it a quasi-sacredness, a sense of originality, while at the same time promoting ideas of common breeding or even racial purity.

The form and function of the state has been changing. In some accounts of globalization, the nation state is depicted as 'withering away' (see **Marxism**), a casualty of globalization, or on the way to becoming one very soon. As globalization accelerates, proliferating transnational linkages seem to undermine the power and efficacy of the state (see **Transnationalism**). It has become increasingly problematic to take the state for granted as a unit of analysis, or even as a broad referent for the term 'society'. As such, while studies of the state were earlier preoccupied with phases of state formation, more recently there has been increasing concern with nation state and nationalism as cultural constructs.

However, though there may be arguments about whether the power of the nation state is on the decline in the face of globalizing pressures, it still demarcates important cultural differences, and postulates an 'us' versus 'them' on the international arena, often jeopardizing regional efforts to constitute an entity larger than the nation state, such as the **European Union** (see **Regionalism**).

National Identity

National **identity** might be described as an identity linked directly to place (or, to be precise, the **nation state**). However, it is only one competing subject position among many others. Today, identity construction is heavily overdetermined, with global, national, regional and local components, as well as gender, race, class and sexuality. The dialectics of the global and the local are said to be producing new conflicts in which choices must be made concerning what features will define national and individual identity (see **Citizenship** and **Hybridity**). Thus, the once assumed correspondence between citizenship, nation and state has been questioned. At the same time, transnational alliances are forging and shaping new identities that transcend state boundaries (see **Cosmopolitanism** and **Cosmopolitan Democracy**).

Neo-liberalism

Neo-liberalism (see **Liberalism**) is the prevailing economic orthodoxy that takes the logic of laissez-faire **capitalism** to the international level, transcending the **nation state**, and argues in favour of unrestricted capitalism, **free trade** (see **Free Trade**) and consumer-based individual ethics (see **Consumerism**). It pushes for a bundle of interconnected policies, including financial and trade **liberalization**, flexible and deregulated labour markets, privatization of the economy, including public utilities, and low levels of public debt, often imposed on countries in transition or those in a **debt crisis** (see **Global Financial Crises**).

Neo-liberalism became the dominant economic ideology in the late 1970s following the breakdown of the Bretton Woods exchange rate mechanism and the abandonment of the post-war Keynesian compromise (see **Bretton Woods System** and **Keynesianism**). The policies of Ronald Reagan in the USA and Margaret Thatcher in the United Kingdom were characterized by a rolling back of the state, with large-scale privatization of government assets, economic **deregulation**, lower corporate taxes and anti-welfarism. With the demise of Communism as a credible challenge, neo-liberalism has now become the 'common sense' doctrine, leading to Francis Fukuyama's pronouncements about the **'end of history'**. In fact, most major political parties in the **G7/G8** countries today advocate a culture of self-help, individual responsibility and entrepreneurship. It is also the doctrine of economic **development** favoured and actively fostered by international financial institutions such as the **International Monetary Fund**.

In terms of international relations, neo-liberalism is often referred to as neo-liberal institutionalism. The neo-neo debate (between neo-liberalism and neo-realism) has dominated academic debate in international relations for the past 30 years. Neo-liberalism widens the concept of **security** to include economic and environmental concerns and, thus, moves away from the almost exclusively geopolitical/military reading offered by neo-realists.

Neo-liberal approaches focus on absolute gains rather than on relative gains, and argue that international institutions and regimes can help reduce international anarchy by constraining state behaviour. Increasing economic and security interdependencies (see **Interdependence**) reduces the utility of the use of military force and, therefore, the risk of war. Long-term co-operation between nation states, it is argued, is both possible and desirable.

For neo-liberals, the deregulation of the economic sector, including liberalization and privatization, are in fact the most important features of globalization.

Neo-liberal hyperglobalizers argue that globalization, an irreversible and 'natural' phenomenon, has rendered the state ineffective. However, in all democratic states the political supremacy of the free market is as yet incomplete and precarious. So far it has not been able to survive periods of protracted economic setback.

Neo-colonialism – *see* Colonialism

Network Society

A term coined by sociologist Manuel Castells, for whom networks constitute the basic units of society and the new social morphology of our societies. Castells sees the interconnected nodes that make up networks as the most apt instruments for a capitalist economy based on innovation, globalization and decentralized concentration. **Capitalism** is now global, and structured to a large extent around, for instance, a network of financial flows. Financial capital needs to rely for its operations and competition on knowledge and information generated and enhanced by information technology (see **Information and Communication Technologies**). Thus, capital accumulation, and its value making, takes place in the global financial markets, enabled by information networks, in the timeless space of financial flows. It is from these networks that capital is then invested globally in all sectors of activity, be they agricultural production, health, education, trade, tourism or information industries.

The diffusion of networking logic, Castells argues, modifies quite considerably the operation and outcomes in all socio-cultural processes, be they production, experience, power or culture. Inclusion or exclusion in networks, and the architecture of relationships between networks, increasingly configure dominant functions and processes, creating new power asymmetries, as power accrues to those who control the switches connecting networks.

Non-governmental Organizations (NGOs)

In a globalizing world, states are seen to be increasingly sharing their powers with, among others, a number of citizens' groups, known as non-governmental organizations (NGOs). NGOs thus consist of a group of people who conduct regular formal or informal meetings and engage in collective activities to achieve specified goals or policy objectives. NGOs are at the forefront of campaigning and lobbying national and international governance institutions to raise awareness and to achieve their policy goals. Indeed, the technologies of globalization have been well adopted and used by NGOs. The **internet**, for instance, has opened up new possibilities and opportunities for NGOs to engage in effective world-wide campaigns against what they see as threats, abuses or non-responsible conduct on the part of businesses or others. NGOs have become a significant part of the international landscape, forming part of an emerging **global civil society** that is more cosmopolitan in general orientation and less attached to individual nation states (see **Cosmopolitanism**).

All NGOs share three main features: they are not for profit; they are committed to non-violent modes of action; and they are independent of national governments. The Red Cross, **Greenpeace** and **Oxfam** are prominent examples of NGOs and illustrate the range of issue areas NGOs are involved in. NGOs with a very significant international dimension are called **international non-governmental organizations (INGOs)**.

NGOs and INGOs work in very diverse areas, and as their numbers and the range of their activities increase, so does their influence. They have created extensive national and international networks (see **Transnational Advocacy Networks**) and have become part of the evolving system of **global governance**. Indeed, some see them as filling the 'democratic deficit' in a situation where, as finance and production become more global, there is no political machinery to deal with citizens' concerns. Many NGOs and INGOs work very closely with international governmental organizations (IGOs), such as the **United Nations (UN)**. NGO and INGO policy networks are particularly strong in **human rights** (see **Amnesty International**), the environment (see Greenpeace) and **development** (see Oxfam). In humanitarian relief efforts, for example, NGOs and INGOs often provide a well-developed organizational infrastructure and expertise while IGOs such as the UN and governmental agencies provide the necessary finances. In war situations, the neutrality of NGOs places them in a good position for conflict mediation and for the distribution of humanitarian aid.

There is no consensus on how many NGOs are currently operating in the world. What is clear, however, is that NGOs deliver more official development assistance than the entire UN system. Government agencies in general regard NGOs as useful partners for the distribution of foreign aid. NGOs are often quicker than governments to respond to new demands and opportunities. In many countries, NGOs are delivering services in urban and rural community development, education, and health care, that faltering governments can no longer manage. And cross-border NGO networks offer citizens' groups unprecedented channels of influence.

So important and established have NGOs and INGOs become that they have received formal recognition by the UN and other international actors. Indeed, many UN conferences on global issues have two centres: one dominated by representatives of nation states and a second attended by **civil society** groups (NGOs and INGOs).

However, for all their strengths, each NGO works for a particular outcome, and tends to be blinkered, judging every public act by how it affects its particular interest. Also, NGOs often have limited capacity for large-scale endeavours, and have to find financial support to sustain themselves, which may compromise their objectives. Since they cannot survive without their grassroots base, they are also sometimes known to compromise the truth to play to the gallery to gain membership and support.

Non-tariff Barriers – *see* Protectionism

North American Free Trade Agreement (NAFTA)

The North American Free Trade Agreement (NAFTA) is a **free trade** agreement (see **Regionalism**; **Common Market**; and **Customs Union**) between the USA, Canada and Mexico. It was negotiated between 1991 and 1993, replacing an earlier agreement between Canada and the USA by extending the free movement of capital, trade and financial services to the south to include Mexico. Its main purpose is the abolishment of barriers to trade and services, including the progressive elimination of customs in many areas of trade (see **Protectionism**).

Compared to the **European Union (EU)**, NAFTA lacks extensive institutionalization. It is characterized by intergovernmental modes of decision-making, so that the administration of agreements remains firmly in the hands of the governments of the three participating states and their representatives. These national representatives meet in the Free Trade Commission, specialized committees and working groups. Unlike the EU, NAFTA has no provisions for regional co-operation in areas other than trade. It is a purely economically-oriented form of regionalism. However, an agreement on labour co-operation was signed in 1993. The agreement focuses on information exchange but does not provide for NAFTA-wide labour standards.

An important impetus for NAFTA was the end of the Cold War. Freed from the constraints of the superpower conflict, dynamics associated with the globalization process became the focus of attention. In the early 1990s there were widespread fears about the formation of a powerful and assertive European trading bloc, a 'Fortress Europe'. NAFTA was at least partly motivated by concerns about the form the EU was about to take.

Together with the EU, the **Association of South East Asian Nations** and **Mercosur**, NAFTA is one of the main regional trading blocs. It is also significant in that it bridges the global South and the global North, uniting the developed and the developing world (see **Developing Countries**). This has implications for the internal structure of NAFTA; its economic diversity could potentially become a problem for internal cohesion. Indeed, the 1997 financial crisis in Mexico put a large strain on NAFTA (see **Global Financial Crises**), though it weathered that test rather well, actively seeking collaborative solutions. (Website: http://www.nafta-sec-alena.org.)

North Atlantic Treaty Organization (NATO)

The North Atlantic Treaty Organization (NATO) is an international governmental organization (IGO) that was established by treaty in April 1949. It is sometimes referred to as the Atlantic Alliance, highlighting one of its main aims: to ensure the USA's defence commitment to Western Europe. The 12 original signatory members of NATO were Belgium, Canada, France, Iceland, Italy, Luxembourg, the Netherlands, Norway, Portugal, the United Kingdom and the USA. Membership expanded when Greece and Turkey joined in 1952, West Germany in 1955 and Spain in 1982. After the end of the Cold War, NATO extended its membership eastwards: in 1999, the Czech Republic, Poland and Hungary joined the alliance and in 2004 Estonia, Latvia, Lithuania, Romania, Slovakia and Slovenia followed.

NATO was founded as a military alliance and as such is a very typical IGO. It was also an ideological grouping, bringing together states with similar political and economic systems and providing a military and ideological counterpart to the Warsaw Pact during the Cold War. As part of a wider **security** strategy, NATO actively aimed to encourage collaboration beyond the military sphere in Western Europe by promoting economic and political co-operation. In terms of security, NATO is based on the principles of deterrence and **collective security**. Article Five of the North Atlantic Treaty states that, 'The parties agree that an armed attack against one of them in Europe or North America shall be considered an attack against them all.' Among other things, it is mandated to safeguard the freedom and security of its member states, to maintain stability in the Atlantic area and in Western Europe, to prevent the occurrence of international crisis, to discuss European security issues, and to promote **democracy, human rights** and **international law**. NATO has a very complex organizational structure combining civilian and military elements. Its highest authority is the North Atlantic Council, on which each member state is represented.

The end of the Cold War has raised serious questions regarding the future of an alliance born out of Cold War frictions. Russia remains a key concern for NATO planners, especially since the recent expansion of NATO membership has brought the association into Moscow's 'backyard'. Thus NATO is developing structures to maintain a dialogue with Russia. Currently, the other main concerns centre around NATO enlargement in Central and Eastern Europe, new areas of involvement (so-called 'out-of-area' operations) such as the former Yugoslavia and Afghanistan, and the future commitment of the USA to NATO and Europe. (Website: http://www.nato.int.)

O

Occidentalism

This term emerged as the reciprocal of the notion of **orientalism**, and suggests a distorted, stereotyped image of Western society, which could be articulated or implicit, held by people inside and outside the West. Behind these renderings, which are shaped by political relationships within the societies in which they exist, is an assumption about how people define themselves and others. One's own social unit and the other's are identified as contrasting elements that are taken to express essences or crucial distinguishing features, such that the resulting characterizations are inevitably negations of each other. (See also **Colonialism**; and **Identity**.)

Offshoring

The spread of global relations has brought some notable shifts in the ways that capital is accumulated, and the key examples cited for this are offshore arrangements and transborder corporate alliances. By moving into the realm of the supraterritorial, or into the **cyberspace** of electronic finance, capital is readily able to escape obligations for taxes or other conditions associated with a particular state jurisdiction, and locate anywhere in the world that offers a better deal. The attraction of offshore centres is that they tend to offer minimal rates of corporate, personal, capital gains, withholding or any other taxes, while at the same time luring capital in with limited regulation and statutory guarantees of confidentiality. States have created offshore zones for both global production processes (see **Export Processing Zones**) and global financial activities.

Offshore financial centres proliferated in the second half of the 20th century, with the Cayman Islands, Luxembourg and Guernsey playing host to a large number of them. Many investment companies also tend to be registered offshore, in Luxembourg, the Bahamas or the Channel Islands.

Organisation for Economic Co-operation and Development (OECD)

The Organisation for Economic Co-operation and Development (OECD) is an example of an international governmental organization. Its membership is open to advanced developed countries which, nominally, have espoused neo-liberal values such as representative **democracy** and a commitment to some form of free market **capitalism** (see **Liberalism**; **Neo-liberalism**; and **Free Trade**).

The predecessor of the OECD, the Organization of European Economic Co-operation (OEEC), was set up in 1948 to administer and co-ordinate European economic recovery after the Second World War. The activities of the early OEEC were deeply rooted in Cold War politics. Although in principle Marshall Aid was open to the Communist countries of Central and Eastern Europe, the conditions attached to the programme meant that effectively these countries were excluded from the inflow of much-needed liquidity. As such, the Marshall Plan strengthened West European American allies in the emerging Cold War against internal and external Communist threats and, additionally, served the USA's own economic interests through rebuilding the **international trade** system and reviving European markets. The OEEC was founded to ensure that European recipients of the **aid** co-operated. Thus, it was the first post-Second World War organization that actively promoted European integration (see **Regionalism** and **European Union**).

In 1961 OEEC membership was extended to include non-European states and reconstituted as the OECD. Its tasks were now expanded beyond the purely economic to include new areas such as technology transfer, the activities of **multinational companies** and relations with other international groupings and organizations. Today, the OECD addresses many issues with regard to the multiple challenges of globalization in the general areas of economics, politics and governance (see **Global Governance**). It helps its member states to promote prosperity and to fight **poverty** through ensuring economic growth, financial stability, trade and investment, technological innovation and **development** co-operation. The OECD has a primarily neo-liberal outlook, as stated in the Paris Convention, and has a clear commitment to economic growth, free trade and development. It makes recommendations to its member states and assists them in co-ordinating their policies to achieve economic growth and development, and is also a very valuable source of economic and statistical information. Internationally, it represents an example of intergovernmental co-operation in the form of a powerful interest group of industrialized countries, with the power to bargain effectively and influence international economic regulations and agreements to the advantage of its member states.

The deep asymmetries in the global economy are made particularly visible through the OECD, as the countries here concentrate an overwhelming proportion of global technological capacity, capital, markets and industrial production. (Website: http://www.oecd.org.)

Organization of Petroleum Exporting Countries (OPEC)

The Organization of Petroleum Exporting Countries (OPEC) is an international governmental organization that was set up in 1960 by Iran, Iraq, Kuwait and Saudi Arabia. Its current membership includes Algeria, Indonesia, Iran, Iraq, Kuwait, Libya, Nigeria, Qatar, Saudi Arabia, the United Arab Emirates and Venezuela. The headquarters of OPEC are in Vienna, Austria. Its principal aims include the establishment of a cartel between oil producers to maintain an oil price level that reflects the interests of OPEC's member states and manages prices and production accordingly. The main instruments of OPEC are the co-ordination and unification of the petroleum policies of its individual member states to devise means to stabilize prices in the international oil market in order to avoid disrupting fluctuations. This implies a steady flow of income for oil-producing countries and a secure supply for the consuming states. OPEC members are in effective control of about two-thirds of the world's oil reserves.

In 1968 OPEC identified two issue areas for its member states in its 'Declaratory Statement on Petroleum Policy'. First, OPEC countries wanted more control over pricing policies. And, second, OPEC countries wanted to be more than just tax collectors in the oil industry, and began to review existing participation agreements. OPEC decisions have a considerable influence on the development of international oil prices, providing OPEC with a substantial leverage in the global economy. In 1973 OPEC acted for the first time in a unified manner by agreeing to increase oil prices unilaterally. This marked the end of an era of cheap oil that had fuelled the

233

booming economies of Western Europe and Japan, and resulted in the first oil shock. In response, the USA and other members of the **Organisation for Economic Co-operation and Development** decided to establish a consumer group to confront the OPEC cartel collectively. The outcome was the establishment of the International Energy Agency. Its original aims were twofold: to ensure a steady supply of oil and to reduce dependency on oil.

However, it was the developing world that suffered the most damage from the increase in international oil prices. **Developing countries** had little ability to diversify into alternative energy sources and no other resources to offset the impact of higher oil prices. OPEC actively encouraged **Third World** countries to take the initiative to renegotiate the international political economy and supported calls in the **United Nations** for a new international economic order. However, oil prices continued to rise throughout the 1970s and peaked after the second oil shock in 1980–81 following the Iranian Revolution. The repercussions of this second oil shock, together with an appreciation of the US dollar exchange rate, initiated the **debt crisis** in the developing world.

Industrialized countries renewed their efforts to explore marginal oil fields, for example in the North Sea, alternatives to oil, and more economical usage of energy. Subsequently, OPEC's share in the energy sector dropped, pointing to the limits in OPEC's control of prices. Higher oil prices resulted in lower oil consumption and, ultimately, in reduced revenues for OPEC members. Additionally, revenues were hurt by the exploration of alternative energy sources and long-term behavioural changes in oil consumption. Not all oil-producing countries are members of OPEC, further reducing the influence of OPEC on international oil supplies. (Website: http://www.opec.org.)

Orientalism

The title of a work by Edward Said, which charged a range of European disciplines and cultural genres with reifying and reducing to stereotypes the Orient in a manner that was complicit with, if not always directly in the service of, the effort to dominate. The obverse of orientalism is **occidental-ism**, which presents a distorted and stereotyped image of Western society. Both oriental and occidental imaginings are products of **colonialism**. Central to the discourse has been the question of representation, of both the 'other' and, by implication, the 'self'. It has thus been a project about both dominance and self-definition.

The term 'orientalism' was conventionally used to describe academic disciplines such as history and comparative philology, which specialized in the study of 'the Orient', with Asia and the Middle East constituting this geographic realm. With the publication of Said's powerful polemic, orientalism emerged as a distinctive body of academic work that raised issues concerning the authoritative representation of colonized ethnic groups. While born in the colonial period, orientalism is seen as a project that has continued long after **empire**, through neo-colonial structures of domination, in all of which the representation of the 'orient' and its people denies them history and agency.

A variant of this discourse is the 'new' orientalism, which might be defined as a populist construction of Islam as a threat to Western civic values, and which treats Muslims as the 'enemy within'.

Oxfam International

Oxfam International is a confederation of 12 independent **aid** and **development non-governmental organizations**. Its mission is to work with local partners on a global scale to reduce **poverty**. Oxfam International has a small secretariat based in Oxford and advocacy offices in Washington, DC, and New York, USA, Brussels, Belgium, and Geneva, Switzerland.

Oxfam Great Britain was founded in 1942 to distribute food for famine relief in Europe. Over the years, Oxfam has developed a host of strategies to combat the causes of famine. Subsequently, Oxfam's activities have included the provision of medicine and medical support, foodstuffs, tools, the sale of **fair trade** produce and crafts from **developing countries** and adequate training to enable people to achieve a certain degree of self-sufficiency. Its main focus is on poverty relief and development, humanitarian relief and national and international campaigning (see **International Non-governmental Organizations (INGOs)**; **Transnational Actors**; and **Transnational Advocacy Networks**).

More recently its issue areas have expanded substantially and now include **international trade**, education, debt and aid, livelihoods, health and **HIV/AIDS**, gender equality, conflict and natural disaster relief, **democracy** and **human rights**, and global **climate change**. Fundraising activities, donations and the management of Oxfam charity shops help finance this INGO. (Website: http://www.oxfam.org.)

P

Pluralism

In its most general sense, pluralism is the affirmation and acceptance of diversity. In philosophy, it is the belief that no single explanatory system or view of reality can account for all the phenomena of life. In politics, it is one of the features of **democracy**, affirming the diversity in the interests and beliefs of the citizenry.

In a globalized world characterized by cultural, ethnic and religious diversity, pluralism refers to the engagement with this diversity (see **Cosmopolitanism** and **Hybridity**). Rather than just passive tolerance, it is the active seeking of understanding across lines of difference. Tolerance in itself, it is argued, does little to remove our ignorance of one another, and given the proximity in which people with cultural, ethnic or other differences live with each other, pluralism is advocated as the way forward since it seeks commitment and dialogue. Thus, in terms of religion, for instance, encounters in a pluralistic society are not premised on achieving agreement on matters of conscience and faith, but on achieving a vigorous context of discussion and relationship.

Pluralism is often used interchangeably with diversity. However, diversity is just plurality, which in itself might be colourful, but also hostile or threatening. Pluralism goes a step further—it seeks to engage with that diversity to create a common society. Given the history of immigration (see **Migration**) and the increasing number of migrants in the world today, pluralism has come to occupy an important position in state discourse. The USA, for instance, has come a long way from exclusion of people who were 'different' on the basis of colour, ethnicity or race, to assimilation, where the emphasis was on suppressing difference to effect uniformity, to pluralism, which seeks an acknowledgement rather than a hiding of the deepest differences between groups.

Post-colonialism

The term refers to the period that begins with the withdrawal of Western colonial rule, from approximately the middle of the 20th century. As such, it tends to connote a historical periodization based on the core period of **colonialism**, and as such, is not able to move away from its associated structural binaries—Western/non-Western, colonizer/colonized, or domination/resistance. The term is also used to connote the persistence of colonial representations of the non-European/non-Western 'other'.

Post-Fordism

The 1970s witnessed a shift away from the Fordist manufacturing system of mass-consumption and mass production (see **Fordism**). Fordism had rested on a 'social contract' between corporate business, organized labour and the government (see **Keynesianism**). Organized labour delivered specialized and motivated workers; corporate business ensured the delivery of high wages and social benefits; and the government ensured union protection, guaranteeing property rights and a wide-ranging welfare net. However, the recession hitting the industrialized world after the breakdown of the **Bretton Woods system** of fixed **exchange rates**, inflationary pressures, increasing competition from manufactures in the developing world and the emergence of a new international **division of labour** put pressure on the Fordist production system. By the 1980s, the comfortable arrangements in the industrialized world between state, capital and workers to maintain high levels of employment, investment and **consumption** had unravelled with the emergence of **neo-liberalism** as the ruling economic orthodoxy.

Priorities now shifted towards flexible accumulation, with innovative technologies and management strategies. The post-Fordist production system is characterized by flexible specialization, constant quality control at all stages of the manufacturing process and competitive differentiation. The production system introduced by the Japanese car-maker Toyota in the 1980s, the so-called just-in-time (JIT) system, exemplifies post-Fordism, and incorporates all its features. In this system, the supplier delivers the components just in time to be assembled. No inventory is necessary and the manufacturer retains a high degree of flexibility in terms of design and production adjustments. As a result, changes in consumer demand can be taken into account very quickly.

The post-Fordist production system significantly altered the face of industrial manufacturing. It reduced the ability to mass produce and stock goods. Employees needed to be more highly skilled in order to take design and managerial decisions on the factory floor if necessary and to respond to changes quickly without the need for additional training. It also changed the investment strategies of **multinational companies**. In order to react to consumer demand speedily, markets, suppliers and assembly lines needed to be geographically closer. As a result, the level of wages by itself became a less significant factor in determining choice of manufacturing location, unlike in Fordism. Wage considerations were now often outweighed by the need for close proximity to potential markets and to reliable suppliers, the availability of skilled labour and specialized technology and infrastructure, though mass production and the factory system continue to exist today alongside post-Fordist production systems such as the JIT method.

In the industrialized world, flexible specialization has resulted in the decreasing importance of trade unions, lower union membership, the rise of flexible contracts in the form of part-time and short-time contracts, lower job security and stagnating or decreasing incomes. Neo-liberalism and glo-balization have thus displaced the dominance of the Fordist system by stressing flexibility, leading to a '**race to the bottom**'. They have pushed for lifting all constraints on the market so that it could speedily respond to altering demand patterns, while employees face deteriorating working con-ditions and employment itself becomes largely temporary or part time, and workers are expected to be flexible in respect of salaries, hours of work, health and safety standards and benefits.

Post-industrial Society

This is a phrase coined by Daniel Bell for a society where work in commodi-fied services predominates over other sectors, class gives way to status, acquired through professional and technical qualifications, theoretical knowledge dom-inates over practical knowledge, technological development is controlled and planned, and the most important technology is not physical but intellectual (see **Commodification**). The post-industrial phase is also characterized by the development of micro-electronic technologies that reduce global distances by enabling the rapid movement of people, ideas and resources across the planet. In cultural terms, post-industrialization implies the production of more mobile and easily tradable products, largely aesthetic commodities.

Post-industrial society is even more steeped in **capitalism** than was its industrial predecessor. Often the terms 'reflexive accumulation' and 'cybernetic capitalism' are also used for it. It is also considered synonymous with **postmodernism**. The fundamental arguments of post-industrialization are not significantly different from the convergence thesis (see **Convergence Theory**). Proponents of convergence argue that the technologies for the production of goods create similarities between societies, and the post-industrial argument suggests that emerging intellectual technologies for the production of services create convergence.

Postmodernism

An anti-universalist, anti-essentialist view of knowledge, that regards all knowledge as bound to its time and place, and contingent upon the view of the person constructing it. It is a rejection of rationalism, and a loss of faith in the Enlightenment project as progress through the application of human reason. At its logical extreme, the relativism of postmodernism makes it possible to assume that all 'knowledges' and theories are equally valid.

Globalization might be said to have ushered in the growth of postmodernist epistemologies in several ways. Intensified interactions between different cultures, for instance, have helped develop the conception of all knowledge as socially and historically relative, particularly, for instance, among migrants and exiles. (See also **Postmodernity**.)

Postmodernity

The jury is still out on whether postmodernity, as a distinct period following **modernity**, actually exists. In globalization theory, postmodernity is considered the latest stage of **capitalism**, characterized by the domination of **multinational companies** in an increasingly globalized marketplace. The service sector continues to grow and dwarf other sectors, and global forms of organization persist and expand at the expense of national ones.

Postmodernity, it is argued, is capitalism in its post-Fordist guise (see **post-Fordism**), hungrily creating new opportunities and arenas in which to operate, still driven by profit. Thus, with new technologies at its command, capitalism has moved from mass production to flexible production systems based on lifestyle and niche marketing. It has created a new aesthetic, based on image industries, in which desires are recreated as needs to bolster demand (see **Consumerism**). Key to the dissemination of such need creation are **advertising** and the visual media, particularly television, and, increasingly, the **internet**, which now operate on a global basis (see **Branding** and **Mass Media**).

For some writers, postmodernity is broadly equivalent to the **post-industrial society**. For others, like **Anthony Giddens**, the current state merely reflects 'late' modernity, representing a continuation rather than a break with modernity. Postmodernity for Giddens is a utopian condition, characterized by a post-scarcity economy, multilevel political participation, especially at the local level, the humanization of technology and global demilitarization. **David Harvey** applies the label postmodernity to global capitalism itself and associated cultural changes. However, by and large, theorists arguing for postmodernism associate it with informationalized, mediatized, virtual, simulated and hyperreal social experiences, all of which suggest the loss of a stable sense of **identity** and knowledge.

Postmodernity is not constructed wholly negatively though. It is seen as welcoming opportunities for greater **pluralism** in knowledge, identities and cultures. It is said to have created a new sensibility, and is celebrated culturally as the end of imperialistic modernism (see **Modernity**). It is associated with the loss of a sense of a common historical past and the flattening out of long-established symbolic hierarchies. As such, it is seen as emancipatory, holding out hope for liberationist, pluralistic and democratic forces. The cultural politics of postmodernity is much more fluid than earlier narratives, such as those of social class, would allow. It is one in which individuals are caught up in economic and cultural flows and communication networks, but through processes of aesthetic invention and reinvention they are able to establish new self-identities of a more or less ephemeral nature.

Poverty

Poverty can be defined as a situation whereby people lack access to material resources such as money, food or shelter and are unable to satisfy their most basic needs. According to the **World Bank**, poverty is defined as living on less than US \$2 a day. Extreme poverty is defined as living on less than US \$1 a day.

Ethical and human arguments central to a critique of globalization have often said that it has made the rich richer and the poor poorer, and that it has dramatically increased **inequality** between and within nations. On the other side are apologists for globalization who argue that the poor who have participated in global trade and exchange have benefited from it, and that among the countries which have opened up to globalization, while inequalities might have increased, there has been an overall reduction in poverty.

Even if it argued that the poor have benefited from globalization, the question remains as to whether it is a fair division of benefits, leading ultimately to the question of distribution and distributive justice, together with the question of whether the poor or disadvantaged receive a fair opportunity and a fair share. These have also been the key concerns of a number of anti-globalization protesters, who are not 'anti-globalization' per se (their protests tend to be among the most globalized events in the world), but who are seeking a better deal for the underdogs of the economy (see **Anti-globalization (Movement)**). And they call for a serious assessment of the adequacy of the national and global institutional arrangements that characterize the contemporary world and shape globalized economic and social relations.

The **International Monetary Fund** and the **World Bank** have been criticized for their standard pro-growth macroeconomic policies that they sell to the world as the most effective route to poverty reduction. Market mechanisms are pointed to as the best means of achieving growth. Thus these global institutions have, it is argued, shifted the discussion away from concerns with equity, to a focus only on growth. Growth here is associated with positive distributional changes in favour of the poor. The examples of Latin America and East Asia are offered at opposite ends of the spectrum, with Latin America having succeeded in macroeconomic stability with limited benefits for poverty reduction, while East Asia succeeded in combining high growth with rapid poverty reduction. And so the real challenge is to make markets work for the poor, with particular attention to enabling factors, such as access to education and health facilities.

The United Nations Development Programme has devised the Human Poverty Index (HPI) to measure the proportion of the population that benefits from **development**. The HPI-1 measures the proportion of the population living in absolute poverty and is calculated for **developing countries**, while the HPI-2 is used for **Organisation for Economic Co-operation and Development (OECD)** countries and includes a relative measure of income to reflect experiences of poverty among those who might be affluent in global terms, but who might not share the overall well-being of the country where they live.

Halving poverty is one of the millennium development goals, the target date for achieving which is 2015. The other goals also relate to poverty and include eliminating hunger, achieving universal primary education, promoting gender equality and empowering women, reducing child poverty, improving material wealth, combating **HIV/AIDS**, ensuring environmental sustainability and developing a global partnership for development.

Protectionism

Protectionism is designed to restrict transboundary exchanges of goods and services (see **International Trade**). The main protective mechanisms can be divided into tariffs and **non-tariff barriers**. Tariffs refer to the application of a particular duty against products or services from abroad. They are comparable to a form of import tax as they increase the price of the foreign product in the country imposing the tariff. Quotas, subsidies, administrative regulations and voluntary export controls are all examples of non-tariff barriers. Quotas are quantitative restrictions designed to limit either the quantity of imported goods or their value. Subsidies refer to certain allowances, cash grants, tax reductions or government contracts designed to foster specific domestic industries in order to increase their competitiveness. Administrative regulations cover a wide field, including all barriers to trade posed by health and safety standards, labour laws, bureaucracy, special marketing requirements, etc. In the case of voluntary export controls, a country voluntarily agrees to limit its exports to another state.

Protectionism is by definition contrary to liberal **free trade** ideas. It is advocated by the mercantilist/neo-mercantilist tradition, writers from the radical tradition and environmentalist leaders in the developing world.

Mercantilist and neo-mercantilist theories advocate the regulation of trade to increase the power of the state and to protect domestic industries from foreign competition. Two arguments against free trade stand out: the infant industry argument and the national **security** argument. The infant industry argument proposes the temporary protection of fledgling domestic industries from foreign competition. Such sheltered conditions ought to be provided until these industries have become competitive and can benefit from **international trade** and **comparative advantage**. The national security argument makes the point that states ought to be self-sufficient in certain sectors for security reasons. An example is the protection of the production of military- and security-relevant technologies in the USA.

Marxist thinkers have influenced radical arguments in favour of protectionism. They emphasize the implications of free trade for social justice and **inequality** (see **Exploitation** and **Anti-globalization (Movement)**). In their view, free trade reflects historical power relations and effectively freezes the current status quo of the international political economy. Instead of promoting **development**, free trade makes it impossible for the global South to develop by systematically discriminating against **developing countries**. The environmental critique argues that free trade contributes to **environmental degradation** since the price for trade commodities rarely takes full costs into consideration. The externalities of trade are excluded. Advocates of labour rights and **human rights** and entrenched interest groups also favour some form of protectionism. The Common Agricultural Policy of the **European Union** illustrates how such groups can lobby to defend their interests and uphold protectionist barriers.

Traditionally, tariffs have been the most widely used form of protectionism. However, since the establishment of the **General Agreement on Tariffs and Trade**, non-tariff barriers have become increasingly popular. Thus, while globalization has fostered international trade, there has been a backlash in the form of protectionist measures, taken by individual states or coming in the form of concerted action by trading blocs or common markets (see **Regionalism**). But despite the persistence of protectionism and restrictions on free trade, markets for goods and services have become increasingly globalized.

Public Goods

Public goods are non-exclusive. If such a good is provided for one, it is accessible to all. It cannot be restricted to anyone and nor can anyone be excluded from it. Thus, the consumption of public goods is available to everyone regardless of individual contributions. They are also non-rival in that the consumption of these goods by one individual does not inhibit the amount of the good available for consumption by others. For example, one person's enjoyment of the benefits of street lighting does not diminish the benefits of street lighting accruing to another. Typical examples of public goods include the provision of defence, knowledge and clean air. The term 'collective goods' is given to public goods provided by public authorities.

Public goods typically generate a free rider problem: individuals can gain by either lowering their contribution to the provision of the public good in question or by refusing to pay for its consumption. If too many individuals apply such a strategy and try to take advantage of the system, the system will fail, i.e. the public good in question cannot be provided any longer. Thus, public goods are related to market failure and the problem of externalities.

A similar problem occurs in the case of the exploitation of common pool resources, e.g. **global commons**. Common pool resource goods are also non-exclusive but they are rival goods. Over-fishing of the oceans, for instance, leads to a depletion of fish stocks, a non-exclusive but ultimately finite resource. The term 'global commons' describes pool resources over which no state can claim exclusive **sovereignty**. Examples include Antarctica, the oceans, the atmosphere and outer space. These resources are managed through multilateral co-operation, **international law** and international treaties (see **Antarctic Treaty System**).

At the domestic level, governments can overcome the free rider or public goods problem by employing their legislative and enforcement authority. At the international level, the problem is slightly more complex due to the absence of a legitimate authority above state level. Indeed, some theorists, most notably realists/neo-realists, argue that the free-rider problem at the international level results in a prisoner's dilemma situation that ultimately undermines the very possibility of multilateral co-operation and the provision of international public goods. However, as neo-liberals and others have aptly pointed out, multilateral co-operation takes place very much because it is in the interest of the participating states to enjoy the benefits of co-operation, i.e. the provision of international public goods. International regimes facilitate such co-operation by establishing the rules of the game, thus making it easier to detect any defection. The principle of **reciprocity** applies in such circumstances.

Generally, co-operation and the provision of international public goods are easier to achieve in small groups than in larger ones. In small groups, the free-riding behaviour of any member is more easily detectable, has a much greater impact and is easier to punish. Examples include regional organizations such as the **European Union** and the **Association of South East Asian Nations**, or the **North Atlantic Treaty Organization**. Global groupings also provide examples, such as the **G7/G8**.

R

Race to the Bottom

Race to the bottom is a common phrase criticizing the implications of trade **liberalization** for environmental standards. Many critics of **free trade** argue that unfettered trade threatens the environment by undermining environmental regulations (see **Ecologism** and **Environmentalism**). In a competitive world where firms are free to locate anywhere, **multinational companies (MNCs)** will move production lines from countries with high levels of environmental protection to those with lower levels of environmental regulation. Given the importance of **foreign direct investment** for the economic **development** of industrialized and **developing countries** alike, an incentive is created for countries to lower their environmental standards in order to remain competitive. It has been claimed that the race to the bottom is contributing to **environmental degradation** world-wide.

The phrase is also often used with regard to wage levels, unionization and health and safety legislation (see **Anti-globalization (Movement)**). MNCs are often blamed for circumventing labour laws by shifting production facilities to countries with lower levels of protection, thereby taking advantage of and actively encouraging exploitative conditions, such as sweatshops in the **Third World** (see **Exploitation**). At the same time, such behaviour puts pressure on the comparatively generous wage levels in the industrialized world. Consequently, the race to the bottom denotes a shift in the balance of power between labour and capital in favour of capital.

Reciprocity

The concept of reciprocity describes a response in kind to another's action. It is a very effective strategy to influence the behaviour of another actor. It uses positive and negative forms of leverage, such as the promise of rewards and the threat of punishment.

Reciprocity can help to ensure international co-operation. The willingness and ability to reciprocate makes it easy for other actors to calculate the benefits of co-operation and the costs of failing to co-operate. Reciprocity can also prevent other actors from undesired action. This captures the essence of deterrence, the threat of punishment if another actor takes a particular course of action.

Reciprocity can be defined as exchanges of roughly equivalent values in which the actions of each party are contingent upon the prior action of the others. So good is returned for good, and bad for bad. A distinction is also made between specific and diffuse reciprocity. The former denotes reciprocal agreements between states and is relevant, for instance, in **international trade** negotiations. Diffuse reciprocity describes the institutionalization of trust in an anarchical international environment. It is at the core of multilateral agreements and international regimes between groups of states where the costs and benefits are not equally distributed at any given time.

Reciprocity finds its application in **international law**, trade relations and in **multilateralism** and international regimes. In international law reciprocity explains why states abide by rules in an anarchic environment that lacks an ultimate authority able to enforce the rules. Long-term advantages of co-operation and compliance may outweigh the short-term benefits of violating the rules. Ensured reciprocity and its inherent 'tit-for-tat' behaviour generate a stable international environment even in the general absence of trust between states.

Reciprocity is also an important concept for the study of international regimes such as trading agreements. It explains the willingness of states to engage in and abide by **free trade** regimes. It gives exporters the incentive to lobby for the **liberalization** of trade. The expansion of international trade has resulted in the creation of a dense web of reciprocal agreements. The extent to which specific direct agreements complement or compete with multilateral, diffuse or indirect agreements is one of the important issues in the debate between **regionalism** and multilateralism.

Region

The definition of what constitutes a region is fraught with difficulty. A region can be empirically identified with data on mutual interactions, similarities of actor attributes, and shared values and experiences. Geographical proximity is one of the main determinants of a region. Many scholars insist that the members of a region also share cultural, linguistic, economic or political ties. The main problem here is to identify the distinctiveness of a particular geographic area as a unit characterized by enhanced political, economic and social interaction. This relates to the question of how different a certain region is with respect to other geographical entities or the international political economy in general.

Different processes of **regionalism** and regionalization at different levels of interaction converge in the making of a region. Economic, political and social forces come together in aligning and shaping a set of new collective norms, principles and identities at the regional level while altering established interests, norms and identities. This is applicable to both regions at the subnational level (micro-regions), and regions at the international level (macro-regions). Regions are becoming important features in an overlapping network of global **multilayered governance**. The processes of **devolution**, integration and regionalism are closely linked with globalization. Indeed, globalization has supported the rise of the regional level of analysis in international relations in many ways. Technological advances associated with the globalization process have certainly enabled the co-ordination of economic, social and political processes across wider territorial spaces and across national boundaries. Globalization has also triggered the reorientation of economic, political and **civil society** actors away from the national level to focus on regional modes of governance (see **Transnational Actors** and **Transnational Advocacy Networks**). At the same time, regions are also forged as a response to globalization as nation states and their governments search for more co-operative means to address some of the difficulties arising from globalization. Economic and financial flows, **security** and environmental issues, **migration** and organized **crime** increasingly require collective regional solutions.

Regionalism

Regionalism is a complex phenomenon that can take the form of micro- and macro-regionalism. Micro-regionalism refers to subnational forms of regionalism. It can, however, include the formation of transborder regions when territorial subunits within several states forge closer exchanges. Micro-regionalism is often associated with the process of **devolution**, the shift of organizational authority from the centre to regional authorities on the periphery. Macro-regionalism, or regionalism between states, denotes formal and state-led projects and processes. It refers also to a body of norms, values and objectives, ideas and a type of **international order** or society. Good examples of these formal regional processes are the intergovernmental conferences determining the shape and direction of the **European Union** or the **Association of South East Asian Nations**. In the contemporary international environment, regional solutions are often sought to address a variety of issue areas. **Security** alliances, free trade areas, customs unions and common markets are typical examples.

Although regionalism and regionalization are often conflated, it is important to clarify some conceptual differences. Unlike regionalism, regionalization is an empirical trend depicting a multidimensional process of intra-regional change that occurs simultaneously at several levels of social, political and economic interaction. It is more spontaneous than formal regionalism and is driven by other actors. While regionalism can be understood as a top-down process imposed and concerted by governments and other public actors, regionalization is a much more unplanned and undirected bottom-up process involving private political and economic actors (see **Transnational Actors** and **Transnational Advocacy Networks**) and **civil society** actors. It is conceivable that public actors too participate in regionalization processes, for instance by actively encouraging transboundary co-operation of private actors.

Regionalism and regionalization are not mutually exclusive concepts. They can and do exist and prosper side by side. Indeed, they tend to complement each other. The more formal process of regionalism, for example, establishes the infrastructure and provides the funds and incentives for regionalization to take place, while informal regionalization can be a push-factor for regionalism and more formal state-oriented or issue-specific regional governance. Thus, regionalization in a way represents a drive for more formal suprastate regulatory mechanisms and regional governance. This notion, that regionalization leads to demands for more formal regionalism, is an intrinsic feature of functional and neo-functional theories.

Regionalism and the associated regionalization processes are not exclusive post-Cold War concepts. Indeed, regional solutions gained somewhat unprecedented popularity after 1945, spearheaded by the newly founded European Communities. This wave of regionalism was influenced by the Cold War and the superpower strategies. Contemporary regionalism, the 'new regionalism', is emerging in a fundamentally different international environment with the end of the Cold War, and in a unipolar world dominated by the USA. Today, regionalism cannot be separated from the globalization process. Regional trade arrangements, for instance, are equally described as protective measures or initiators of increasingly freer global trade. Regionalism is often conceived of as a way of 'negotiating' globalization. Some scholars interpret regionalism as the creation of social buffers against the potentially disruptive and disturbing effects of globalization. Thus, regionalism can be regarded as a contradiction of globalization, or a response to counter the implications of globalizing processes by serving protectionist tendencies (see **Anti-Globalization (Movement)**; **International Trade**; **Free Trade**; and **Protectionism**). At the same time, however, regionalism and globalization are complementary. Technologies related to globalization enable the co-ordination of large-scale regional processes. Regionalism has also fostered the dissolution of previously sovereign space, transborder activities and regional governance, and, in many cases, has been an effective mechanism for administering and creating global norms, such as notions of universal **human rights**, trade rules or technical standards. (See also **Integration**; **Common Market**; **Customs Union**; and **Free Trade Area**.)

Rio Conference – *see* United Nations Conference on Environment and Development (UNCED)

Risk (Risk Society)

Two globalization theorists are known for their work on risk—**Anthony Giddens** and **Ulrich Beck**. For Giddens, risk is characteristic of societies that are future-oriented; that see the future as a territory to be conquered. Modern **capitalism** is quintessentially future-oriented, forever calculating future profit and loss, so that risk becomes a continuous process, together with its antithesis, insurance. Giddens cites the example of a **welfare state** as an example of a risk management system. Risk is also critical to modern economies: when positively embraced, it is the source of the energy that creates wealth.

For Beck, risk is at the centre of his analysis of contemporary social change. Present-day society, at least in the industrialized world, has moved beyond concerns about immediate well-being, and the production and distribution of physical goods to make well-being possible. It has moved on now to take cognisance of the damage and the negative side effects that have emerged with the growth of welfare, such as **environmental degradation** and pollution. Managing these risks has become the central concern of affluent societies.

There are several ways in which present-day risks are different from those faced in earlier times. First, they are a direct fall-out of industrialization; indeed, they multiply as industrialization proceeds and derive from over-production. Second, they are not all perceptible to the senses, nor are they localized. There is the added danger that as high-risk industries globalize, not even science can come to the rescue and calculate the risks entailed. What is also characteristic of the contemporary experience of risk is that it is politically and scientifically reflexive. Risk itself thus becomes a globalizing force as it universalises and equalizes, affecting everybody in the world, regardless of nationality or class. The only answers to risk are supranational ones: strategic arms reduction talks, earth summits, etc.

Robertson, Roland

Roland Robertson is seen as a key architect of the sociology of cultural globalization. He introduced the idea of globalization as both the compression of the world and the intensification of consciousness of the world as a whole through the ever-increasing proliferation of global connections and our understanding of them.

First, with globalization there is an accelerated coming together. However, one of the paradoxes of globalization is that while there is convergence, there is also simultaneous fragmentation. Thus, in an increasingly globalized world, there is heightened civilizational, societal, ethnic and regional self-consciousness. As such, rather than being about unity, globalization is about a simultaneous increase in diversity at various levels.

Second, globalization is not just the spread of global forces and relations, it is also the spread of an idea, of a heightened global consciousness, or a sense of interconnectedness. He distances himself from **world systems theory**, which, he believes, ignores the complexities and contradictions in contemporary cultural globalization. He uses the terms 'globality' and the 'global human condition' to describe this globe-oriented and globe-encompassing perspective. He talks of a discourse of globality (globe talk) consisting largely in the shifting and contested terms in which the world as a whole is defined, and which is a vital component of contemporary global culture. Thus, globalization is at once objectively experienced and sub-jectively interpreted.

Globalization, in Robertson's view, predates **modernity** and the rise of **capitalism**. Indeed, he presents five phases of globalization in Europe. He does, however, concede that the process currently being witnessed is quali-tatively different from earlier manifestations, in that modernization has accelerated the process of globalization and permeated contemporary con-sciousness. At its heart lies the 'glocal', defined as the creation and incor-poration of locality. These processes themselves largely shape, in turn, the compression of the world as a whole. The global and the local comingle to produce the 'glocal', with borders becoming highly porous and indeed eroded. (See also **Glocal(ization)**.)

S

Security

Security can be defined as the absence of threat. Beyond that, however, the subject remains rather contentious. Problems begin with the object of security. Who or what needs to be secured? There is also dispute regarding what exactly the nature of the threat being talked about is.

Security, in an international relations perspective, has centred on the survival of the **nation state** as an intact political and territorial entity. It is linked to the use of military force to defend the state and its territorial integrity against external threats. This is reflected in the debate between the realist/neo-realist and liberal/neo-liberal schools of thought (see **Liberalism** and **Neo-liberalism**) that dominated the development of international relations theory until the 1980s. Realism, for example, ties the interpretation of security to the anarchic international system, where there is no overarching power guaranteeing security or the rule of law above the level of the sovereign state. Thus, the sovereign state becomes the only locus of security for the individual. However, the anarchic structure of the international system creates a security dilemma, based on distrust, and a mismatch between perceptions and intentions. Insecurity and war are endemic and natural for realists and neo-realists. Indeed, war is often seen as having a positive function, initiating change. Under such conditions security is achieved via self-help.

The liberal/neo-liberal school of thought, while accepting certain premises of the realist tradition such as the anarchic structure of international relations and the resulting security dilemma, is none the less more optimistic. Accordingly, long-term co-operation achieved through the establishment of international institutions and international regimes can help enhance international security. The economic interdependencies generated by **international**

trade also help to create a level of relative security among trading partners. The liberal school also emphasizes the role of norms and rules, the spread of liberal **democracy** and the importance of **collective security** in this context.

The debate between realism/neo-realism and liberalism/neo-liberalism dominated international relations for much of the Cold War and focused on issues related to external threats to state security. Two points of critique stand out here. First, even during the heyday of the Cold War, states were subject to internal as well as external security threats. The second point of critique concerns the object of security—the state. During the 1980s, **postmodernism**, critical theory and gender-based approaches found their way into international relations, putting forward concerns about a state-centric concept of security, calling for a focus instead on individual security concerns.

And it is here that the human security paradigm gained ground. Human security can be defined as the absence of threats to individuals such as violence, hunger, thirst, disease and oppression. Human security has several dimensions and includes economic, food, health, personal, environmental and political security. The rise of the human security paradigm was supported by two factors. First, in the post-Cold War environment, the threat and actual instances of conflict between two or more major states have become rather rare occurrences. Of much greater concern are instances of civil war, ethnic cleansing, and internal strife, as the examples following the break-up of Yugoslavia or the massacres in Rwanda illustrate. And, second, all too often it is the state itself that becomes a threat to the security of its citizens. **Human rights** violations by government authorities are a regular feature in many states in the contemporary era. Indeed, all too often human rights violations and the restriction of civil liberties are justified in the name of state security. This is not only restricted to some authoritarian regimes in the so-called **Third World**. The 'war on terror' following the 9/11 attacks on the World Trade Center has been used by many governments in the West to systematically roll back civil liberties. The abrogation of the Convention against Torture, if deemed necessary for national security, or the Guantá-namo Bay detention centre, are two notorious examples of US anti-terrorist measures.

The state security angle stands almost in direct contrast and contradiction to the human security principle. This is reflected at the international level in the conflict between communitarian notions (see **Communitarianism**) of **sovereignty** and non-intervention and the ideas of universal human rights and **humanitarian intervention**, based on cosmopolitan principles (see **Cosmopolitanism**).

Globalization has further eroded the traditional security concept based on the nation state. First, the globalization process has led to the dissolution of the strict dividing line between the domestic and international spheres. Issues of international security can all too easily develop domestic consequences, e.g. by triggering a wave of refugees or disturbing vital economic supply lines. Second, globalization leads to the creation of new security actors. The revolution in the **information and communication technologies** and the transport sector has also facilitated the emergence of international or even global **terrorism**, thus removing it from its previous primarily local context. And, third, globalization has increased the salience of **identity** issues, creating new challenges for security, a topic that has been taken up by Samuel Huntington in his **clash of civilisations** theory.

Sovereignty

A key concept in the contemporary globalization discourse and political and international relations theory, and a defining feature in the organization of world politics dominated by sovereign nation states. Political and international relations theory points to two dimensions of sovereignty: an internal and an external one. In its internal dimension it is the ultimate legitimate authority over a well-specified population and a clearly demarcated territory. In its external dimension, a sovereign entity accepts no higher authority than itself. The modern (Westphalian) nation state embodies both dimensions: a sovereign state does not accept any internal equal or external superior.

Several implications follow for international relations. The existence of sovereign states implies, necessarily, anarchic international relations since it precludes any authority above state level. Equally, the principle of sovereignty as a key feature of international relations leads to the doctrine of sovereign equality of all states and to non-intervention in the domestic affairs of individual states.

The concept of sovereignty has a long history and is closely related to the rise of the Westphalian state. Philosophers such as Jean Bodin and Thomas Hobbes understood sovereignty as the unrestricted power of monarchs to create, declare and enforce law. Such sovereign power was necessary in order to overcome the insecurity arising out of the anarchic condition of the 'state of nature', a theoretical construct describing a situation where people live outside the restraints of **civil society**. Under such conditions of perfect anarchy, humanity's worst instincts would reign freely, creating a **security dilemma** and a state of perpetual warfare of all against all. There would be no common concord, no co-operation, no moral life, and no commerce. There would be no guarantees that agreements would be honoured and potential long-term gains could not be realized. Indeed, in the 'state of nature' life would be 'solitary, poor, nasty, brutish and short'.

It is in order to overcome the security dilemma inherent in the 'state of nature' that people agree to a transfer of power to a sovereign authority. In return, the sovereign provides a measure of order and security. Ironically, this only transfers the problem to another level. Another 'state of nature' is created—this time between states rather than between people. Thus, at the international level sovereign states are only restricted by their own capabilities (and those of others).

With the Peace of Westphalia (1648), the concept of sovereignty began to acquire its external dimension. It denotes the beginning of the modern state, the Westphalian state, the formally recognized exclusive territorial jurisdiction of monarchs. The doctrine of non-interference undermined rival extra-territorial claims such as those from the Catholic Church or the Holy Roman Empire. From Europe, the Westphalian state with its key characteristic, sovereignty, was exported throughout the world.

Today, sovereignty and the associated doctrine of sovereign equality are cornerstones of **international law** and the contemporary international system. It is enshrined in the **United Nations (UN)** Charter. However, the concept has been subject to many misconceptions. For instance, it is important to understand that the doctrine of sovereign equality is merely a legal and theoretical notion. Sovereignty has never been absolute. Interdependencies, the reciprocal nature of international law, international agreements and treaties, and membership of **international organizations** such as the UN have always restricted sovereignty. All states are to a greater or lesser extent penetrated by extra-territorial forces.

In the contemporary globalization debate, sovereignty has become a key issue. According to some commentators, sovereignty is being eroded by a combination of factors, such as increased economic interdependencies, the growing influence of **multinational companies** and the expanded authority of international governmental organizations such as the **International Monetary Fund** or the **World Bank**. The **European Union**, with supranational powers, is the biggest challenger to traditional conceptions of sovereignty. Hyperglobalizers, such as Kenichi Ohmae, have heralded the dawn of a post-Westphalian age, characterized by the end of the sovereign nation state. Such notions may also be supported by developments in international law. **Human rights** norms, for instance, increasingly conflict with the norm of non-intervention in the domestic affairs of sovereign states (see **Humanitarian Intervention**).

Other scholars, however, have pointed out that sovereignty is not a static but a dynamic concept. States are not only reacting to the forces of globalization, but are also instrumental in shaping the international environment that facilitates globalization in the first place. Both the state and sovereignty have undergone a long historical development, a development that is still ongoing. Rather than being eroded, sovereignty is increasingly being shared and even extended through participation in the ever-growing number of **international non-governmental organizations** and the emerging network of multilevel **global governance**. The post-Westphalian interpretation of globalization, therefore, it is argued, is largely a myth and sovereignty, while changing, remains the primary organizing principle of international relations.

Structural Adjustment

Structural adjustment is a term related to the conditionalities attached to **International Monetary Fund (IMF)** and **World Bank** assistance, recommending domestic and international economic policy changes for **developing countries**. In return for IMF loans, recipient countries agree to undertake so-called structural adjustment programmes entailing the liberalization of their economies to **international trade** and foreign investment (see **Multinational Companies**), the reduction of state subsidies, privatization of state-owned enterprises, **deregulation** of economic activity, including the removal of price and capital controls, and stringent budget constraints and export orientation (see **Debt Crisis** and **Neo-liberalism**).

There is a longstanding debate as to whether structural adjustment programmes initiated necessary reforms in developing countries or whether they reflected the interests of creditors, leading to the wholesale **exploitation** of much of the **Third World** (see **Anti-globalization (Movement)** and **World Systems Theory**). Criticism focuses on the consequences of structural adjustment programmes, including reduced local purchasing power due to lowered wages as national currencies are devalued, the elimination of tariffs, quotas or other controls on imports (see **Protectionism**), thereby slowly displacing domestic producers by foreign competition, cuts in government spending on education, health care and the environment, and withdrawal of price sub-sidies on basic necessities, such as food grains. The IMF uses such measures to increase foreign exchange earnings to facilitate debt repayment. It seeks to ensure that the money lent to a country is not spent for politically popular but unproductive purposes, like subsidizing food. It tries to ensure that infla-tion does not eat away all progress, and that the economy is stable enough to attract investment. In addition, it demands steps to curtail corruption.

However, the conditionalities, directly and indirectly, most severely impact on the poorest and most vulnerable sections of the population, thereby not only putting the brakes on any **poverty** reduction that may have been achieved, but also exacerbating inequalities within the society (see **Race to the Bottom**). Imposing structural adjustment policies also raises questions con-cerning interference in the **sovereignty** of countries receiving IMF help.

Structural adjustment programmes have come in for severe criticism. Indeed, the 1980s, which saw the **debt crisis** and the implementation of a number of structural adjustment programmes around the world, is referred to as the 'lost decade'. The United Nations Development Report (1997) states that structural adjustment programmes, in many instances, tried 'to balance the economy at the cost of unbalancing people's lives'. During the 1990s, the IMF and the World Bank have begun to shift their focus away from structural adjustment towards the new goals of poverty reduction and **sustainable development**.

Sustainable Development

The term 'sustainable development' was first adopted by the Agenda 21 programme of the **United Nations**. According to the 1987 Brundtland Report, sustainable development is a process of 'developing' that meets the needs of the present without compromising the ability of future generations to meet their own needs. The report and the concerns expressed in it were a reaction to **environmental degradation**. The term reflects the knowledge that the earth's resources are finite, and that current patterns of growth are not sustainable. It is intertwined with the need to effect economic growth in the long term, meeting the basic needs of all, and extending to all the oppor-tunity to fulfil their aspirations for a better life. However, sustainable development can only be pursued if population size and growth are in har-mony with the changing productive potential of the ecosystem. It is not suggesting a fixed state of harmony, but a process of change in which the exploitation of resources, the direction of investments, the orientation of technological development, and institutional change are made consistent with future as well as present needs.

Some people now object to the term 'sustainable development' as an umbrella term, since it implies continued **development**, and insist that it should be reserved only for development activities. 'Sustainability' itself is nowadays used as an umbrella term for all human activity, and sustainable societies are supposed to be rooted in 10 core principles: **democracy**, subsidiarity (power at the local level), ecological sustainability, common heritage, **human rights**, jobs/livelihood/employment, food security and food safety, equity, diversity and the precautionary principle (whereby the proponents of a product or practice bear the burden of proving it is safe before it is used/implemented).

In the international arena, however, environmental and economic regimes seem to play out in contradiction to each other. While the environmental regime is concerned with the protection of the natural heritage for this and future generations, the economic regime is concerned with equal rights to exploit it. Environmental agreements are based on respect for natural limits; economic agreements on the right to carry through economic expansion successfully. The two also address very different systems of responsibility and **accountability**, with the environmental regime addressing sovereign states (see **Sovereignty** and **Nation State**), while economic agreements assume transnationally active corporations that are not accountable to states.

T

Tariffs – *see* **Protectionism**

Terrorism

At a very basic level terrorism can be defined as the threat or the use of violence to achieve political goals. It denotes the application of force as leverage in political bargaining processes. Beyond that there is little consensus and no established definition of terrorism. Indeed, the definition of what constitutes terrorism is often politically motivated. This is best captured by the proverbial saying that one man's freedom fighter is another man's terrorist.

There are, however, certain characteristics that set terrorism apart from other uses of force. The violence used in terrorist attacks is usually directed against non-combatants. It comes in various forms, such as hijackings, hostage-taking, assassinations, bombings and other indiscriminate attacks targeting civilians. The aim is to terrorize and demoralize civilian populations, to spread domestic discontent in order to facilitate change and to achieve the political objectives of those engaged in terrorist activities. Thus, the primary goal is to create a climate of fear, to spread instability and social unrest. Terrorism is often seen as a tool of the otherwise powerless and marginalized. It depends on the amplification of a relatively small amount of power and its impact is largely of a psychological nature. The efficacy of terrorist methods depends to a large extent on how far they have been able to capture the attention of civilian populations.

Terrorism is not a new phenomenon. State and non-state actors have used terrorist tactics in the past. The legions of the Roman empire, for instance, were known to put to the sword every man, woman and child of any rebellious community, to set an example and to create an atmosphere of terror in neighbouring communities. Another historical example is that of the Jewish Sciarii, who engaged in a systematic campaign of terror against the Roman empire. Later, in the 11th and 12th centuries, a Muslim sect called the Assassins used targeted assassinations to defend their beliefs. In the 19th century, anarchists aimed for the complete destruction of the state and anything that contributed toward this goal was regarded as moral. From these examples it is clear that both state and non-state actors have been known to employ terror tactics. States themselves have often used force with the specific aim of terrorizing civilian populations. Much of the literature, however, makes an analytical distinction between terrorism as an illegitimate act of violence by non-state actors and acts of war or acts of repression by state actors.

Terrorism is used as a tool to draw attention to the grievances of particular groups. Its causes can be political, ideological, ethnic or religious, and its ultimate goal is political change. However, due to the indiscriminate and often extreme nature of its attacks, terrorism often fails to generate the widespread support necessary to facilitate change and is, therefore, ultimately ineffective.

Globalization is connected to terrorism in many ways. Indeed, in many responses to terrorism, the depth and direction of globalization seem to be at issue. First, the same technologies that are linked to the spread of globalization have also changed the nature of terrorism. The increase in air travel, for example, has transformed terrorism from being a localized occurrence into an international threat. The development of new **information and communication technologies**, the advent of satellite television and the extension of media coverage has enabled terrorists to co-ordinate their attacks more effectively and multiplied the shock effect of terrorist attacks, as they now reach a much wider audience. Ironically, however, the extension of media coverage also poses a problem for terrorists. They now need to find a way of sustaining the interest of viewers—no mean achievement in a world characterized by information overload on a daily basis. Hence, terrorists appear to devise ever more spectacular attacks, increase the number of casualties, and even to acquire **weapons of mass destruction**.

Second, globalization, perceived as **Americanization** and **cultural homogenization**, leads to a pronouncement of **identity** issues. Particular communities may feel increasingly threatened by Western norms and values, leading to conflict between different civilizational blocs (see **Clash of Civilizations**).

Terrorism, therefore, can appear as a backlash against perceived **Westernization** or cultural homogenization.

Third, contrary to the neo-liberal logic of economic globalization (see **Neo-liberalism**), not everyone benefits from the **deregulation** and liberalization of trade and financial flows and the **global division of labour**. According to some theorists, globalization is the latest version of Western **imperialism** (see **Colonialism**; **Dependency Theory**; **Empire**; and **Marxism**), which is entrenching the divide between the global North and the global South, and perpetuating inequalities while also generating new ones on a global scale. Such a reading sees terrorism as a tool of the economically dispossessed—a reaction to the unequal distribution of wealth.

Fourth, economic globalization generates rising expectations that are increasingly difficult to meet. Failing to satisfy these new expectations of **consumerism** may lead to a feeling of disenfranchisement among certain populations which, again, may resort to terrorism as an outlet for their frustrations.

The global *jihad* propagated by Osama bin Laden's al-Qa'ida network denotes a new trend in terrorism. This apparent reaction to **modernity** appears to be driven by seemingly religious motivations and is, therefore, seen as a reaction against the perceived spiritual oppression of Muslims by the secular West.

Third Cultures

Cultural flows are seen to produce both homogeneity and heterogeneity, creating hybrid transnational third cultures (see **Hybridity**) that are not simply a sum of the bilateral exchanges between nations. Third cultures are sets of practices, bodies of knowledge, conventions of lifestyles that have developed in ways that are increasingly independent of nation states. Thus, new global processes and flows simply make available new cultural possibilities, making the world at once seem more culturally singular and, simultaneously, a more diverse place. They do not, however, create 'a' global culture; they merely make possible forms of social interaction not tied to place or limited in time.

Third cultures are particularly visible among people whose geographical mobility and professional culture allow them something of a cosmopolitan orientation. Indeed, here third cultures might be seen to perform a mediating function. Increased cultural flows, however, do not necessarily produce greater tolerance and **cosmopolitanism**. Indeed, there may be a retreat from the 'threat' of cultural disorder through a reassertion of ethnic, religious or other identities.

Third World

This term, a remnant of the Cold War, was used to refer to countries that did not belong to either the West (First World) or to the Soviet bloc (Second World), with the Third World consisting of developing or non-aligned countries (see **Developing Countries** and **Development**). This tripartite distinction lost its meaning with the collapse of the Berlin Wall and the events that followed in 1989, eliminating the Second World. Meanwhile, many countries of the so-called Third World, such as those in south-east Asia, were entering a phase of rapid economic growth. Today, the term is broadly used to denote poorer regions of the world, especially former colonies of Western states (see **Colonialism**). In the post-Cold War world, however, the tripartite division into First, Second and Third World has given way to binaries such as North-South, developing-developed, rich-poor or a continuum, such as industrialized/industrializing-non-industrialized. Indeed, with economic activity increasingly becoming localized in regions below the level of the nation, 'developed' and 'developing' sectors or the North and South are no longer contiguous with national boundaries. Thus, parts of the earlier Third World are on the pathways of transnational capital and belong to developed sectors of the economy, while parts of the First World marginalized in the new global economy may contain pockets that show levels of **poverty** and deprivation commonly associated with the Third World. It is for this reason that a case is now made for 'the end of the Third World'.

Time-Space Compression

Attributed to **David Harvey**, the term suggests the objectification and universalization of concepts of space and time that have allowed time to annihilate space. It refers to the manner in which the speeding up of economic and social processes has experientially shrunk the globe, so that distance and time no longer appear to be major constraints on the organization of human activity. Harvey argues that the pressures of technological and economic change have continually collapsed time and space, resulting in the annihilation of space by time—through the reorganization of time in such a way as to overcome space, leading to a change in the very pace of life as time taken to do things and the experiential distance between different locations become shorter.

When people in two different locations across the globe are able to experience the same event simultaneously, then space might be said to have been annihilated by time compression. Or, to give another example, the world shrinks as the speed of transport increases. With the **mass media**, images generated are lost the moment they are consumed (see **Consumerism**). Thus, insofar as images have no past or future, human experience becomes compressed into an overwhelming presence.

This compression, however, is not a gradual and continuous process, but something that takes place in short bursts due to what Harvey calls capitalist overaccumulation (see **Capitalism**). With each step, the time taken to do things reduces and this in turn reduces the experienced distance between different points in space.

Feminist geographer Doreen Massey discusses the power-geometry of time-space compression. She overlays social differentiation onto time-space compression to argue that different social groups and individuals are placed in very distinct, highly complicated and varied relations to these flows and interconnections—with some the initiators of these flows and movements, some in charge of it and able to control it, others at the receiving end of it, and still others effectively trapped or imprisoned by it. She underlines that mobility and control over mobility both reflect and reinforce power relations.

Time-Space Distanciation – *see* Giddens, Anthony

Trade System

International actors engaging in **international trade** have created a trade system regulating the cross-border movements of goods, capital and services. The contemporary trade system endorses a neo-liberal vision (see **Neo-liberalism**) pushing for the progressive removal of tariff and **non-tariff barriers** to trade. The predecessor of the contemporary trade system with its emphasis on **free trade** can be found in the 19th century. It was in this period that the doctrine of free trade emerged (see **Comparative Advantage**). Advocated by people such as David Ricardo and Richard Cobden, the superpower of the day, Great Britain, signed on to a free trade system. The record of this system, however, is one of mixed success. Some states, most notably Germany and the USA, preferred protectionist policies to catch up and surpass Britain's economic power (see **Protectionism**). The First World War all but destroyed the international free trade system. The final blow was delivered by the economic upheaval of the 1920s, which led many states to abandon free trade **liberalism** for more isolationist policies.

The current trade system has its origins in the aftermath of the Second World War and the Bretton Woods institutions (see **Bretton Woods System**). Among other things, Bretton Woods paved the way for the foundation of the **General Agreement on Tariff and Trade (GATT)** in 1947, which has brought major reductions in customs, duties, quotas and other measurers that previously inhibited international trade. Following the Uruguay Round of multilateral trade talks, the GATT gave way to the **World Trade Organization (WTO)**. The WTO represents the main institution of the international trade system. Compared to the GATT, it has greater competences to enforce existing trade agreements and to negotiate new measures for **liberalization**. In addition to the WTO, various regional arrangements also exist to reduce restrictions to trade between their members.

The current international trade system differs from its predecessor inasmuch as it has become much more polarized. Neo-liberal globalization, so the critics of the current free trade agenda argue, is leading to an ever-increasing gulf between the industrialized world, the global North, and **developing countries**, the global South (see **Anti-globalization (Movement)** and **World Systems Theory**). The current trade system reflects an institutionalization of a particular constellation of power and interests. It benefits the global North and disadvantages the global South.

Traditionalism – *see* Deglobalization

Trafficking

Human trafficking refers to people being moved by compulsion, or against their will, for the purposes of **exploitation**. Sometimes people might appear to move willingly, but they do so because they are misled about the object of their travel. For instance, women are sometimes promised jobs in entertainment or care, but upon arrival at their destination find they are required to work in the sex industry with little choice but to comply. Trafficked adults and children have little protection. It is testimony to the intense **poverty** that drives people to look for better opportunities elsewhere, and in that process, to become vulnerable to exploitation.

In a broader sense, trafficking refers to the trade in illegal items such as organs, narcotics or illegal arms (see **Arms Trade**). Organ trafficking, for instance, often links the upper strata of biomedical practice to the lowest reaches of the criminal world, through organ brokers. Global power and wealth hierarchies are reflected here too, with movement from the rest to the West, from black and brown to white, from female to male.

Transnationalism

The term describes a condition in which, transcending distance and the presence of international borders, certain kinds of relationships are forged and sustained. This globally intensified space sustaining relationships might span large parts of the planet, and constitute largely virtual arenas of activity. An area of increasing academic interest, transnationalism could refer to social movements, **capital flows**, political activity, families and public cultures spanning nation states.

Long-distance networks certainly predate the nation as we know it today. What is different in a globalized world is the intensity and simultaneity with which the ties, interactions, exchanges and mobility function in real time, aided by new telecommunication technologies.

Discourses on transnationalism and globalization tend to diverge significantly, primarily in the key assumptions they make about the role of the state in the production of meaning, **identity** and social outcomes. While the globalization discourse focuses on social processes that are decentred from specific national territories, and tends to see the state as withering away, transnational social relations are seen to be anchored in, while also transcending, one or more nation states. Borders continue to have significance though they might be transgressed by transnational practices. Thus, while states and globalizing processes are often seen as antagonistic to each other, they are mutually constitutive for transnationalism.

Studies on transnationalism have often tended to ponder the effects of transnationalism and the limits to the idea of **citizenship**. For instance, Benedict Anderson, in his conceptualization of 'imagined communities', warns of the danger in the 'long distance **nationalism**' practised by transnational political diasporas. On the other hand, some states themselves have transnationalized the meaning of nationhood by actively promoting the reincorporation of emigrants into national projects through migrant remittances and investments.

Transnational Actors

In a broad sense, any **civil society**, political or economic actor from one country who has a relation with an actor from another country or with an international organization is a transnational actor. Transnational actors constitute the third main element in the international system and the global economy after the **nation state** and international governmental organizations (IGOs). However, unlike states and IGOs, transnational actors are organizations with a private membership, if they are organizations at all. **International non-governmental organizations** and **multinational companies** are the most organized and numerous versions of transnational actors.

Transnational actors are sustained by a range of modes of social organization, mobility and communication, and the structures or systems of relationships these engender are often described as networks (see **Transnational Advocacy Networks**). Also included here are ethnic diasporas (see **Diaspora**) and new migrant populations, as well as illegal and violent social networks, including international **crime** syndicates and internationally operating terrorist networks (see **Terrorism**), human smuggling and **trafficking**.

Transnational bonds, however, do not have to be cemented by exclusive territorial claims; they may be equally held together or recreated through the mind, through cultural artefacts, and through a shared imagination. It is contended that transnationalism changes people's relations to space by creating 'social fields' that connect and position some actors in more than one country. Not all immigrant groups or individuals, however, have the same frequency, depth and range of transnational connections.

Transnational Advocacy Networks

Transnational advocacy networks are transnational political spaces where different national and international actors meet for the purpose of joint enterprise. They are sets of actors working internationally on an issue who are bound together by shared values, a common discourse and dense exchanges of information and services. Transnational advocacy is active across a wide range of issues, including **human rights**, the environment, gender issues and women's rights, infant health, the rights of indigenous people, work practices and unfair trade practices. They foster the spread of transnational networks and establish links between different **civil society** actors within domestic societies, across national borders and within **international organisations**. Transnational advocacy networks provide opportunities for information exchange and dialogue among these diverse actors. These actors can include national and **international non-governmental organizations**, research and civil society lobby organizations, local social movements, religious groups, churches, the media, trade unions and consumer organizations, and parts of international governmental organizations (IGOs), as well as parts of national governments.

Transnational advocacy networks are committed to social change. As such they are very similar to social movements. What sets them apart are the different tactics they employ in order to achieve their goals. Unlike social movements, transnational advocacy networks are able to mobilize activists and specialists with direct access to national and international policy-making élites, while social movements rely on methods of overt confrontation, such as mass demonstrations (see **World Social Forum** and **Zapatista Movement**). Transnational advocacy networks have the ability to mobilize information strategically in order to influence political decision-makers. Their characteristics enable them to promote international norm convergence and to monitor compliance.

Transnational Corporations – *see* Multinational Companies (MNCs)

U

United Nations (UN)

The United Nations (UN) is an international governmental organization. It came into being as the result of negotiations between the allied powers during the Second World War and was an attempt to learn from the failures of the League of Nations and to regulate international relations after the War. The UN Charter can be regarded as the written constitution of the UN. It is a multilateral treaty and an important source of **international law** (see **Multilateralism**). It also contains the primary objectives of the UN: (1) to maintain international peace through **collective security**; (2) to promote international co-operation in economic and social affairs; (3) to promote respect for **human rights** and universal freedoms.

In many ways, the UN is the successor of the League of Nations. It is a second attempt to reform the international arena by regulating the relations among states in a fundamentally anarchic environment. However, the founding fathers of the UN had learned from the failure of the League and considered the shortcomings of the interwar liberal reform programme (see **Liberalism**). Nowhere is this more apparent than in the Security Council and the veto powers of its five permanent members, which reveals a commitment to bring in the great powers such as the USA. In addition, the Security Council has stronger executive powers compared to the League of Nations.

The six principal organs of the UN are the General Assembly, the Security Council, the Economic and Social Council, the **International Court of Justice**, the Trusteeship Council and the UN Secretariat. Like the League, the UN is based on the principles of **sovereignty** and collective security. The Security Council is arguably the most important institution of the UN. It comprises 15 members, five of which have permanent membership and enjoy veto rights. Representatives of all member states meet at regular intervals in the General Assembly, which gathers annually to discuss international issues. It also serves as a supervisory body over other international agencies related to the UN. These specialized agencies include the **International Monetary Fund**, the **World Bank**, the United Nations Educational, Scientific and Cultural Organization, the World Health Organization, the United Nations International Children's Emergency Fund, the United Nations High Commission for Refugees, the Food and Agriculture Organization and the United Nations Environment Programme.

The UN has a long history of maintaining international peace through peace keeping and preventative diplomacy. However, Cold War realities effectively paralysed the Security Council and, thus, curtailed collective security operations. None the less, the UN remained active, particularly in the world-wide processes of **decolonization**, which rapidly expanded UN membership. Decolonization transformed a western European state system based on national sovereignty into a truly global one. The end of the Cold War triggered new hopes and raised expectations of an increased role for multilateral institutions such as the UN in international relations. Fuelled by successful UN intervention in the Gulf War in 1991, US President George Bush went so far as to proclaim the dawn of a 'new world order' guided by international law and a new confidence in multilateralism.

However, after this first wave of optimism the UN has arguably foundered rather than flourished. It appears that the doctrines of sovereignty and non-intervention, central to the UN, make it difficult to adjust to the nature of many post-Cold War conflict scenarios where active intervention in the internal affairs of states might be required to prevent and put a halt to raging civil wars, genocide and large-scale **human rights** abuses (see **Humanitarian Intervention**). Many voices call for a substantial reform of the UN, especially with regard to the Security Council, whose permanent membership reflects historical convenience rather than the realities of power distribution in today's world.

Nevertheless, the UN has not been entirely unsuccessful. Its network of functionally specialized agencies has changed the very nature of international relations by creating patterns of overlapping interdependencies (see **Interdependence**). In that respect it may represent the first step towards a 'working peace system' as envisaged by the functionalist theory of David Mitrany. Functionalist theory proposes that international co-operation is easier to achieve in technical low politics areas, such as the international political economy, environmental issues and human rights issues. However, co-operation will eventually spill over into areas of high politics, such as foreign policy and **security** matters. Arguably, this can be a long process. It is here that globalization may actually aid the UN project. This can happen in two ways. First, the forces of globalization foster technical co-operation in low politics areas where the need for internationally and globally recognized standards and procedures, rules and regulations has resulted in the creation of a web of institutions with overlapping membership and competencies. And, second, globalization aids the dissolution of Westphalian notions of sovereignty and the emergence of a system of **global governance** where **international organizations** such as the UN find themselves in a very prominent position (see **Multilayered Governance**). Some commentators speak in this context of the emergence of a post-Westphalian state where territorial sovereignty is no longer a defining factor. **Homogenization** will further dissolve Westphalian constructions, supporting instead cosmopolitan notions of human rights and universal freedoms (see **Cosmopolitanism**). (Website: http://www.un.org.)

United Nations Conference on Environment and Development (UNCED)

Environmental degradation, such as air, river and marine pollution, desertification, resource depletion and **climate change**, is transnational in character and can have global implications. As such, it requires concerted efforts at the international level. In June 1992, the United Nations Conference on Environment and Development (UNCED) met in Rio de Janeiro, Brazil, and proclaimed the Rio Declaration on Environment and Development. Also known as the Earth Summit, the Rio conference represented the outcome of growing concerns regarding economic **development** and growth and its environmental implications.

Concerns for the environment had been mounting gradually since the 1970s. The Earth Summit represented the culmination of concerted international efforts to address environmental problems, and the emerging responses included a Framework Convention on Climate Change, a Convention on Biological Diversity, a Forestry Convention and a Convention to Combat Desertification.

The Framework Convention on Climate Change (FCCC) was a response to alarming signs suggesting that changes in the global climate were caused by human industrial activity—the emission of so-called greenhouse gases, such as CFCs, carbon dioxide and methane—and was prepared to be ready for signing at the Rio conference. Concerns about the rapid extinction of species and the loss of habitat were the subject of the negotiations on the Conventions for Biological Diversity. The loss of rainforests and large-scale deforestation through commercial logging operations and land clearing for agricultural purposes were also discussed. However, these negotiations became deadlocked on account of the resistance of some **developing countries**, which argued their sovereign right to use natural resources, such as forests, obtaining on their national territory (see **Sovereignty** and **Nation State**). As such, the Forestry Convention failed, and was later replaced by a set of Forestry Principles emphasizing sovereign rights to exploit forests. Another convention, the Convention to Combat Desertification, addressed the issue of increasing desertification, especially in Africa, and aimed to co-ordinate international action to combat land degradation and provide a code of good practice for marginal land.

At the centre of the UNCED was the search for a consistent approach to further economic and social development, while seeking to prevent further environmental degradation in the process. This found expression in the concept of **sustainable development**. The two main documents of the Earth Summit, the Rio Declaration and Agenda 21, are focused on achieving sustainable development, an anthropocentric perspective on environmental issues. The Rio Declaration outlines general principles to guide action on development and the environment. Agenda 21, on the other hand, contains a much more detailed programme of action on sustainable development.

The Rio conference proved to be one of the biggest ever held. About 150 states and 45,000 delegates attended. The conference managed to agree on the Rio Declaration, Agenda 21 and Forest Principles. The FCCC and the Convention on Biological Diversity were signed. The Convention to Combat Desertification was completed and ready for signature only in 1994.

The Earth Summit represented an important step in the direction of the development of an environmental ethic based on cosmopolitan principles (see **Ecologism**; **Environmentalism**; and **Cosmopolitanism**). Underlying this was the realization that the best way to develop the political will for international co-operation on environmental (and other) matters was to foster a global ethic of international responsibility. Loyalties ought to transcend the fixation on particular political communities, such as sovereign states, in order to respond effectively to the challenges of environmental management.

However, communitarian notions (see **Communitarianism**) centred round state sovereignty and national interests were still very much in evidence. The

271

1997 **Kyoto Protocol** to the FCCC ran into similar difficulties. Several industrialized countries, including the USA, Australia, Canada and Japan, were reluctant to support any obligations requiring emissions reduction. Developing countries and transition economies raised objections that Kyoto obligations would severely impede development and industrialization efforts. Perhaps the most notorious example of the clash between a developing cosmopolitan ethic and communitarian notions of state sovereignty was the 2001 withdrawal of the US signature from the Kyoto Protocol, on the grounds that it was contrary to US economic interests. (For further information, see: http://www.un.org/geninfo/bp/enviro.html.)

W

Wallerstein, Immanuel – *see* **World Systems Theory**

Washington Consensus

The Washington Consensus describes an agreement between the **World Bank**, the **International Monetary Fund** and the US Treasury Department on what constitutes the best set of policies to promote economic **development**. It proposes a policy framework broadly based on trade and capital market liberalization, fiscal austerity, rapid privatization, widespread **deregulation** and the downscaling of government (see **Neo-liberalism**).

Initially, the Washington Consensus policies were intended to counter the problems in Latin America in the 1980s (see **Debt Crisis**). Governments had run large budget deficits, which were exacerbated by inefficient state-owned enterprises. High protectionist barriers (see **Protectionism**) had stifled competition and loose monetary policies led to inflation. However, although developed to respond to the idiosyncracies of Latin America, the economic policies of the Washington Consensus (privatization, budget austerity and trade liberalization) became the ruling mantra of development and were introduced all over the developing world (see **Structural Adjustment**). These policies have often proved to be inappropriate for countries in early stages of economic development or in transition economies. In other cases they aggravated the effects of economic, social and financial crises (see **Global Financial Crises**). Critics have pointed out that Washington Consensus policies have become ends in themselves rather than means to more equitable and sustainable growth. Partly as a response, a post-Washington Consensus is emerging. The World Bank, for instance, has begun to move away from the Washington Consensus towards **poverty** alleviation policies and **sustainable development**.

Weapons of Mass Destruction (WMD)

Weapons of Mass Destruction (WMD) refer to three different categories of weapons systems: nuclear weapons, biological weapons and chemical weapons. These arms categories distinguish themselves from other weapons systems through the unparalleled damage and immense loss of life they can cause if deployed.

WMD have a significant deterrence potential. At the same time they pose many challenges to the international system. Biological and chemical weapons are relatively cheap and easy to manufacture. They are sought by many states for their perceived deterrence effect. But their low cost and ease of manufacture creates the real danger that they might be acquired and deployed by rogue states or terrorist groups with the explicit aim of creating as many casualties as possible.

WMD have been the focus of many **arms control** (see **Arms Trade**) efforts and several international arms control regimes have been established to control the spread and deployment of biological, chemical and nuclear weapons. However, there are limits to non-proliferation and rogue states and non-state actors are a serious problem for policy-makers.

Welfare State – *see* Keynesianism

Westernization

A form of theorizing based on positing a monolithic West driving forces of **development** and modernization. It is seen as apparently reducing non-Western life to a pathological response to Western domination. (See also **Americanization**; and **Cultural Imperialism**.)

World Bank

The World Bank (also known as World Bank Group) is one of the world's largest sources of **development** assistance. It is another name for the International Bank for Reconstruction and Development (IBRD) and its four associated agencies–the International Finance Corporation, the International Development Association, the Multilateral Investment Guarantee Agency and the International Centre for Settlement of Investment Disputes. It is an **intergovernmental organization** and has its origin in the establishment of a new international economic order following the Second World War. It came into existence as part of the Bretton Woods agreements (see **Bretton Woods System**) in 1945 with the mission to facilitate the rebuilding of European economies shattered by the Second World War.

With the recovery of Europe, the World Bank began focusing its activities on **developing countries**. Its underlying strategy has been to foster the creation of an economic infrastructure which would 'kick start' development. It provides long-term loans and grants, and offers technical assistance to developing countries. Its financial help and technical expertise is used in many different areas, ranging from infrastructure projects (such as roads, hydroelectrical dams) to reform of the health and education sectors, as well as economic development in general.

Membership of the World Bank is restricted to the members of the **International Monetary Fund (IMF)**. Financial contributions from its member states provide a substantial part of the funds of the World Bank, and like the IMF, the World Bank has a system of weighted voting, thus giving power to states making the largest financial contributions. In addition, funds are also raised on the private capital markets.

The World Bank has repeatedly been the subject of criticism for being a tool of the USA and the West (see **Anti-globalization (Movement)**). In addition, it has been critiqued for its underlying neo-liberal philosophy (see **Neo-liberalism**), focusing on free market solutions despite sufficient evidence that **structural adjustment** policies, such as privatization, **free trade** policies and budgetary discipline, are often harmful to development.

Over time, and with an increasing body of evidence against some of these approaches, the World Bank has been changing its stance. For instance, it now accepts that some controls over short-term speculative flows are necessary to protect national economies. In recent years, it has extended its agenda and moved from a concentration on economic growth as the best path to development to **poverty** reduction strategies. Partly in response to its critics, the Bank has also begun to invest heavily in **sustainable development** projects. It now emphasizes growth that is stable, sustainable and equitable, while also seeking to ensure wider participation in its projects. (Website: http://www.worldbank.org.)

World Economic Forum (WEF)

The World Economic Forum (WEF) is a Geneva-based international association bringing together representatives from business and industry, and national policy-makers and academics, with international and transborder interests. Its annual meetings are usually held in Davos, Switzerland. The WEF was inaugurated in 1971 and has organized hundreds of local, national and international meetings between chief executives of large companies and political leaders in order to discuss and shape the national and international economic order under the banner of 'entrepreneurship in the global public interest'. For example, the WEF was instrumental in launching the Uruguay Round of **international trade** negotiations, which culminated in the setting up of the **World Trade Organization**. The WEF has also promoted links between local and global capital in India, China, Latin America and post-Soviet Russia, and even attempted conciliation in, for instance, the Arab–Israeli and Greco–Turkish disputes.

According to its critics, particularly in the anti-capitalist and **anti-globalization** movements, the WEF is a lobby group for interests of an increasingly globalizing big-business élite, and is seen as a bastion of economic **neo-liberalism**. It is seen as an example of the formation of a new international capitalist class of business executives, politicians and bureaucrats. Furthermore, critics point to the influence an unelected and unaccountable association such as the WEF can have on **global governance**. Partly in response to the criticism directed against it, the WEF has invited representatives from leading **international non-governmental organizations**, such as **Amnesty International** and **Oxfam**, to take part in its meetings. The WEF is also seeking other ways to temper its image, with its directors stating that the globalized economy must not become synonymous with free market on the rampage.

The WEF is a good example of how the globalization process is providing particular interest groups with the incentive and opportunity to form international and even global alliances. If the WEF can be regarded as an international meeting place for an increasingly globalized capitalist élite, its counterpart, the **World Social Forum**, is an annual meeting held by left-wing members of the anti-globalization movement to discuss alternative forms of globalization. (Website: http://www.weforum.org.)

World Social Forum (WSF)

The World Social Forum (WSF) is an open meeting place for social movements, **non-governmental organizations (NGOs)**, national and **transnational advocacy networks** and other **civil society** organizations opposed to economic **neo-liberalism**, financial **capitalism**, **imperialism** and the current organization of the international economy. It aims to provide a venue for the diverse members of the **anti-globalization movement** to co-ordinate campaigns, exchange ideas, debate issues, formulate proposals, network and to organize global strategies.

The WSF was set up to counter the alleged élitist and undemocratic processes symbolized by the **World Economic Forum (WEF)**. It held its first meeting in Porto Alegre, Brazil, in January 2001, and began its construction of a programme for globalization from below with the slogan, 'Another world is possible'. Since its inception it has become a permanent process seeking alternatives to what its proponents believe to be a hegemonic neo-liberal world order. It has so far had a significant political impact by sparking a wide-ranging international debate on the future of **global governance**, and the lack of **accountability** in emerging governance structures. The WSF claims to be non-governmental, non-confessional and non-party as well as pluralistic and diverse. Like the WEF, it is neither an international governmental organization nor an NGO. (Website: http://www.forumsocialmundial.org.br/.)

World Systems Theory

Economic historian Immanuel Wallerstein coined the term 'world system' to refer to a largely self-contained and self-sufficient unit which has the capacity to develop independently of the social processes and relationships internal to its component states or societies. There are three possible types of world system—world empires, in which several cultures are unified under a single government; world economies, in which a multiplicity of states are joined by a common economic system; and world socialism, a utopian state characterized by a unified political-economic system which integrates multiple cultures.

While being Marxist-Leninist in orientation (see **Marxism**), world systems theory provides a global level of analysis. The whole global structure is seen as one of overlapping hierarchies. Here, trade and exploitative relations constitute the primary mechanism for **capitalism** and global integration. The focal point of pressure in the world economy is the state structure. Three different forms of state structure are described: (a) core states that have strong governments, well integrated with the national culture; (b) peripheral states that are weak, poor, and invaded cultures; and (c) semi-peripheral states with moderately strong governments, but low technologies, making them dependent on the core states.

The conceptual pairing of core and periphery, defined by asymmetrical relations, is critical to this theory. Capitalism creates the global market and a **global division of labour** between core and peripheral zones, and relations between these are marked by unequal exchange, with capital-intensive goods produced at the core being indirectly exchanged for labour-intensive goods produced in the periphery. Indeed, capitalism expands on the back of this unequal exchange, leading to the underdevelopment of periphery zones (see also **Dependency Theory**).

Wallerstein used world systems theory to voice his protest against global **inequality**. He demonstrated that the world is constituted as a capitalist system, dominated by **multinational companies** that operate independently of political arrangements, and that can achieve economic domination over them. These corporations set up global linkages and systems of exchange so that the globe is increasingly constituted as a single market for commodities, labour and capital. (See also **Developing Countries**; and **Development**.)

World Trade Organization (WTO)

The World Trade Organization (WTO) was established in 1995 to replace the provisional **General Agreement on Tariffs and Trade (GATT)**. The GATT included a series of treaties and administered a series of international negotiations to facilitate free trade at the international level. The WTO was the outcome of the last GATT round of trade negotiations beginning in 1986, more popularly known as the Uruguay Round of negotiations.

The GATT was originally drawn up in 1947 with the intention of establishing an intergovernmental organization (IGO) responsible for **international trade**. However, the agreement to establish an International Trade Organization was not ratified and hence the GATT evolved as a compromise, acting as a standby until the foundation of the WTO. During its existence, the GATT established a set of rules and norms to govern international trade and to remove tariffs and **non-tariff barriers** to international trade (see **Free Trade**; **Protectionism**; and **Trade System**). After lengthy negotiations, the loosely structured GATT was transformed into the WTO, which has the status of an IGO and includes the GATT agreements, focusing mainly on trade in goods, while also introducing a General Agreement on Trade in Services.

The main functions of the WTO are: to administer WTO trade agreements; to provide a forum for trade negotiations; to handle trade disputes;

to monitor national trade agreements; to offer technical assistance and training for **developing countries**; and to facilitate effective co-operation with other **international organizations**.

The WTO and the GATT have often been criticized for facilitating the spread of neo-liberal globalization (see **Neo-liberalism**). First, the WTO agenda setting appears to be partial towards the interests of the rich developed countries and large **multinational companies**, resulting in imbalanced and biased rules of trade. One example often mentioned by critics is the failure of the WTO to remove **non-tariff barriers** and subsidies from the heavily protected agricultural sectors in Western Europe, the USA and Japan. Second, environmental protection, labour standards, health and safety standards, **human rights** issues and national interests are all deemed secondary to its chief concern, which is free trade. And, finally, there is the issue of participation. The development of the global political economy has over the last 50 years enhanced the role of international organizations such as the WTO, entrusting them with ever-increasing powers in shaping international norms and expectations. However, only states can be WTO members, and the WTO agenda is driven by governments. This raises the problem of transparency and wider participation in international decision-making processes and democratic governance at the international level. Public dissatisfaction with the decision-making procedures, for instance, was part of the driving force behind the massive protests at the ministerial conference in Seattle, USA, in 1999—see **Anti-globalization (Movement)**. (Website: http://www.wto.org.)

World Wide Web

The world wide web (www) is a flexible network of networks within the **internet** where institutions, businesses, associations and individuals can create their own 'sites' or 'home pages' with a variable collage of text and images. The construction of world wide webs was enabled by software technology first developed in Mosaic, a web browser software programme invented in 1992 by students in Illinois's National Center for Supercomputing Applications. This allowed groupings of interests and projects on the net, creating organizing structures and communities almost totally divorced from physical locations, thus making for meaningful interactions. The world wide web transformed the chaotic browsing that had been the earlier norm. In the 1990s, the web quickly gained acceptance as a key infrastructure for business and governments.

X

Xenophobia

Xenophobia literally is the fear and distrust displayed towards strangers in general and foreigners especially. Its origins are in the Greek words *xeno* (stranger, foreigner) and *phobia* (fear). It is typically used to describe hostility towards outsiders, those who are different. There is a close connection with some of the more extreme versions of **nationalism** and ethnocentrism and it is often linked to isolationist and protectionist policies (see **Protectionism**).

In the wider globalization discourse the right wing of the anti-globalization camp (see **Anti-globalization (Movement)**) is partly driven by xenophobic fears. While the anti-globalization movement is often regarded as being deeply anti-capitalist and coming from the left, critique from the right of the political spectrum cannot be ignored. Xenophobia is associated with particularist protectionism, a collective term for a wide spectrum of critics who blame globalization for many of the economic and social problems faced by national societies. They are motivated by a fear of reduced living standards (see **Race to the Bottom**), a loss of national **identity** and culture through foreign influences and the loss of national **sovereignty**. They denounce **free trade** agendas, the power of **multinational companies** and international institutions, the perceived **Americanization** of national cultures and the general permeability of national borders to transnational influences.

Particularist protectionism can be observed world-wide. Examples include Pat Buchanan in the USA, Jörg Haider's Austrian Freedom Party or Jean-Marie Le Pen's National Front in France. They style themselves as protectors of the interests of the working class and the nation against corrupt corporate élites, free trade and immigration. Usually, their policies combine economic nationalism and proposals on how to deal with the 'foreigner problem', including issues of immigration, refugees and imported labour.

Xenophobic trends in conjunction with globalization can be seen in many countries and are not uncommon even among the established political middle ground, their key indicators being attempts to restrict international refugee and labour **migration**. Nor is xenophobia restricted to industrialized countries in the global North. Islamic **fundamentalism** or Hindu nationalism fall into the same category.

Z

Zapatista Movement

The Zapatista Movement is a democratic popular movement of resistance against neo-liberal globalization (see **Neo-liberalism**) and **globalism** in Mexico. It had its origins in a rebellion in the Mexican state of Chiapas in 1994. The residents of Chiapas, mostly people of indigenous heritage, found themselves increasingly economically marginalized as a result of neo-liberal policies such as those epitomized by the **North American Free Trade Agreement (NAFTA)**.

The Zapatistas, as they are commonly known, draw their name from Emiliano Zapata, a leading figure of the Mexican Revolution which broke out in 1910. Zapata's army fought for agrarian reform and land distribution and included legendary figures such as Pancho Villa. Today's Zapatista movement skilfully employs this revolutionary heritage. Its aims are not dissimilar to those of the original Zapata, including agrarian and social reform. It is a grassroots movement made up primarily of indigenous people protesting against the implementation of NAFTA, seeking the restoration of political and economic rights for Mexico's disenfranchised indigenous people and combating the destructive consequences of economic neo-liberal globalization. The Zapatistas were concerned that increased marketization would intensify social polarization, while also making it increasingly difficult to follow an autonomous, more ecologically-sensitive **development** trajectory.

Unlike particularist protectionists, however, the Zapatista Movement aims to confront neo-liberal economic globalization on a global scale—see **Anti-globalization (Movement)**. To this end, it has successfully used computer-mediated communication technology to establish a global electronic network of solidarity and to challenge neo-liberal globalization in word and action. Indeed, for their globalization of protest, the Zapatistas have been called the 'first informational guerrillas'.

The Zapatista Movement is part of the wider anti-globalization movement and is an example of universalist **protectionism**. Universalist protectionists include an increasing number of national and **international non-governmental organizations** and **transnational advocacy networks** concerned with environmental protection, **fair trade**, **human rights**, gender issues and labour standards. These groups challenge neo-liberal globalization and focus on constructing a new **international order** based on the global redistribution of wealth and power. They are guided by concerns for equality and social justice and push for 'globalization from below', favouring marginalized people.

BIBLIOGRAPHY

Albrow, M. *The Global Age: State and Society beyond Modernity.* Cambridge: Polity, 1996.

Amin, S. 'The Challenge of Globalization', in *Review of International Political Economy*, Vol. 3, No. 2, 1996.

—— *Capitalism in the Age of Globalization: the Management of Contemporary Society.* London: Zed Books, 1997.

Amoore, L., and Langley, P. 'Experiencing Globalization: Active Teaching and Learning in International Political Economy', in *International Studies Perspectives*, Vol. 2, No. 1, 2001.

Anderson, B. *Imagined Communities.* New York: Verso, 1993.

Appadurai, A. *Modernity at Large: Cultural Dimensions of Globalization.* Minneapolis: University of Minneapolis Press, 1996.

Appadurai, A. (Ed.). *Globalization.* Durham and London: Duke University Press, 2001.

Applebaum, R. P., and Robinson, W. I. *Critical Globalization Studies.* Oxford: Routledge, 2005.

Archibugi, D., and Held, D. *Cosmopolitan Democracy.* Cambridge: Polity Press, 1995.

Archibugi, D., Held, D., and Koehler, M. *Re-Imagining Political Community.* Stanford University Press, 1998.

Axford, B. *The Global System.* Cambridge: Polity Press, 1995.

Balassa, B. *The Theory of Economic Integration.* London: Allen and Unwin, 1961.

Barber, B. *Jihad vs. McWorld.* Ballantine, 1996.

Barker, C. *Television, Globalization and Cultural Identities.* Milton Keynes: Open University Press, 1999.

Barnet, R. J., and Cavanagh, J. *Global Dreams: Imperial Corporations and the New World Order.* New York: Touchstone Press, 1994.

Basch, Linda, Glick Schiller, Nina, and Szanton Blanc, Cristina. *Nations Unbound: Transnational Projects, Postcolonial Predicaments, and Deterritorialized Nation States.* Langhorne, PA: Gordon and Breach, 1994.

Bauman, Z. *Globalization.* Cambridge: Polity, 1994.

Baylis, J., and Smith, S. *The Globalization of World Politics – An Introduction to International Relations.* Oxford: Oxford University Press, 2005.

Beck, Ulrich. *Risk Society: Towards a New Modernity.* London: Sage, 1992.

—— *What is Globalization?* Cambridge: Polity, 2000.

Bello, W. *Deglobalization: Ideas for a New World Economy.* London: Zed Books, 2002.

Beneria, L. *Gender, Development, and Globalization: Economics as if All People Mattered.* New York: Routledge, 2003.

Bergsten, C. F. 'Globalizing Free Trade', in *Foreign Affairs*, Vol. 75, No. 3., 1996.

Beyer, P. *Religion and Globalization.* London: Sage, 1994.

Beynon, J., and Dunkerley, D. *Globalization: The Reader.* London: The Athlone Press, 2000.

Bhabha, Homi. *The Location of Culture.* London: Routledge, 1993.

Bhagwati, J. *In Defense of Globalization.* Oxford: Oxford University Press, 2004.

Bircham, E., and Charlton, J. *Anti-Capitalism: A Guide to the Movement.* London: Bookmark Publications, 2001.

Bisley, N. *Rethinking Globalization.* Basingstoke: Palgrave Macmillan, 2007.

Booth, K., and Dunne, T. *Worlds in Collision: Terror and the Future of Global Order.* London: Macmillan, 2002.

Boyer, M. C. *Cybercities: Visual Perception in the Age of Electronic Communications.* New York: Princeton University Press, 1996.

Brecher, J., Costello, T., and Smith, B. *Globalization from Below.* Southend Press. 2000.

Bull, H. *The Anarchical Society – A Study of Order in World Politics.* London: Macmillan, 1977.

Bullman, U. 'The Politics of the Third Level', in Jeffrey, C. (Ed.), *The Regional Dimension of the European Union: Towards a Third Level in Europe?* London: Frank Cass, 1997.

Burbach, R. *Globalization and Postmodern Politics.* London: Pluto Press, 2001.

Cairncross, F. *The Death of Distance – How the Communications Revolution Will Change Our Lives.* London: Orion Business, 1998.

Castells, M. *The Rise of the Network Society: The Information Age – Economy, Society and Culture: Volume 1.* Oxford: Blackwell Publishers, 2000.

—— *The Internet Galaxy.* Oxford: Oxford University Press, 2001.

Castels, S., and Davidson, A. *Globalisation and Citizenship.* Basingstoke: Macmillan, 2000.

Centre for Civil Society (http://www.lse.ac.uk/collections/CCS/publications/Default.htm).

Cerami, C. A. 'The US Eyes Greater Europe', in *The Spectator*, 5 October 1962.

Cerny, P. G. 'Globalization and Other Stories: The Search for a New Paradigm for International Relations', in *International Journal*, Vol. 51, 1996.

Cha, V. D. 'Globalization and the Study of International Security', in *Journal of Peace Research*, Vol. 37, No. 3, 2000.

Cheng, S. J. A. 'Rethinking the Globalization of Domestic Service', in *Gender and Society* 17 (2): pp. 166–86, 2003.

Chomsky, N. *World Orders, Old and New.* London: Pluto Press, 1994.

—— *Failed States: The Abuse of Power and the Assault on Democracy.* London: Penguin, 2006.

Clark, I. *Globalization and Fragmentation: International Relations in the Twentieth Century.* Oxford: Oxford University Press, 1997.

—— *Globalization and International Relations Theory.* Oxford: Oxford University Press, 1999.

Cooperrider, D., and Dutton, J. E. *Organizational Dimensions of Global Change.* London: Sage, 1999.

Council for Asia-Europe Cooperation. *Strengthening International Order – The Role of Asia-Europe Co-operation.* Tokyo: Japan Center for International Exchange, 2000.

Cox, K. R. *Spaces of Globalization: Reasserting the Power of the Local.* New York: Guilford, 1997.

Danaher, K., and Burbach, R. *Globalize This!* Common Courage Press, 2000.

Demers, D. *Global Media.* Hampton Press, 1999.

Duménil, G., and Lévy, D. 'The Neoliberal (Counter-)Revolution', in Saad-Filho, A., and Johnston, D. (Eds), *Neoliberalism: A Critical Reader.* London: Pluto Press, 2005.

Dunford, Michael, and Grieco, Lidia. *After the Three Italies: Wealth, Inequality and Industrial Change.* Blackwell, RGS-IBG Series, 2005.

Dunning, J. *Explaining International Production.* London: Unwin Hyman, 1998.

—— *Multinational Enterprises in a Global Economy.* Wokingham: Addison-Wesley, 1993.

Dunning, J. H. *Governments, Globalisation and International Business.* Oxford: Oxford University Press, 1997.

Eisenstein, Z. *Global Obscenities: Patriarchy, Capitalism and the Lure of Cyberfantasy.* New York University Press, 1998.

Ellwod, W. *The No-Nonsense Guide to Globalization.* London: Verso, 2001.

Escobar, A. *Encountering Development: The Making and Unmaking of the Third World.* New York: Princeton University Press, 1995.

Falk, R. *Predatory Globalization.* Cambridge: Polity, 1999.

—— 'Globalization-from-Below: An Innovative Politics of Difference', in Sandbrook, R. (Ed.), *Civilizing Globalization: A Survival Guide.* Albany: State University of New Press, 2003.

Featherstone, M. *Global Culture: Nationalism, Globalization and Modernity.* London: Sage, 1990.

Featherstone, M., Lash, S., and Robertson, R. *Global Modernities.* London: Sage, 1995.

Friedman, J. *Cultural Identity and Global Process.* London: Sage, 1994.

Friedman, M. *Capitalism & Freedom.* Chicago: University of Chicago Press, 1962.

Friedman, T. *The Lexus and the Olive Tree: Understanding Globalization.* New York: Farrar, Straus and Giroux, 2000.

Frobel, F., Heinrichs, J., and Kreye, O. *The New International Division of Labour.* Cambridge: Cambridge University Press, 1980.

Fukuyama, F. 'The End of History?', in *National Interest*, Vol. 16, 1989.

Gaddis, J. L. '*Toward the Post-Cold War World*', in *Foreign Affairs*, Vol. 70, No. 2, 1991.

Germain, R. *Globalization and its Critics: Perspectives from Political Economy.* Basingstoke: Macmillan, 1999.

Giddens, A. *The Consequences of Modernity: Self and Society in the Later Modern Age.* Cambridge: Polity, 1990.

—— *The Third Way: The Renewal of Social Democracy.* Cambridge: Polity, 1998.

—— *Runaway World: How Globalization Is Reshaping Our Lives.* New York: Routledge, 2000.

Gills, B. *Globalization and the Politics of Resistance.* London: Macmillan, 2000.

Gilpin, R. *The Challenge of Global Capitalism: The World Economy in the 21st Century.* Princeton: Princeton University Press, 2000.

—— *The Global Political Economy.* Princeton: Princeton University Press, 2001.

Goldmann, K. *Transforming the European Nation State.* London: Sage, 2001.

Gray, J. *False Dawn: The Delusion of Global Capitalism.* London: Granta, 1998.

Greene, O. 'Environmental Issues', in Baylis, J., and Smith, S. (Eds), *The Globalization of World Politics – An Introduction to International Relations.* Oxford: Oxford University Press, 2005.

Griffiths, M., and O'Callaghan, T. *International Relations – The Key Concepts.* New York: Routledge, 2002.

Guehenno, J. M. 'The Impact of Globalisation on Strategy', in *Survival*, Vol. 40, No. 4, 1999.

Hall, S. 'The Question of Cultural Identity', in Hall, S., Held, D., and McGrew, T. (Eds), *Modernity and its Futures.* Cambridge: Polity, 1992.

—— 'New Cultures for Old', in Massey, D., and Jess, P. (Eds), *A Place in the World? Places, Cultures and Globalization.* New York: Oxford University Press, 1995.

Hannerz, Ulf. *Transnational Connections: Culture, People, Places.* Cambridge: Polity, 1995.

Hardt, M., and Negri, A. *Empire.* Cambridge, MA: Harvard University Press, 2000.

Harrison, G. 'Introduction: Globalisation, Governance and Development', in *New Political Economy*, Vol. 9, No. 2, 2004.

Harvey, D. *The Condition of Post-Modernity: An Enquiry into the Conditions of Global Change.* Oxford: Blackwell Publishers, 1989.

—— 'Neoliberalism as Creative Destruction', in *The ANNALS of the American Academy of Political and Social Science*, Vol. 610, No. 1, 2007.

Hay, C. 'What's Globalization Got to Do with It? Economic Interdependence and the Future of European Welfare States', in *Government and Opposition*, Vol. 41, No. 1, 2006.

—— 'International Relations Theory and Globalization', in Dunne, T., Kurki, M., and Smith, S. (Eds), *International Relations Theories – Discipline and Diversity.* Oxford University Press: Oxford, 2007.

Held, D. *Democracy and the Global Order: From the Modern State to Cosmopolitan Governance.* Cambridge: Polity, 1995.

—— *Democracy and Globalization*, MPIfG Working Paper 97/5 < http://www.mpi-fg-koeln.mpg.de/pu/workpap/wp97–5/wp97–5.html > (accessed 19.09.2006).

—— *Debating Globalization.* Cambridge: Polity, 2005.

Held, D., and McGrew, A. (Eds). *Governing Globalization: Power, Authority, and Global Governance.* Cambridge: Polity, 2002.

Held, D., and McGrew, A., with Goldblatt, D., and Perraton, J. 'Managing the Challenge of Globalization and Institutionalizing Cooperation through Global Governance', in Kegley, Jr, C. W., and Wittkopf, E. R. (Eds), *The Global Agenda – Issues and Perspectives.* New York: McGraw-Hill, 2001.

Held, D., McGrew, A., Goldblatt, D., and Perraton, J. *Global Transformations: Politics, Economics and Culture.* Cambridge: Polity, 1999.

Hettne, B. 'Globalization, the New Regionalism and East Asia', in Tanaka, T., and Inoguchi, T. (Eds.), *Globalisation and Regionalism.* Hayama: United Nations

University, Global Seminar '96 Shonan Session. < http://www.unu.edu/unupress/ globalism.html > (accessed 04.12.2000).

—— 'Globalization and the New Regionalism: The Second Great Transformation', in Hettne, B., Sapir, A., and Sunkel, O. (Eds), *Globalism and the New Regionalism.* New York: St. Martin's Press, 1999.

—— 'Globalisation, Regionalisation and Security: The Asian Experience', in *European Journal of Development Research*, Vol. 14, No. 1, 2002.

Hettne, B., Sapir, A., and Sunkel, O. *Globalism and the New Regionalism.* New York: St. Martin's Press, 2002.

Hettne, B., and Söderbaum, F. 'Theorising the Rise of Regioness', in Breslin, S., Hughes, C. W., Phillips, N., and Rosamond, B. (Eds), *New Regionalism in the Global Political Economy.* London: Routledge, 2002.

Heywood, A. *Key Concepts in Politics.* Basingstoke: Palgrave, 2000.

Higgott, R. A., Underhill, G. R. D., and Bieler, A. *Non-state Actors and Authority in the Global System.* London: Routledge, 2000.

Hirst, G., and Thompson, P. *Globalization in Question: The International Economy and the Possibilities of Governance* (2nd edn). Cambridge: Polity, 1999.

Hobsbawm, E. *Nations and Nationalism Since 1780* (2nd edn). Cambridge: Cambridge University Press, 1992.

Hoogvelt, A. *Globalization and the Postcolonial World.* London: Macmillan, 1997.

Hughes, C. W. 'Globalisation and Security in the Asia-Pacific – An Initial Investigation', University of Warwick, Centre for the Study of Globalisation and Regionalisation, Working Paper No. 61/00.

Huntington, S. P. 'The Clash of Civilizations', in *Foreign Affairs*, Vol. 72, No. 3, 1993.

—— *The Clash of Civilizations and the Remaking of World Order.* New York: Simon and Schuster, 1996.

Hutton, W., and Giddens, A. *Global Capitalism.* The Free Press, 2000.

Hveem, H. 'Explaining the Regional Phenomenon in the Era of Globalization', in Stubbs, R., and Underhill, G. (Eds). *Political Economy and the Changing Global Order.* Oxford: Oxford University Press, 2000.

Hymer, S. *The International Operation of National Firms.* Cambridge, MA: MIT Press, 1976.

—— *The Multinational Corporation: A Radical Approach.* Cambridge: Cambridge University Press, 1979.

Jeffrey, C. *The Regional Dimension of the European Union: Towards a Third Level in Europe?* London: Frank Cass, 1997.

Jenkins, B. ' The Europe of Nations and Regions', in Sakwa, R., and Stevens, A. (Eds), *Contemporary Europe.* Basingstoke: Macmillan, 2000.

Kagan, R. *Paradise and Power: America and Europe in the New World Order.* London: Atlantic Books, 2003.

Kaldor, M. *New and Old Wars: Organized Violence in a Global Era.* Stanford: Stanford University Press, 1999.

—— *Global Civil Society: An Answer to War.* London: Polity, 2003a.

— 'The Idea of Global Civil Society.' *International Affairs* 79, No. 3, pp. 583–93, 2003b.

Keck, M., and Sikkink, K. A*ctivists Beyond Borders: Advocacy Networks in International Politics.* Ithaca: Cornell University Press, 1998.

Kegley, Jr, C. W., and Wittkopf, E. R. *The Global Agenda – Issues and Perspectives.* New York: McGraw-Hill, 2001.

Keohane, R. O. *After Hegemony – Cooperation and Discord in the World Political Economy.* New Jersey: Princeton University Press, 1984.

—— *Neorealism and its Critics.* New York: Columbia University Press, 1986.

Keohane, R. O., and Nye, J. *Power and Interdependence: World Politics in Transition.* Boston: Little Brown, 1977.

—— 'Globalisation: What's New? What's Not? (And So What?)', in Held, D., and McGrew, A. (Eds), *The Global Transformations Reader: An Introduction to the Globalization Debate* (2nd edn). Cambridge: Polity, 2003.

Khor, M. *Remarks to the International Forum.* New York: November, 1995.

—— *Rethinking Globalization.* Zed Books, 2001.

Kilminster, R. 'Globalization as an Emergent Concept', in Scott, A. (Ed.), *The Limits of Globalization: Cases and Arguments.* London: Routledge, 1997.

King, A. *Global Cities.* London: Routledge, 1990.

Klein, N. *No Logo.* New York: Picador, 1999.

—— *Fences and Windows: Dispatches from the Front Lines of the Globalization Debate.* New York: Picador, 2002.

Kopfman, E., and Youngs, G. *Globalization: Theory and Practice.* London: Pinter, 2001.

Krasner, S. *International Regimes.* Ithaca: Cornell University Press, 1983.

Krugman, P. *The Return of Depression Economics.* New York: Norton, 2000.

Kuper, A., and Kuper, J. *The Social Science Encyclopaedia.* London: Routledge, 1999.

Lash, S., and Urry, J. *Economies of Signs and Space.* London: Sage, 1994.

Lechner, F. J., and Boli, J. *The Globalization Reader* (2nd edn). Oxford: Blackwell Publishing, 2004.

Lipsey, R. G. 'Globalisation and National Government Policies: An Economist's View', in Dunning, J. H. (Ed.), *Governments, Globalisation and International Business.* New York: Oxford University Press, 1997.

Lomborg, Bjorn (Ed.). Global Crises, Global Solutions. Cambridge: Cambridge University Press, 2004.

Lutz, Helma. 'At Your Service Madam! The Globalization of Domestic Service', in *Feminist Review* 70(1): pp. 89–104, 2002.

Mansfield, E. D., and Milner, H. V. 'The New Wave of Regionalism', in *International Organization*, Vol. 53, No. 3, 1999.

Maull, H. W. (Ed.) 'Governance in the Age of Globalisation: Implications for the ASEM Agenda', in Council for Asia-Europe Co-operation, *Strengthening International Order – The Role of Asia-Europe Co-operation.* Tokyo: Japan Center for International Exchange, 2000.

Micklethwait, J., and Wooldridge, A. *A Future Perfect: The Challenge and Hidden Promise of Globalisation.* London: Heinemann, 2000.

Milward, A. *The European Rescue of the Nation-State.* London: Routledge, 1993.

Mittelman, J. H. *Globalization.* London: Lynne Rienner, 1996.

The Globalization Syndrome. Princeton: Princeton University Press, 2000.

—— *Whither Globalization: The Vortex of Knowledge and Ideology.* London: Routledge, 2004.

Mittelman, J. H., and Johnston, R. 'The Globalization of Organized Crime, the Courtesan State, and the Corruption of Civil Society', in *Global Governance*, Vol. 5, No. 1, 1999.

Monbiot, G. *The Age of Consent*. London: Perennial, 2004.

Munck, R. 'Neoliberalism and Politics, and the Politics of Neoliberalism', in Saad-Filho, A., and Johnston, D. (Eds), *Neoliberalism: A Critical Reader*. London: Pluto Press, 2005.

Naess, A. *Ecology, Community and Lifestyle*. Cambridge: Cambridge University Press, 1976.

Naisbitt, J. *Global Paradox: The Bigger the World-Economy, the More Powerful its Smallest Players*. London: Brealey, 1994.

Navarro, V. 'The Worldwide Class Struggle', in *Monthly Review*, Vol. 58, No. 4, 2006.

O'Brien, R. *Contesting Global Governance: Multilateral Economic Institutions and Global Social Movements*. Cambridge: Cambridge University Press, 2000.

Ohmae, K. *The Borderless World: Power and Strategy in the Interlinked Economy*. London: Fontana, 1990.

—— 'The Rise of the Region State', in *Foreign Affairs*, Vol. 72, 1993.

—— *The End of the Nation-State: The Rise of Regional Economies*. London: Harper-Collins, 1996.

Palley, T. I. 'From Keynesianism to Neoliberalism: Shifting Paradigms in Economics', in Saad-Filho, A., and Johnston, D. (Eds), *Neoliberalism: A Critical Reader*. London: Pluto Press, 2005.

Peige, S. *Regions and Development: Politics, Security and Economics*. London: Frank Cass, 2000.

Perrons, Diane. *Globalisation and Social Change: People and Places in a Divided World*. London and New York: Routledge, 2004.

Polanyi, K. *The Great Transformation*. Boston: Beacon Hill Press, 1957.

Preibisch, P. *Towards a New Trade Policy for Development*. New York: United Nations, 1964.

Reich, R. *The Work of Nations*. New Work: Alfred A. Knopf, 1991.

Ritzer, G. *The McDonaldization of Society: An Investigation into the Changing Character of Contemporary Social Life*. London: Sage, 2000.

—— *The Globalization of Nothing*. London: Sage, 2004.

Robertson, R. *Globalization: Social Theory and Global Culture*. London: Sage, 1992.

—— 'Glocalization: Time-Space and Homogeneity-Heterogeneity', in Featherstone, M., Lash, S., and Robertson, R. (Eds), *Global Modernities*. London: Sage, 1995.

Robertson, R., and Garrett, W. R. *Religion and Global Order*. New York: Paragon House, 1991.

Robertson, R., and White, K. *Globalization: Critical Concepts in Sociology*. London: Routledge, 2003.

Robins, K. 'Globalization', in Kuper, A., and Kuper, J. (Eds), *The Social Science Encyclopaedia*. London: Routledge, 1999.

Robinson, W. I. 'Social Theory and Globalization: The Rise of a Transnational State', in *Theory and Society*, Vol. 30, No. 2, 2001.

Rodrik, D. *Has Globalization Gone Too Far?* Washington, DC: Institute for International Economics, 1997.

Rostow, W. W. *The Stages of Economic Growth.* Cambridge: Cambridge University Press, 1960.

Rupert, M. *Ideologies of Globalization: Contending Visions of a New World Order.* London: Routledge, 2000.

Said, E. W. *Orientalism.* New York: Vintage, 1979.

Sandbrook, R. *Civilizing Globalization: A Survival Guide.* Albany: State University of New Press, 2003.

Sassen, S. *Losing Control? Sovereignty in the Age of Globalization.* New York: Columbia University Press, 1996.

—— *Globalization and Its Discontents: Essays on the New Mobility of People and Money.* New York: The New Press, 1998.

—— *The Global City: New York, London, Tokyo* (2nd edn). Princeton: Princeton University Press, 201.

Scholte, J. A. 'The Globalization of World Politics', in Baylis, J., and Smith, S. (Eds), *The Globalization of World Politics – An Introduction to International Relations.* Oxford: Oxford University Press, 1997.

—— 'Global Civil Society', in Woods, N. (Ed.), *The Political Economy of Globalization.* London: Macmillan, 2000.

—— *Globalization – A Critical Introduction.* Basingstoke: Palgrave, 2000.

Scott, A. *The Limits of Globalization: Cases and Arguments.* London: Routledge, 1997.

Sell, S. 'Structures, Agents and Institutions: Private Corporate Power and the Globalization of Property Rights', in Higgott, R. A., Underhill, G. R. D., and Bieler, A. (Eds), *Non-state Actors and Authority in the Global System.* London: Routledge, 2000.

Sen, A. *Development as Freedom.* Oxford: Oxford University Press, 1999.

Shaw, M. *Global Society and International Relations: Sociological Concepts and Political Perspectives.* Cambridge: Polity, 1994.

—— *Politics and Globalisation: Knowledge, Ethics and Agency.* London: Routledge, 1999.

Shiva, V. 'WTO is Dead, Long Live Free Trade: Globalization and its New Avatars' (http://www.ifg.org/pdf/WTO%20is%20Dead.pdf), 1996.

Sideri, S. 'Globalisation and Regional Integration', in Peige, S. (Ed.), *Regions and Development: Politics, Security and Economics.* London: Frank Cass, 2000.

Smith, A. *The Wealth of Nations* (New York: Penguin, 1983).

Smith, A. D. 'Towards a Global Culture', in Theory, Culture and Society 7(2–3). London: Sage, 1990.

Soros, G. *George Soros on Globalization.* New York: Public Affairs, 2002.

Spybey, T. *Globalization and World Society.* Cambridge: Polity, 1996.

Starr, A. *Naming the Enemy: Anti-Corporate Movements Confront Globalization.* London: Zed Books, 2000.

Steger, M. *Globalism.* Rowman and Littlefield Publishers, 2002.

Steger, M. B. *Globalization – A Very Short Introduction.* Oxford: Oxford University Press, 2003.

Stiglitz, J. *Globalization and its Discontents.* London: Penguin, 2002.

Strange, S. 'Big Business and the State', in *Millennium*, Vol. 20, No. 2, 1991.

—— 'Rethinking Structural Change in the International Political Economy: States, Firms and Diplomacy', in Stubbs, R., Underhill, G. R. D. (Eds), *Political Economy and the Changing Global Order*. London: Macmillan, 1994.

—— *The Retreat of the State. The Diffusion of Power in the World Economy*. Cambridge: Cambridge University Press, 1996.

—— *Mad Money*. Manchester: Manchester University Press, 1998.

Stubbs, R., and Underhill, G. *Political Economy and the Changing Global Order*. Oxford: Oxford University Press, 2000.

Tanaka, T., and Inoguchi, T. *Globalisation and Regionalism*. Hayama: United Nations University, Global Seminar '96 Shonan Session. < http://www.unu.edu/unupress/globalism.html > (accessed 04.12.2000).

Tomlinson, J. *Cultural Imperialism*. London: Pinter Publishers, 1991.

—— *Globalization and Culture*. Chicago: Chicago University Press, 1999.

Tsing, Anna. 'Inside the Economy of Appearances', in Appadurai, A. (Ed.), *Globalization*. Durham and London: Duke University Press, 2001.

Varia, Nisha. 'Globalization Comes Home: Protecting Migrant Domestic Workers' Rights', in *Human Rights Watch World Report*, pp. 1–13, 2007.

Väyrynen, R. *Post-Hegemonic and Post-Socialist Regionalism: A Comparison of East Asia and Central Europe*. University of Notre Dame, The Joan B. Kroc Institute, Occasional Paper #13:OP:3, 1997.

—— *Globalization and Global Governance*. Rowman and Littlefield, 1999.

Vernon, R. 'International Investment and International Trade in the Product Cycle', in *Quarterly Journal of Economics*, Vol. 80, No. 2, 1966.

Wallerstein, I. *The Capitalist World Economy*. Cambridge: Cambridge University Press, 1979.

—— *The Decline of American Power: The US in a Chaotic World*. New York: New Press, 2003.

Walzer, M. *Toward a Global Civil Society*. Providence, RI: Berghahn, 1998.

Waters, M. *Globalization*. London: Routledge, 1995.

Weiss, L. *The Myth of the Powerless State*. Ithaca: Cornell University Press, 1998.

Went, R. *Globalization: Neoliberal Challenge, Radical Responses*. London: Pluto Press, 2000.

Wolf, Martin. *Why Globalisation Works: The Case for the Global Market Economy*. New Haven and London: Yale Nota Bene, Yale University Press, 2005.

Woods, N. *The Political Economy of Globalization*. London: Macmillan, 2000.

World Bank. *Globalization, Growth and Poverty: Building an Inclusive World Economy*. Washington, DC: World Bank, 2000.

LIST OF ENTRIES AND CROSS-REFERENCES

A

Accountability
Acid Rain
Acquired Immune Deficiency
  Syndrome (AIDS)
Advertising
African Union (AU)
Agribusiness
Aid
Air Pollution
Al-Jazeera
Americanization
Amnesty International
Andean Group
Antarctic Treaty System
Anti-globalization (Movement)
Appadurai, Arjun
Arms Control
Arms Trade
ARPANET
ASEAN Regional Forum (ARF)
Asia-Europe Meeting (ASEM)
Asian Financial Crisis
Asia-Pacific Economic Co-operation
  (APEC)
Association of South East Asian
  Nations (ASEAN)
Autarky
Automatic Teller Machine (ATM)

B

Ballistic Missile Technology
Bank for International Settlements
  (BIS)
Beck, Ulrich
Beggar-thy-Neighbour Policies
Beijing Declaration
Biodiversity

Bond-Rating Agencies
Bové, José
Brahimi Report
Branding
Bretton Woods System
Bush Doctrine

C

Cable News Network (CNN)
Capital Controls
Capital Flows
Capitalism
Caribbean Common Market
  (CARICOM)
Carnegie Endowment for International
  Peace
Casino Capitalism
Centre-Periphery
Chomsky, Noam Avram
Citizenship
Civil Society
Clash of Civilizations
Climate Change
Club of Madrid
Club of Rome
Coca-Colonization
Collective Goods
Collective Security
Colonialism
Commodification
Commodities
Commodity Chains
Common Market
Communitarianism
Comparative Advantage
Concentration of Capital
Conservatism
Consumer Culture

295